Discovering Shakespeare:

A *Festschrift* in Honour of Isabel Holden

Editor, Daniel Wright

The Shakespeare Authorship Research Centre
at Concordia University

Edward de Vere, 17th Earl of Oxford

CONCORDIA
UNIVERSITY

TABLE OF CONTENTS

Many thanks to all who contributed so much to make this tribute to Isabel Holden possible, among whom, in addition to the contributors of the articles within, we must particularly acknowledge those so instrumental to the production of this volume. Without their participation, the project could not have gone forward — Robert Prechter, Sally Webb, Steve Jackson and Adam Leyrer. Kudos all 'round! Well done! Isabel would be proud of you!

Foreword

I've heard it said — and I firmly believe it — that our highest purpose in life is to plant seeds for trees to grow, under the shade of which trees we will never sit. No one exemplified that philosophy more than Isabel Holden.

It has been one of the great privileges of my life that I got to know Isabel Holden and observe the enchantments she could conjure in her dedication to transform the world into the magical place she knew it could be, if but we could make provision and time for entry into a world of wonder. She was so many things — one would require a book the size of the OED to list her virtues — but perhaps what I most treasured in Isabel was her commitment to the future. She was passionate in her support for education, and at every opportunity she made it possible for others to study and learn.

I first met Isabel when she swirled into the very first Shakespeare authorship conference that I assembled at Concordia University in the 1990s. She was clad in earthy tweeds and thick wool to stave off the April cold of the Pacific Northwest which, at that changeable time of year, is so often like the brisk chill that nips at one's fingers and ears in her native New England. She was one of the most energetic and passionate participants in the conference, and her enthusiasm for this annual event — the first of its kind in academia — was inspirational.

Accordingly, it is with great gratitude to Isabel, in tribute to a life so well lived, that I wish to dedicate this select compilation of papers that have been presented by so many fine minds in recent years at the annual Shakespeare Authorship Studies Conference at Concordia University. Challenging ideas invigorated Isabel, and I hope these essays stir new thoughts and invite studied reflection in those who will read them with the kind of careful attention we know Isabel would give them.

To me and many others, Isabel was the Grand Dame of Oxfordianism, the herald of a summons to engage and re-engage the works of Shakespeare with the conviction that, illumined by the light cast upon them by one's recognition of their true author and his purpose, the poems and plays of England's inimitable poet-playwright might seize us with fresh excitement and rouse us to new appreciation for the genius of these works' artful witness to truths that could only be spoken by one endowed with the gift to say what no other could utter in a manner no other could master.

Those of us who, in so many ways, derive so much of our dedication to the study of Shakespeare to Isabel, owe it to Isabel, therefore, to "take the plunge" and swim in the heady swirl of a sea of research, argument and insight that promises those who also dare to dive in an incomparable joy — the shock and the bliss of discovery — stunning discovery like that of Bassanio which comes from opening a box that may appear dull and leaden but which contains, concealed within, treasure that promises to transform one's life.

Hail and farewell, Isabel! Your memory is always with us, and the quest you so vigorously and rapturously pursued continues!

Daniel Wright
The Shakespeare Authorship Research Centre
Concordia University
Portland, Oregon

A Eulogy

In Commemoration of the Life of Isabel Holden

Charles Francis Topham de Vere Beauclerk

It's a great privilege to have been asked over to the United States to honour Isabel today. I knew that the iron in her soul would draw me here willy-nilly, and so it has… .

Isabel was a woman of discretion and modesty, who, if she intended something, preferred to do it before speaking; hence, her life as a leading Shakespearean heretic—despite her considerable influence in this field—may be unknown to many of you. But it is in this role that I wish to speak of Isabel today.

There was, it's true, a martial quality to Isabel's bearing and temperament, yet there was something unbroken too, a certain wildness perhaps—very rare in the world today—and a former age might well have seen her in the guise of crusader or knight errant. Even in her own home, one got the impression that she was just passing through, a soldier on campaign perhaps or some scholar-gypsy, the bohemian and the Amazon coming together with delightful improbability. She always seemed to be pacing her hall on the top of the hill, drawing off her gloves or thrusting her whip into the umbrella stand as a fresh gust of wind blew in under the door. Shy and intensely private though she was, nothing could stop Isabel bolting on her armour one more time if the cause beckoned. I can see her now, lance couched, visor down, ready for the charge. And yet, as all her admirers will aver, she was the invisible knight, working to great effect behind the scenes.

I first met Isabel in 1989 at Oxford University where she appeared without warning at one of the De Vere Society lectures. She sat near the back in a tweed suit and hat, with her sister, Constance St. John, identically attired. A genial recluse, we spoke briefly after the event. Several months later, I received a letter from her, suggesting the unthinkable: that I give a lecture on the Earl of Oxford at the Folger Shakespeare Library in Washington D.C. It was like asking the Archbishop of Canterbury to preach the Gospel at Mecca. (As I would soon learn, Isabel took a perverse joy in swimming against the tide.) Intrigued by the sheer folly of her proposal, I readily agreed, not imagining that anything could come of it. I had not reckoned with the Holden tenacity.

A year went by, and then, out of the blue, a formal letter of invitation arrived from the Director of the Folger, Werner Gundersheimer, asking me to speak at that august institution. Isabel, herself a Friend of the Folger and well in with the Library's administrators—the Trustees of Amherst College—had pulled it off! That one lecture was to change my life profoundly, and Isabel was responsible for arranging dozens more through her contacts at schools and colleges throughout New England over the coming years. Around the same time she alerted Roger Stritmatter, now Dr. Stritmatter, to the existence of Oxford's Geneva Bible at the Folger. His subsequent dissertation on the annotations in that Bible proved a watershed in Oxfordian studies, and Stritmatter himself became the first student to earn a Ph.D. by crossing the Shakespeare Authorship minefield. I'm told he still has both his legs!

Isabel came to the belief that the Earl of Oxford was Shakespeare late in life, and despite the depth of her knowledge and the force of her conviction, she was never dogmatic or uncharitable in stating the case for de Vere. The academy, with its entrenched beliefs and vested interests, was not the enemy in Isabel's book; rather it was a hive of potential converts, and armed with her gruff charm, she set to work with a will, inviting members of the English faculty from Smith to dinner on the hill, careful to put them at their ease before letting the tiger out of the cupboard. She even took a Shakespeare course at Smith College so as to introduce some of her heterodox ideas to less free-thinking souls. She corresponded too with a number of leading Shakespeare scholars, including Eric Sams, whose work on *Edmund Ironside* was of particular interest to her. Through her reading and correspondence with others, she was always taking the subject in new directions and helping to expand the consciousness of the movement.

Isabel was a pollinator of ideas, a sort of Johnny Appleseed of the Oxfordian world, who enjoyed introducing people both to each other and to new concepts, and to this end she presided over a literary salon which met on the hill once a month. A paper would be presented on some aspect of the Shakespeare-Oxford question, followed by discussion. These motley gatherings were convivial occasions, which Isabel chaired in her own vague yet forthright manner, by turns enthusiastic and offhand. If by chance there was a lull in the conversation, she would terrify some novice by turning to him with a well-aimed "And what have you got to say for yourself?" If, on the other hand, she felt that the speaker was wandering from the point or being too clever, she would retire to the pantry and make a tremendous din with the dishes in a shameless attempt to drown him out!

Isabel's scholarly instincts were excellent, and often ahead of the game. She saw early on the significance of the so-called apocryphal plays for the Oxfordian case, hence her exploration of *Edmund Ironside*. She was also a champion of Lady Mary Wroth, the niece of Sir Philip Sidney, whose prose romance, *The Countess of Montgomery's Urania*, may yet contain vital clues to the Authorship mystery. And in the last couple of years she had nosed out a trail in 16th-century Ferrara, a city-state south of the Veneto, leading—she believed—to the lady who inspired Shakespeare's creation of Portia in *The Merchant of Venice*. All her spe-

cial interests were reflected in this final caper, from alchemy to Renaissance feminism.

Though fiercely independent and something of a loner, Isabel was always generous in sharing knowledge and ideas, and 87 Round Hill Road became a hub and refuge for Shakespearean dissidents. We bathed in "the cool streams of her liberality"—to steal a phrase from Thomas Nashe—and relished "the high countenance she showed to scholars." There was always some fugitive soul up in the creaky attic overlooking those blue Holyoke mountains -- including myself once. Even Isabel made sure that the old coaching house (for so it is) was never more than a staging-post on her quest, for she never ceased to dream of finding that elusive path leading to the heart of the Shakespeare mystery, or—better still—of putting someone else onto it.

Whatever her forbidding exterior might suggest, Isabel was a wonderfully warm person, in the profoundest sense of one whose nature springs from deep within. Undoubtedly a fighter, she was much more than that: she was, without cavil or qualification, truly herself, and in so being gave others the courage to be more fully themselves. One had the feeling that she had something very special up her sleeve—a little bit of magic perhaps—and it is surely in Isabel's brand of self-effacing integrity that our future as a race, if we have one, reposes. "No law is sacred to me," said Emerson, "but that of my nature." Isabel more than understood this; she embodied it.

I last saw Isabel last winter. There had been a number of guests for supper, and, yes, the conversation turned on the Shakespeare question, with Isabel talking fondly of her lady from Ferrara. Before bed, a friend and I accompanied her on her walk with the dogs. Thick flakes of snow fell, would you believe it, from a starry sky. On the way back she stopped in the parking lot just down from her house, and gave us both a big shock by suddenly drawing a sword from her sturdy-looking cane and making as if to carbanado some imaginary foe. "Steady on, old girl," I murmured feebly. But she was laughing like a kid—a kid of 92! It seemed she had a few wild oats left to sow.

It wasn't that Isabel was ill at ease in the modern world; rather, she chose to defy it by holding fast to her vision of the true and the beautiful. Who here hasn't seen her in that extraordinary horse-drawn fly—rather like a giant tea-cup—whizzing along the Vermont lanes in full equestrian gear, whip poised, a half-net over her face, like some trespasser from a lost age of romance? It was an unforgettable sight.

And Isabel was an unforgettable person. Northampton will be a ghost town without her. I almost feel like a ghost myself, returning here today.

To end, I'd like to recite a sonnet by the young Robert Frost which to me evokes that spirit of self-reliance and adventure that was such an inspiring element of Isabel's nature:

Into My Own

One of my wishes is that those dark trees,
So old and firm they scarcely show the breeze,
Were not, as 'twere, the merest mask of gloom,
But stretched away unto the edge of doom.

I should not be withheld but that some day
Into their vastness I should steal away,
Fearless of ever finding open land,
Or highway where the slow wheel pours the sand.

I do not see why I should e'er turn back,
Or those should not set forth upon my track
To overtake me, who should miss me here
And long to know if still I held them dear.

They would not find me changed from him they knew—
Only more sure of all I thought was true.

Farewell Isabel, and on behalf of us all, thank you.

© Charles Beauclerk, 12th October 2007, Northampton, Mass.

The Shakespeare Authorship Question — A Suitable Subject for Academia?

William Leahy, Ph.D.
Head of School (English), Brunel University

This last academic year has been something of a turning point for me. I began the year in the usual way, researching my specialist area of Renaissance processional literature while turning out the odd journal article concerning Shakespeare's history plays. Various deadlines loomed, as they are prone to do, and the near future promised continuing success, albeit of a fairly rudimentary kind. Yet, here I stand as the end of the academic year approaches posing what, for me and for most Shakespearean academics, has traditionally been a ridiculous if not impossible question. The Shakespeare Authorship Question—a suitable subject for academia? It is understandable, given the nature of the questioning environment at this, Concordia University's annual Shakespeare Authorship Studies Conference, that many would feel this question I have posed is a merely rhetorical one, which will be answered with a resounding "Yes!" However, as an academic working within an institution and a discourse with certain well-defined constraints, it is important for me, whatever conclusion I reach, to make an appropriately academic case for what I say and for what I shall propose. In the initial section of this paper, I wish to trace the events of the past academic year that led me to where I stand today, but I want also, in the subsequent section, to make an academic case for my claim that the Shakespeare Authorship Question is, indeed, a suitable subject for academia and that, in this context, the Authorship Question's time has come.

In June 2005, I was asked to write a short article for an English fortnightly magazine concerning the latest controversy involving Shakespeare and Authorship. Mark Rylance, Artistic Director at Shakespeare's Globe Theatre in London, had made the claim—not new as it turned out—that Shakespeare's works had very possibly been written by a team of authors headed by Francis Bacon. In this article, I cited the usual academic objections to such a claim, as well as expressing myself in the typical ironic tone adopted by academics when asked for their opinion on the Authorship Question in general. In my defence, it is worth pointing out that I also took the opportunity to ridicule the "fact of Stratford"; its theme-park ambience and the many "half-truths" on which it is built. Writing this article sparked an interest in the subject for me, one that led me to attend a conference at the Globe on the Authorship Question a few weeks later. It was here that my attitude began to change and that I began to understand certain things. First, I began to get a grasp on the fact that the Authorship Question gives rise to a good deal of conflict, a conflict in which the opposing sides are clearly demarcated. On the one side are, generally, those non-academics who believe that the Authorship Question is, at the very least, a legitimate question. On the other is the Academic Establishment who will have no truck with the Question and regard it as illegitimate in those terms. Second, I began to understand that the Question is not purely one of isolated individuals doing their own, unconnected research. This is a world populated by groups and texts which have shared beliefs and shared interests. Third, I came to realise that it is a global phenomenon which generates vast quantities of both online and paper research. Fourth, and perhaps most importantly, I came to realise that this phenomenon has a history stretching back to the lifetime of Shakespeare himself.

Not long after this conference I was asked to write another article, this time for the *Times Higher Educational Supplement*. As I wrote it, I felt that certain things had changed in me, the most noticeable of which was my dropping of an ironic tone when discussing the Authorship Question. That is not to say that I began to make a case for another author of Shakespeare's work. Rather, I suggested that many of the perceptions of those involved in the Authorship Question (the vast majority of whom were non-academics) needed to be treated with more respect by the Academic Establishment. I felt this to be the case for two reasons. First, much of the research that has been done and is being carried out as we speak is of the highest quality. It is true that much other research carried out in the name of the Authorship Question is somewhat weak in an academic sense, and this causes some of the better research to be undermined. However, as stated and without wishing to sound pompous (as an academic), much of the research is of an academic standard. Second, I feel that orthodox Shakespeare criticism is, to some extent at least, indebted to the sorts of ideas that the non-academic Authorship researchers have been suggesting for many years. One such important area—one which I concentrated upon in my article—is that of Shakespeare and collaboration. One does not have to look too far back to find orthodox Shakespeare criticism stating that very few of the works were written in collaboration. Furthermore, this criticism generally insisted that if collaboration did take place in one or two plays, the plays generally were poor and the sections that made them poor were not written by Shakespeare. It is worth saying that many conclusions such as these were based on poor research, of the type that orthodox scholars routinely accuse non-academics of producing. Equally significant, however, is that fact that many of the plays are now considered to have been produced in collaboration, as was normal among playwrights at the time, and they are none the worse for it. To my mind, this development within the field

of Shakespeare criticism has been one effect of serious inquiry into the Authorship Question and the research carried out in its name. This effect is one that remains unacknowledged by the Academic Establishment, however. It was difficult to communicate all of these ideas in one short article, but as I said, my ideas on this subject were beginning to crystallise.

As luck would have it, the next step in this process occurred in-house, in my own institution. My newly appointed Head of School (to which office I have since succeeded) was seeking to make a splash within the institution by suggesting many new graduate programmes in English and other subjects in order to increase our postgraduate numbers. As one can imagine, trying to carve out a unique Shakespeare niche for oneself in a London university is difficult. All of the major universities in London run at least one Shakespeare MA, and many of them are very well established and are run by well-known academics. I approached our Head of School with an idea to run a Shakespeare and Authorship MA which would be the first of its kind, not just nationally, but in the world. When he heard this, he went for it at once, without, to his credit, making any of the typically ironic comments regarding the nature of the subject. Colleagues generally were more sceptical, and one or two were hostile. However, the mere fact that it would be the first of its kind in the world and that it could, therefore, recruit well won the day. As strange as it sounds, the Shakespeare Authorship Question was seen as a potential "earner." Since then, the first major administrative hurdle in approving the course has been cleared and a program of study is in place. As a preface to this, I am running a year 3 module: "Shakespeare: The Return of the Author," from this September onwards.

In order to formalise my burgeoning interest in the area and in seeking to broaden the institutional basis for the subject, my next step was to contact a number of academics, actors, journalists and various specialists with a view to setting up a so-called research network into the Authorship Question. This culminated in a funding bid to the Arts and Humanities Research Council of the UK which, if successful, will provide £30,000 over two years in order to set up seminars and discussions with interested parties and will culminate in a major international conference, the publication of an edited collection of articles and the launch of a paper journal specifically about the Authorship Question. I await the outcome of that bid with excitement and trepidation.

This is where I am now in academic and institutional terms. In theoretical terms, I have some work to do in order to convince my academic colleagues that this is the way to go. For I have set myself the task of bringing the Authorship Question into academia, legitimating its status within the institution and removing the stigma that academics attach to the whole subject. This is not to suggest that all the work carried out by non-academics is not enormously valuable or indeed needs the legitimating approval of academia. On the contrary, it is my desire to enlighten academia, to broaden the horizons of many in the institution, to demonstrate that the Shakespeare Authorship Question is a phenomenon that bears analysis. In short, that the Shakespeare Authorship Question is a legitimate question. What follows is the academic case I shall make.

I stated that the year 3 course I wish to run is entitled "Shakespeare: The Return of the Author." I have chosen this title for specific reasons, as it strikes me as one which encapsulates a contemporary cultural reality. Many academics and, I am sure, non-academics were surprised at the publication in 2004 of Stephen Greenblatt's biography of Shakespeare, *Will in the World*. This surprise was based in a perceived about-turn in Greenblatt's critical practice, in the sense that he seemed to legitimate a type of discourse that has traditionally been considered by academia as lacking in scholarly rigour. Scholars generally agreed that details of Shakespeare's life were sketchy, to say the least, and that to fill in the gaps to the extent that Greenblatt

does was questionable. Greenblatt has not been alone in this, however. 2005 saw the publication of James Shapiro's *1599: A Year In the Life of William Shakespeare*, another text which, to all intents and purposes, fills in the enormous gap of the known movements and events of Shakespeare's life in this particular year with *pure supposition*. Shapiro manages to do this by inserting many historically verified occurrences in and around the supposed important events of Shakespeare's day-to-day existence for this one year of 1599. Greenblatt is much more ambitious in that he fills in the gaps for the entire life of Shakespeare (and, indeed, Shakespeare's father, wife, children and a couple of neighbours). However, the important point that needs to be made here is the fact that these academics, among the most renowned of their generation, have turned to this genre *at this point in time*.

In many senses, these works by Greenblatt and Shapiro are not the first of their kind. Richard Wilson's *Secret Shakespeare*, though defined as an academic book—whereas Greenblatt's and Shapiro's books are seen to be more of the genre of popular biography— is essentially a certain kind of Shakespeare biography, one which wears its agenda very clearly on its sleeve. However, I feel it is true to say that all Shakespeare criticism is, to some extent or other, a negotiation of the biography—both known and supposed— of Shakespeare. One need merely scan the introductions to various editions of the plays (the Arden series, for example) to see all sorts of references to what Shakespeare must have been thinking, how he must have seen the world, how various events must have affected him and so on. In this sense, then, it becomes clear that Greenblatt, Shapiro, Wilson et al are not really doing anything new or radical in terms of their critical trajectory. What is new is that they are dropping the old pretence of academic objectivity, *laying to rest the idea that facts ought to outweigh supposition in academic treatises*, rejecting what has become the conventional, unquestioned belief in the idea of the "Death of the Author."

This notion of Roland Barthes regarding the author—as a mere conduit of language and therefore unable to control or even greatly affect interpretation of the text—as essentially missing and therefore unimportant became something of an unquestioned tenet of poststructuralist criticism. Literary critics whose views adhered to the general constraints of this kind of criticism, such as New Historicists and Cultural Materialists, found Barthes' perception to be most enabling in their own work, one of the outcomes being the new attention paid to context that very much defined the practices of these schools. Thus, we have the notorious essays of the New Historicists which, controversially at the time, linked all sorts of apparently non-related historical events and texts to the actual literary text they were examining—very often a work of Shakespeare's. The prioritisation of context became a conventional academic practice in this field, and the author was, on the surface at least, relegated to a position of mere scribe. However, a brief review of Greenblatt's earlier work reveals that, while espousing the "Death of the Author," he always found a special place for Shakespeare. One need merely reconsider, for example, the implications of Greenblatt's assertions that Shakespeare's drama was "a primary expression of Renaissance power" ("Invisible Bullets" 45), or that his plays functioned to "impose normative ethical patterns on the urban masses" (*Renaissance Self-Fashioning* 254). In these assertions, Greenblatt is providing Shakespeare with agency, stating that, as an author, Shakespeare is attempting to do certain things with his writing and, furthermore, that he succeeded. *In this scenario, the author is not dead*; he is very much alive and attempting to manipulate his audience according to his own ideological agenda. Greenblatt's latest work carries this idea to its natural destination. For, with his production of a biography on Shakespeare, Greenblatt merely makes explicit what had been sub-textual in his earlier work. Like the biographies written by Shapiro and Wilson then, Greenblatt's text marks an explicit ac-

knowledgement of the primary place of the writer in academic criticism, and in doing so heralds the "Return of the Author." The repercussions of this for both academic and non-academic work in general, and the Shakespeare Authorship Question in particular, are profound.

One of the reasons I believe that the Authorship Question is one that ought to have academic standing is that it produces its own, well-populated genre. By this I mean that, since its inception, the Question has given rise to books, journals, collected editions, magazines and, more recently, an enormous electronic body of work that is explicitly about the Authorship Question itself. This historical body of work is itself worthy of academic examination as a discrete and vibrant genre which reflects evolving cultural, social and political developments. For this reason I feel that academia ought, if for no other reason that I suggest, to turn its attention to the important textual history of the Authorship Question. It is worth reiterating here that I would go further in terms of genre because, as I stated earlier, all works of criticism concerning Shakespeare are, to a greater or lesser extent, negotiations of the facts of his life. However, returning to the primary genre generated by the Authorship Question itself, it is true to say that the dominant element of this genre is that of biography, both of Shakespeare and of other writers. Generally speaking, the facts of the lives of the writers, whether of Shakespeare or any other, are matched to the facts of the plays and poems, and conclusions are then drawn. This is, of course, precisely the methodology of Greenblatt, Shapiro and Wilson. The conclusions may well be different, but the ways in which these conclusions are reached are the same. Whether the texts are by non-academics, therefore, or by some of the most respected scholars in the world of Shakespeare criticism alive today, the methodologies used are identical. For one school, the author has returned and is again knocking on the door of the academic establishment. For the other school, the "non-academic," the author has never been away. But given the commensurability of methodology, it is apparent that the Shakespeare Authorship Question, as an academic entity, ought also to be knocking on the door. The practice indulged in by academics themselves suggests that the Authorship Question's time has come.

The fact that the methodologies and the resultant texts of both the Academic Establishment and those non-academics working in the field are so similar brings into stark contrast the basis upon which the Authorship Question remains on the margins of academic acceptability. It is true to say, and we have all experienced it in one form or another, that academics in general have little time for the Authorship Question, regarding it as silly at best and as a time-wasting, meaningless hobby at worst. Time and again it is possible to read of academics who reject the question out of hand, often in a most aggressive and contemptuous manner. It is true to say, and this is another aspect of the subject which fascinates me, that the Authorship Question gives rise to passions—on both sides—that research into almost any other subject singularly fails to do. However, returning to my main point, it is therefore true to say that academics very often reject the Authorship Question despite the fact that many (non-academic) researchers in the field use the same methodology as they and produce research which is every bit as scholarly as their own. Academic research which suggests, as it has repeatedly, that Shakespeare was a proto-feminist, a proto-Marxist, a monarchist, a Puritan, or whatever, is no more or less academic than research which believes that Shakespeare did not write certain plays or that someone else did. This suggests that the research undertaken under the rubric of the Authorship Question is rejected by academics not because of its methodology or even its conclusions. It is rejected because it is, simply put, produced by non-academics. It is outside of the discourse, outside of the game. This point is proved by the academic acceptance of Richard Wilson's claim, in *Secret Shakespeare*, that Shakespeare

was a Roman Catholic, the evidence being one occurrence of the name "Shakeshafte" in the accounts of a noble family who lived nowhere near Stratford. *Wilson's thesis is no more convincing, in terms of evidence, than thousands of texts produced by non-academics considering the Authorship Question.* Indeed, it is more questionable in many ways. But he is an academic and the game requires that only the official players can play. Supporters are not allowed on the field.

If we continue to concentrate on this point a little longer, we come to realise that, in fact, much academic Shakespearean criticism is, at the very least, highly questionable. Indeed, one need merely revisit Greenblatt's defining and hugely influential work to understand this. Is he really saying, as he seems to be in *Renaissance Self-Fashioning*, that given the evidence in plays such as *The Merry Wives of Windsor*, Shakespeare is writing in order to "foster psychic mobility in the service of Elizabethan power" (253)? Is he certain, again given the evidence, that in writing plays such as *Coriolanus* Shakespeare approached "his culture … as dutiful servant" (253), content to support the reconstitution of State power? As many academics would say when considering the works generated within the field of the Shakespeare Authorship Question, the evidence does not, it would seem, support the conclusions except, perhaps, in the mind of the critic. That would be fine and we could leave it at that, of course—except, as we all know, Greenblatt's work and his conclusions have been enormously influential; indeed, they very much have determined what it has been possible to say within academic Shakespearean criticism for a couple of decades at least.

While Greenblatt had his many supporters, there was academic criticism both of his methodology and his conclusions throughout the 1980s and 1990s. However, he was never marginalised or ridiculed by his critics, and his conclusions were never dismissed out of hand. Rather, countless academic essays and articles appeared that refuted Greenblatt's conclusions using alternative evidence and drawing alternative conclusions. Thus, although Greenblatt's initial conclusions could be said to be both questionable and extraordinary in many ways, they were taken seriously and argued against rationally. It is precisely this that I wish to demand for the Shakespeare Authorship Question: Not that the conclusions drawn by any one scholar practising within its constraints must be accepted or liked, but only that they are not rejected out of hand due to prejudice rather than rational examination. The conclusions often will be extraordinary and questionable, but if they are, then they should be questioned; they should be given the same treatment that Greenblatt's extraordinary conclusions are given.

That Greenblatt's work of the 1980s and 1990s is so different from his latest work, *Will in the World*, does signify, as I have already said, a reorientation of focus in terms of Shakespeare studies in academia. This shift has much to do with the turn away from the kinds of political criticism embodied in the likes of New Historicism and Cultural Materialism and the recent turn toward something new. The areas of concern which have dominated Shakespeare studies in academia over the last thirty years or so - Shakespeare and Post colonialism, Shakespeare and Feminism, Shakespeare and Theory and so on—have begun to subside, and there is something of a void or, at least, a transitional gap in which various new types of criticism are appearing. Thus, one reads of the "New Textualism" or "Post-New Historicism" and so on. This gap, however, signifies an opportunity for the types of criticism done under the name of the Shakespeare Authorship Question. By this, I do not simply mean the type of research that nominates an alternative author, although that must have its place. I also mean research into areas of Shakespeare and collaboration and into the cultural and political processes that have made Shakespeare what he is today in our societies. So when I see the opportunity for the Authorship Question within academia, I conceptualise that opportunity in the wid-

est sense, as one which could see the entire refiguring of the ways in which Shakespeare and Shakespeare studies are viewed in the twenty-first century.

The task that is being set here is a great one, without doubt. There is a call for academia to review the way it goes about things and to open itself to legitimate questions. It is worth considering the fact that refusing to legitimate the Shakespeare Authorship Question within academia is perhaps understandable given what is at stake; perhaps Shakespearean scholars have resisted legitimizing the Authorship Question because it could undermine the whole edifice of which they are a part. There may be an understandable sense of threat on their part. Furthermore, the edifice is not only academic, but also has an economic base which will be enormously difficult to refigure. This is something I have considered before, and I wish to quote here an extended section of the article, which attempted to be humorous, that first expressed my interest in this subject. In it, I wished to outline the resistance that exists to any notion of an alternative to Shakespeare, a resistance embodied in

> Stratford-upon-Avon, the chocolate box town in "Shakespeare Country" with shops called *Julius Cheeser*, *Henry the Fitter* and *As You Like Kit*.... This resistance is hardly surprising given the fact that, as is clear from ambling through the streets of Stratford, there is simply too much at stake. For Shakespeare is an industry, a global brand whose name, like that of Nike or Shell, will be protected by those who have an interest in this industry and who simply cannot have their brand maligned or undermined. The same is true of academia. Hundreds of courses are run every year with titles such as "Shakespeare" or "Shakespeare and History" or "Shakespeare and Hats" that to suddenly give in to the idea that Shakespeare was some-

body else is simply unthinkable. Imagine the reaction of the publishing companies when faced with all of those books to pulp! There would be mass suicide in universities and publishers the world over and Stratford would become a ghost town of roving wild dogs feeding upon the thousands of dumped boxes of Shakespeare Éclairs, Tempest Toffees and Coriolanus Cough Drops. The many American and Japanese tourists would find somewhere else to go; a Bacon fun park perhaps, or 'Marlowe's Marvellous Merrieworld' (43-44).

The tone is, as I said, ironic, but the point is a serious one. The Shakespeare Authorship Question, in economic terms, threatens the efficacy of the brand and is therefore resisted. In academic terms, both the practice and the status of many individuals and groups are at stake giving rise to the same resistance. The methodology used and the conclusions reached by those working under the name of the Shakespeare Authorship Question are not the reasons for this resistance, although it is always claimed that they are. The differences between research that is academically sanctioned and work that is not has little to do with the quality of the research and much to do with having the power to judge this research. For those in academia who are standing in judgment, the entire subject of the Shakespeare Authorship Question threatens this power.

Universities are traditionally institutions at which, to use a cliché, "the truth is sought." While this is indeed a cliché, for most academics it contains the kernel of the reason for which they came to academia in the first place. Years spent within the institution, pledging much time and effort to the efficacy of one's research, can cloud this initial desire and deform the reasons for this investment. My desire is for Shakespeare scholars to rediscover this initial spark and to admit to

the provisional nature of their own subject. Is one's area of research so precious that one will deny the possibility of its compromised nature merely to ensure its continuation? I am certain that the vast majority of Shakespeare scholars would answer such a question with a resounding "No!" The MA program I wish to begin is the first step in a process which, I hope, will allow both students and academics the sort of self-reflexivity that will enable them to confidently and resoundingly say "No!" and will allow them, when faced with the question, "Is the Shakespeare Authorship Question a suitable subject for academia?" to answer with a resounding "Yes!"

Works Cited

Barthes, Roland. "The Death of the Author." Ed. and Trans. Stephen Heath. London: Flamingo, 1984. 142-148.

Greenblatt, Stephen. *Renaissance Self-Fashioning*. Chicago: The University of Chicago Press, 1984.

—. "Invisible Bullets: Renaissance Authority and its Subversion, *Henry IV* and *Henry V*." Eds. Jonathan Dollimore and Alan Sinfield. Manchester: Manchester University Press, 1985. 18-47.

—. *Will in the World: How Shakespeare Became Shakespeare*. London: Pimlico, 2005.

Leahy, William. "The Business of Bill." *New Statesman* 134/4745 (June 2005): 42-44.

—. "Bard, by any name, is still sweet." *Times Higher Educational Supplement* 1701 (June 2005). 14.

Shapiro, James. *1599: A Year in the Life of William Shakespeare*. London: Faber & Faber, 2005.

Wilson, Richard. *Secret Shakespeare: Studies in Theatre, Religion and Resistance*. Manchester: Manchester University Press, 2004.

Edward de Vere's *Antony and Cleopatra*

Michael Delahoyde, Ph.D.
Assistant Professor of English, Washington State University

Upon receiving distressing news about Antony, Cleopatra utters to her lady-in-waiting, "I am pale, Charmian" (2.5.59)—not "I feel faint" nor even a self-contradictory "I am struck speechless." "I am pale" indicates that Cleopatra is objectifying herself, making a pronouncement as if she were watching herself from the vantage point of one of her own many awestruck spectators.

Shakespeare's Cleopatra is a drama queen, literally and colloquially. The historical Cleopatra, due to Roman propaganda vilifying her, serves still as a prototype for all patriarchal hatchet jobs on women in power. But the Cleopatra of Shakespeare's *Antony and Cleopatra* is the original "diva," and we would not have Scarlett O'Hara or *All My Children*'s Erica Kane without Shakespeare's dramatic portrait. It's a complex phenomenon of characterization to try to explain, involving outrageous egomania, or "narcissistic exuberance" (Bloom 551), made tolerable through an ironic self-awareness, but when played correctly it's cheeky and charming. Any frustrated theater major who believes in reincarnation insists that s/he lived as this Queen of the Nile, although apparently the historical Cleopatra was rather unprepossessing; yet she obviously knew how to enter a room, how to generate a mystique, and how to scintillate.

And, with the concurrent character study of Mark Antony that the play offers, Shakespeare gives us a look at the first self-aware celebrity couple. The very first scene of the play begins with two of Antony's soldiers who, like skulking tabloid reporters, snipe about the diva and the current "Mr. Cleopatra" but also help elevate their initial entrance into an event, with the histrionic announcement, "Behold and see" (1.1.13). Of course, this proto-photo-op, like Antony's

"dotage" according to the commentators, already "O'erflows the measure" of spectacle (1.1.1-2) with Cleopatra's posse in tow and what will eventually become the cliché of the obligatory fanning eunuchs.

That my celebrity-culture analogy here is several hundred years anachronistic justifies to one Stratfordian why my skepticism regarding the absence of any letters from Will Shakspere—not one saved by any early celebrity-signature hound—is the "lamest" bit of Oxfordiana ever to contribute to his apoplexy. Granted, gladly (notwithstanding Shakspere's own son-in-law Dr. Hall's journal recording of his Drayton sighting—big deal!); but then what inspired Shakespeare to write this play? Are we again to exercise our already overstrained Greenblattian imagination and picture Stratford Will late one afternoon in early February of 1607 realizing that he just had to resurrect a 1640-year-old story because of its gripping geopolitical tensions and its snazzy battles on land and sea which the dramatist doesn't even try to represent on stage? Or that though historically remote, geographically irrelevant, and dramaturgically recalcitrant.... But, let me not be guilty of a straw-man argument against the custodians of the straw-man playwright. Here are specific explanations for *Antony and Cleopatra* on the part of the orthodox critics, all of them abstract and bloodless. "The whole play is an exposition of *concordia discors*," says Waddington (qtd. in Deats 20), as if that's a kind of compelling creative stimulus not to be denied. Similarly paradoxical, Marilyn French declares the play Shakespeare's "broadest and most realistic study of constancy," featuring two characters remembered for their inconstancy (251-252). Harold C. Goddard, who usually is found to be brilliantly insightful and down-to-earth, calls *Antony and Cleopatra* "a study in the power of personality versus the impersonality of power" (II 185); but that's as far as it goes in terms of any motive for the writing of the play. The stultifyingly orthodox Stanley Wells, Stratford's Shakespeare Trust front-man, considers the play an illustration of another abstract though at least more human principle: tragedy "brought about by the clash between the demands of a private love-relationship and those of the outside world" (302). While other critics cannot decide whether the play is "a condemnation of irresponsible lust" or "a celebration of a magnificent passion transcending traditional moral laws" (qtd. in Deats 1), we may guess that Rabkin and Adelman send Harold Bloom into fits by declaring that the play functions "not only as a study in ambivalence, but—in an anticipation of both Derrida and deconstruction—as a study in indecidibility" (qtd. in Deats 11).

Despite the many such pronouncements put forth to account for the play, none can convince anyone that these abstractions come anywhere near the true impulse for Shakespeare's undertaking. Honest attempts towards interpretation, often by these same orthodox critics, keep coming back to the main characters. Wells has misgivings about that fact, since the "central characters invite us not so much to identify with them as to wonder at them; an impression that is reinforced by the fact that they are given virtually no soliloquies in which to reveal themselves to the audience" (300). But the much-lauded Mark Van Doren distinguished *Antony and Cleopatra* among the Shakespeare tragedies in terms of the characters vis-à-vis their general contexts: "The intensity of Hamlet, Othello, Lear, and Macbeth was derived from their respective predicaments; the intensity of Antony and Cleopatra seems to be generated in themselves" (237). So, towards determining the actual sources of inspiration behind this play, the impulse to consider real-life persons represented by the main characters is—though characteristically Oxfordian!—the most sensible.

Thinking the play a product of the early 1600s, attempts have been made by a few orthodox scholars to identify Antony and Cleopatra with Essex and Queen Elizabeth, but to most this seems "far-fetched" since they didn't "forsake Empire to follow sensuality," and the Rebellion does not match the play's politics (Morris 272), although Fulke Greville destroyed an *Antony and Cleopatra* play of his own after the Essex Rebellion "because he feared that his characters Antony, Cleopatra, and Caesar might be construed as portraits of Essex, Queen Elizabeth, and Robert Cecil" (Jiménez 3). Even so, can there be serious doubt that Elizabeth at least partly lies behind the portrait of Shakespeare's Cleopatra?

> [B]oth were queens regnant, both used courtship as a mainstay of their statecraft, and both attained apotheosis of a sort as female deities. . . . Both treated courtiers and maids of honor roughly; both affected illness or other shams to give false impressions; both were marvelously facile in foreign languages; both governed their kingdoms with skill; both desired amusement and revelry; both wore gorgeous apparel; both were witty. . . . Both used feminine wiles to gain political advantage; both were consummate actresses, but both could show the woman behind—or within—the queen. (Rinehart 81, 83)

Echoing Enobarbus' praise of Cleopatra— "Age cannot wither her, nor custom stale / Her infinite variety" (2.2.234-235)—Lytton Strachey, in his biography of Elizabeth, acknowledged, "The variations in her own behaviour were hardly less frequent than nature's" (qtd. in Clark 351).

There are more precise parallels too, literally striking ones. Scenes of the play closely resemble a few at the Elizabethan royal court. For example, a messenger brings news of Antony, sending Cleopatra into histrionic agonies: "Antonio's dead!" (2.5.26). After

Cleopatra's microscopic examination of any available nuances in body language or visage, the messenger is finally able to report that Antony married Octavia. Cleopatra utters the line, "I am pale, Charmian" (2.5.59), but then pitches a fit and slaps the messenger about: "the Folio directs that Cleopatra 'Strikes him down,' 'Strikes him,' and 'She hales him up and downe.'" And "for these aspects of her character, too, Shakespeare had not far to look for a model. His own queen, brilliant and captivating, was yet capable of undignified spurts of rage, hysterical nerve storms, and public flirtation" (Morris 275). Ambassadors such as the Spanish Mendoza and other witnesses continually refer to her tantrums (Morris 275-276). Cleopatra's outburst is paralleled by "Elizabeth's slapping her maids of honor and boxing the ears of even more important persons. Elizabeth once handled a maid of honor so roughly, 'telt liberall bothe with bloes and yevell words', that she broke the maid's finger" (Wilson 107, qtd. in Rinehart 85).

Although distraught, Cleopatra seems to have the resourcefulness to have her ladies grill the messenger for information about Antony's new wife: "the feature of Octavia, her years, / Her inclination;... / The color of her hair" (2.5.112-114). Some scenes later (3.3), Cleopatra herself solicitously interrogates the messenger she had terrorized earlier. She wants to know about Octavia's height, voice, gait, the shape of her face, hair color, and so forth. Cleopatra twists his description so that she can declare Octavia "dull of tongue, and dwarfish" (3.3.16).

Not published until 1683, Sir James Melville's *Memoirs* record incidents occurring in 1564 between this emissary of Mary, Queen of Scots and Queen Elizabeth: "He describes in detail Queen Elizabeth's anxious inquiries about the appearance and accomplishments of her dreaded rival" (Morris 272; cf. Rinehart 82ff).

How are these undignified parallels accounted for? Stratfordians can say only that William Shakspere "must have seen and heard the queen, besides hearing continual talk about her" (Morris 271). Another back-pedals:

> It is not, of course, claimed that Shakespeare had heard of Elizabeth's inquiries about her rival.... It is merely suggested that in two scenes where Cleopatra's conduct has been stigmatized as unregal, Shakespeare came uncannily close to contemporary examples of queenly behavior....
> (Muir 200)

What rubbish. Would this not have been sufficient to have Shakspere dragged in for a questioning, mutilation, branding and imprisonment, if he were the playwright?

The Oxfordian solution may not be the only resolution to these issues, but it is the only explanation that can account for numerous other features and nuances of *Antony and Cleopatra*, and it provides the only satisfactory answer as to why this play came into existence.

We turn to Antony, the "masker and reveler" as he is called in *Julius Caesar* (5.1.62). Concerning the historical events between about 40 BCE and 30 BCE when Antony and Cleopatra died, Shakespeare's universally acknowledged source for *Antony and Cleopatra* is *The Life of Marcus Antonius* from *Plutarch's Lives*, translated from Greek to French and, in 1579, from French to English by Thomas North (Asimov 317ff). Although Oxford's purchase of Plutarch's works in French, along with the famous Geneva Bible and a volume of Chaucer, was recorded by Cecil in 1570 (Anderson 41), North's translation seems to be the greater influence. More than North's sometimes ambiguous material for which Shakespeare either provides hints of explanation (such as Cleopatra's diplomacy to Octavius' messenger) or which he leaves enigmatic (Antony's emotional behavior before his men), the playwright also adopted details from North's translation: references to "bankets" (banquets), for example, and the famous passage in which Enobarbus describes Cleopatra's grand entrance on her luxurious barge, which is nearly a verse transcription of North's account.

A reading of North, however, also reveals a wealth of materials not included in the play but which would have caught Oxford up inextricably in Antony's story. It is ultimately impossible for de Vere not to have identified with Antony. Plutarch's biography of the Roman fallen hero begins with Antony's high-profile family background. Almost immediately, we hear of Antony's first troubles:

> Now Antonius being a fayer younge man, and in the pryme of his youth: he fell acquainted with Curio, whose friendship and acquaintance (as it is reported) was a plague vnto him. For he was a dissolute man, giuen over to all lust and insolence, who was to haue Antonius the better at his commaundement, trained him on into great follies, and vaine expences vpon women, in rioting & banketing. So that in short time, he brought Antonius into a maruelous great det, & too great for one of his yeres. (397)

Oxford's financial struggles from early on and the disapproval he met with for his bohemian periods—attributable in great part to Cecil, both the disapproval and the debt—would have struck a familiar chord during Oxford's first reading of this biography. As early as 1573, Cecil was prudishly bitching in letters about the company the young Oxford was keeping (Nelson 114).

Antony's travel to Greece and his military exploits next would have inspired de Vere's envy. But he could take comfort in a biographical parallel simply involving a substitution from martial to literary arts:

> Futhermore, things that seeme intollerable in other men, as to boast commonly, to ieast with one or other, to drinke like a good fellow with euery body, to sit with the souldiers when they dine, and to eate and drinke with them souldier-

like: it is incredible what wonderfull loue it wanne him amongest them. . . . But besides all this, that which most procured his rising and aduauncement, was his liberalitie, who gaue all to the souldiers, and kept nothing for him selfe. (399)

With his literary circle of the late 1570s as his "soldiery," this describes Oxford as well as it does Antony. Records show Oxford's former servants acknowledging "his swete liberality" (Nelson 326).

Even though, as Plutarch reports, once back in Rome Antony supposedly committed untold "great insolencies" and outrages, was guilty of the "greatest faultes [and] deserued most blame":

> Caesar notwithstanding, when he returned from the warres of Spayne, made no reckoning of the complaints that were put vp against him: but contrarily, bicause he found him a hardy man, & a valliant Captaine, he employed him in his chiefest affayres, and was in no whit deceiued in his opinion of him. (401)

Charlton Ogburn acknowledges of Oxford that "none other of her subjects was accorded such latitude by the Queen" (qtd. in Nelson 493). Even his detractors noted the favoritism Oxford enjoyed through the 1570s from England's "Caesar"—Elizabeth. This was recognized first in the early '70s, but even in 1579 Fulke Greville certifies for the record that Oxford is "Superlative in the Princes favour" (qtd. in Nelson 189).

How could Oxford not see himself as a modern-day Antony when he read about the lifestyle Antony enjoyed in Rome?

> In this house they did nothing but feast, daunce, & maske: and him selfe passed away the time in hearing of foolish playes, or in marrying these plaiers, tumblers, ieasters, & such sort of people. (403)

... or even away from Rome?

> Antonius liuing merily & quietly abroad . . . he easely fell againe to his old licentious life. For straight one Anaxenor a player of the citherne, Xoutus a player of the flutes, Metrodorus a tombler, and such a rabble of minstrels & fit ministers for the pleasures of Asia (who in finenes & flattery passed all the other plagues he brought with him out of Italie). (411)

If Oxford did not already replicate Antony in the social sphere, then he must have modelled himself after the Roman captain once having read Plutarch:

> He had a noble minde, as well to punish offendors, as to reward well doers: and yet he did exceede more in geuing, then in punishing. Now for his outragious manner of railing he commonly vsed, mocking and flouting of euerie man: that was remedied by it selfe. For a man might as boldly exchaunge a mock with him, & he was as well contented to be mocked, as to mock others. (412)

When did de Vere undertake his mission to raise the practice of railing to a fine art? We know he was accused of launching into rails, and former servants Faunt and Wotton testify to his "raginge deameanore" in 1573 (qtd. in Nelson 96). Though panicked and attempting to save his own traitorous neck, Arundel's sixth point of accusation against Oxford specified his "raylinge at Francis Sowthwell for commending the Qwenes singeinge one night" (qtd. in Nelson 207) and, more generally, Arundel claims that "in raylinge of all estates he over runnes him spareinge no woman be she never so virtuous nor any man be he never so honourable, and this beast beinge never restrained from this libertie of raylinge" (qtd. in Nelson 204). We know Shakespeare appreciated the sublime dramatic

beauty of a devastating rail, of vituperatory abuse, such as Kent's assessment of Oswald in *King Lear* as

> A knave, a rascal, an eater of broken meats; a base, proud, shallow, beggarly, three-suited, hundred-pound, filthy worsted-stocking knave; a lily-liver'd action-taking, whoreson, glass-gazing, superserviceable, finical rogue; one-trunk-inheriting slave; one that wouldst be a bawd in way of good service, and art nothing but the composition of a knave, beggar, coward, pandar, and the son and heir of a mungril bitch; one whom I will beat into clamorous whining, if thou deni'st the least syllable of thy addition. (2.2.15-24)

So, in numerous ways, including idiosyncratic personal behavior, Oxford found himself reflected in Antony. In the play, with lines such as Antony's "If I lose my honor, / I lose myself" (3.4.22-23), we see the results of Oxford's projection of himself into the character.

There can be little doubt as to the identity of his latter-day Cleopatra, particularly when we read this Plutarchan passage:

> For Caesar and Pompey knew her when she was but a young thing, & knew not then what the worlde ment: but nowe she went to Antonius at the age when a womans beawtie is at the prime, and she also of best iudgement . . . Now her beawtie (as it is reported) was not so passing, as vnmatchable of other women, nor yet suche, as vpon present viewe did enamor men with her: but so sweete was her companie and conuersacion, that a man could not possiblie but be taken. And besides her beawtie, the good grace she had to talke and discourse, her curteous nature that tempered her words & dedes, was a spurre that pricked to the quick. Furthermore, besides

all these, her voice and words were maruelous pleasant: for her tongue was an instrument of musicke to diuers sports and pastimes, the which she easely turned to any language that pleased her. (412-413)

No one who knew her, or even who knows her through historical biographies, could fail to think of Elizabeth here. In addition to the Cleopatra/Elizabeth parallels described earlier, Shakespeare is "dubious about Cleopatra's decision to attend the battle, and, indeed, to 'appear there like a man' (as it was said, after the fact, that Queen Elizabeth had done at Tilbury at the time of the defeat of the Spanish Armada, costumed like 'an androgynous martial maiden')" (Garber 736). A 1959 biography of Queen Elizabeth by Elizabeth Jenkins says that Oxford "dazzled the Queen and absorbed the attention of her leisure moments" (qtd. in Ogburn 503); so with Cleopatra representing Elizabeth and himself inhabiting the Antony character, the Ovid enthusiast in de Vere must have thrilled at Plutarch's note about the public reaction to the Antony and Cleopatra match: "there went a rumor in the peoples mouthes, that the goddesse Venus was come to play with the god Bacchus, for the general good of all Asia" (413).

If Eva Turner Clark is right in detecting early versions of *Antony and Cleopatra* and *The Merchant of Venice* in Stephen Gosson's reference to *Ptolome* and *The Jew* as being two exceptionally good plays performed at The Bull in 1579 (349), perhaps being prepped for court production (357), then Oxford's first impetus in writing the play was a Plutarch-inspired glorification of the relationship between Queen Elizabeth and himself. Indeed, even beyond the celebrity couple, the setting of the play really is Elizabeth's court: "the women of the Egyptian court have functions similar in most respects to those of Elizabeth's attendants" (Brown 136). Consider the tone of Charmian's first line: "Lord Alexas, sweet Alexas, most any thing Alexas, almost most

absolute Alexas, where's the soothsayer that you prais'd so to the Queen?" (1.2.1-3). This is not the utterance of a slave. It is that of an idle aristocratic gentlewoman, haughtily posing as world-weary. Furthermore, Queen Elizabeth's chief gentlewoman of the Privy Chamber, Blanche Parry, "made a special study of palmistry" and occasionally told the fortunes of maids of honor (Wilson 7-8; qtd. in Rinehart 85), so this scene of the play echoes court pastimes. Thus, according to the Stratfordian view, at the same Mermaid Tavern—or "Mermaid University" as Joseph Sobran calls it with appropriate sarcasm (7)—in which William Shakspere knocked back the tankards of sack and picked up his legal knowledge, French, natural history, medicine, music, angling, all things Italian, astronomy, horticulture, the nasal inflections of Naples and the vocabulary of falconry, were apparently also circulating thorough accounts—virtual transcriptions—of the doings at the royal court!

Anticipated Oxfordian objections to the somewhat static interpretation of the play as presented so far lead us, however, to another dimension. L. L. Schücking finds that "Cleopatra at the end of the play is totally inconsistent with the character depicted in the first three acts" (qtd. in Muir 198). "In the first acts, she is a courtesan, rather than a queen. We have 'an exhibition of all the arts of harlotry.' Another critic declares that 'she owes more to a study of prostitutes than to a knowledge of how even the worst queens behave'" (Muir 198-199). Antony's obsession with Cleopatra may also strike some as too gruesome to be a representation of Oxford's feelings for Elizabeth. "These strong Egyptian fetters I must break, / Or lose myself in dotage," he frets (1.2.116-117). "Like a right gypsy, hath, at fast and loose, / Beguil'd me to the very heart of loss" (4.10.46-50). As Stanley Wells notes, "Antony's sense of shame at the hold that Cleopatra exerts over him resembles at times the self-disgust of the persona of the sonnets' relationship with his dark lady" (302-303). And I believe, at least in her first iteration, the Dark Lady was Anne Vavasor, the maid-of-honor with whom de Vere had an affair and an illegitimate son, for which he and she were imprisoned. To Antony, Cleopatra is the "serpent of old Nile" (1.5.25); and the 16th-century portrait of Anne Vavasor certainly shows her looking serpentine. The elder Ogburns, in *The Oxfordian*, also feel that "the Egyptian Queen was partially Anne Vavasor" (259), the original "Dark Lady" in Oxford's life (263).

One of my former students, Natanya Moore, had this impression on reading the play:

> Not until Antony and Cleopatra end up trapped "aloft" in her monument does Cleopatra mention her son. One historical detail omitted from Shakespeare's play is that Cleopatra's son was considered by the Romans to be illegitimate. I can't help being reminded of de Vere and Vavasor in the Tower with their illegitimate son. Vavasor had been a lady-in-waiting to Elizabeth, and the main female character in the play second to Cleopatra is her lady-in-waiting, Charmian.

> Perhaps de Vere is pointing out Elizabeth's lack of empathy. After all, she was often accused of being illegitimate, not only by her sister Mary but also by her own father. Henry VIII passed several acts declaring her illegitimate, then legitimate again, and back and forth. Although Cleopatra's son is a very minor detail in the play, perhaps de Vere was trying to say, "Hey, Elizabeth! I was bewitched by a dark lady! I know now that I erred, and that my affair with Anne is doomed, but don't forget there is a child to consider." (Moore)

I do think that the play functions, in perhaps its first revision, as an appeal to Elizabeth for compassion and understanding. As Mark Anderson explains, "Much of Shake-speare is thus a palimpsest" (124). The elder Ogburns recognize this: "In our opinion, *Antony and Cleopatra* was drastically revised more than once, and while . . . the Egyptian Queen was partially Anne Vavasor to Oxford's Antony, she was in the last all Elizabeth, with the great drama becoming an epic of Lord Oxford's tragic relationship with his Queen" (Ogburn and Ogburn 259). Thus, Cleopatra works alternately *and often simultaneously* as Elizabeth and Anne Vavasor in a multi-layered result of refashioning of the play. During a performance of the play in the early 1580s, Elizabeth would have recognized herself as Cleopatra—she took plays and entertainments personally (Marcus 144)—and, knowing the play came from Oxford, would also have recognized Vavasor as Cleopatra. I believe that Oxford hoped Elizabeth could see that her situation was not very different from that of her disgraced maid-of-honor and therefore would be compelled to show some mercy.

It becomes inescapable, once we accept the palimpsest notion, that there must have been at least one additional significant revision of the play, resulting in a level reflecting situations in the later years of Oxford's life. When a messenger brings Antony news that Fulvia is dead, Antony laments, "There's a great spirit gone!" (1.2.122). This is just one of many moments in the Shakespeare canon when a character realizes that he did not sufficiently appreciate his wife while she was alive, a phenomenon that Oxfordians have seen as autobiographically reflecting de Vere's regrets over his treatment of his wife Anne Cecil, who died in the late 1580s (Sobran 188). Like Brutus, Posthumus, and apparently Oxford, Antony also receives news of his wife's death while away (187). This parallel would indicate a layer of the play as we now have it being written later than the late 1580s, and I would posit probably at least the late 1590s, due to the treatment of Octavius. The antagonist in *Antony and Cleopatra* may, as the elder Ogburns think, originally have represented Leicester (264). But regarding Antony's next wife in the play, Octavia, Octavius magnanimously states to Antony, "A sister I bequeath you, whom no brother / Did ever love so dearly" (2.2.149-150). Goddard notes that although Octavius objects to the idea of Antony's giving up a kingdom for a "whore," he's willing to fork over a sister for an empire (186), but the greater importance for us here is the brother-in-law relationship.

> Oxford writes of his family and Burghley's as being "knit in alliance." Shakespeare uses the same metaphor more than a dozen times. In *Antony and Cleopatra*, Antony and Octavius Caesar are said to be "forever knit together" by Antony's marriage to Octavia. (Sobran 277)

The brother-in-law Oxford would be thinking of, then, is very likely Robert Cecil. More damning is Octavius' command to a comrade after Antony's death:

> Go with me to my tent, where you
>   shall see
> How hardly I was drawn into this
>   war,
> How calm and gentle I proceeded
>   still
> In all my writings. Go with me,
>   and see
> What I can show in this.
>
>   (5.1.73-77)

In other words, Octavius will immediately set down a revised history as the official record, and at least it's a minor comfort to know that Oxford recognized the empire-building Cecilian tactic. Indications are, then, that in the final version of Antony and Cleopatra, de Vere was thinking of Robert Cecil in the role of Octavius. Despite their shortcomings, even the embarrassing features of both Antony and Cleopatra,

> there is no doubt which side Shakespeare is on. For him . . . an age of chivalry is yielding to one of calculators, sophists, and economists. He is thinking not of Rome but of

England, where upstarts, Puritans, and businessmen are taking over, and the old nobility may soon be extinct. The play may be read as a kind of elegy for Oxford's class and the people it could produce. (Sobran 170)

The elder Ogburns detect traces of the earlier version of the play in which Octavius as antagonist represented Leicester (264), but in the final version, long after Leicester's death and with the ascendancy of Robert Cecil, Leicester was marginalized into the late Julius Caesar role (1166). Cleopatra makes Charmian insist that Antony, not Julius Caesar, is the one true love of her life, and she dismisses the earlier affair as having come during "My salad days, / When I was green in judgment, cold in blood" (1.5.73-74). She uses the phrase not as we do to mean times of romantic poverty or colorful youth, but rather as an image of inexperience and passionlessness. "It is tempting, though unhistorical, to think of her as the original 'Caesar salad.' Alas, that Caesar was a Mexican restauranteur of the 1920s" (Garber 744).

Though indirectly self-eulogizing, Oxford has Cleopatra offer more noble words after the death of Antony: "In his livery / Walk'd crowns and coronets; realms and islands were / As plates dropp'd from his pocket" (5.2.90-92). But Oxford's legacy, as encrypted within this play, truly comes in the playwright's expansion of the role of Plutarch's simple "contrieman" who brings figs to Cleopatra (Plutarch 455). Cleopatra's death is vague in Plutarch's account. That an asp had been among the figs is only a hypothesis, and no snake is found in the tomb afterwards (Plutarch 455). In Shakespeare's version, the man is allowed in, and Cleopatra asks him if he has in his basket "the pretty worm of Nilus there / That kills and pains not" (5.2.243-244). The "worm"—an obsolete Anglo-Saxon term for serpent—is indeed present, and "his biting is immortal" (5.2.246-247). This man is cast as a "clown," and leaves only after some quibbling, wishing Cleopatra "all the joy of the worm" (5.2.260, 279). Richard Whalen has thoroughly explained this enigmatic scene as referring to the immortalizing effects of the efforts of the Queen's "worm," or "Ver." And this reading of the passage confirms what Thomas Nashe had said about de Vere; in his pamphlet *Strange News*, he warns Gabriel Harvey about crossing Oxford:

> Mark him well. He is but a little fellow, but he hath one of the best wits in England. Should he take thee in hand again—as he flieth from such inferior concertation—I prophesy that there would be more gentle readers die of a merry mortality, engendered by the eternal jests he would maul thee with, than there have done of this last infection [plague]. I myself . . . enjoy but a mite of wit in comparison of his talent. (qtd. in Anderson 260)

With the pen as his weapon, Oxford can do considerably more than just shake a spear.

Cleopatra escapes in death, presumably joining Antony on the other side, and even Octavius Caesar's offers a valedictory: "No grave upon the earth shall clip in it / A pair so famous" (5.2.359-360; qtd. in Ogburn 90). Thus, in the end, as I suspect it was at first, *Antony and Cleopatra* serves as a tribute to Elizabeth and the playwright. The elder Ogburns call it a "memorial" (1171) to "the epic of their romance" (1178), so perhaps we might even consider *Antony and Cleopatra* a kind of "monument," as it were. As individuals, Antony and Cleopatra can seem to be a bit much to take, but in the end, and in retrospect, they're certainly preferable to insecure administrators, petty and grasping little Caesars. Historian Lucy Hughes-Hallett explains the phenomenon:

> For all that they [Antony and Cleopatra] were both quite evidently ambitious and energetic workers in government and politics, Cleopatra and her lover, in their Dionysiac

association, are imagined to have slipped the net of social duty. This is what makes them seem so threatening, so abominable to the Apollonian Roman, a type of which Octavius proudly proclaimed himself the prime example. It is also what made their story so attractive. For the dutiful, well-regulated Apollonian, limiting himself to "moderation in all things," must always feel a fleeting envy of the Dionysiac, whose way seems so easy, so self-indulgent, even though it leads in the end to what is, for the Apollonian, the ultimate horror, the annihilation of the self. (98)

We may lament that political forces suppressed de Vere's identity and tried to obliterate his every connection to the Shakespeare works. Though powerful administrators fretted that empires were at stake, an even more powerful imagination, fueled in part by actual lived experiences and human relationships, succeeded in creating a more impressive realm—one that many of us continue working towards restoring to its rightful lord.

Works Cited

Anderson, Mark. *"Shakespeare" By Another Name*. New York: Gotham, 2005.

Antony and Cleopatra. The Riverside Shakespeare. 2nd ed. Boston: Houghton, 1997. 1395-1439.

Asimov, Isaac. *Asimov's Guide to Shakespeare*. New York: Gramercy, 1970.

Bloom, Harold. *Shakespeare: The Invention of the Human*. New York: Riverhead, 1998.

Brown, Elizabeth A. "'Companion Me with My Mistress': Cleopatra, Elizabeth I, and Their Waiting Women." *Maids and Mistresses, Cousins and Queens: Women's Alliances in Early Modern England*. Ed. Susan Frye and Karen Robertson. Oxford: Oxford UP, 1999. 131-145.

Clark, Eva Turner. *Hidden Allusions in Shakespeare's Plays*. Ed. Ruth Loyd Miller. Port Washington: Kennikat, 1974.

Deats, Sara Munson. "Shakespeare's Anamorphic

Drama: A Survey of *Antony and Cleopatra* in Criticism, on Stage, and on Screen." *Antony and Cleopatra: New Critical Essays*. Ed. Sara Deats. New York: Routledge, 2005. 1-94.

French, Marilyn. *Shakespeare's Division of Experience*. New York: Summit, 1981.

Garber, Marjorie. *Shakespeare After All*. New York: Pantheon, 2004.

Goddard, Harold C. *The Meaning of Shakespeare*. Vol. 2. Chicago: U of Chicago P, 1951.

Hughes-Hallett, Lucy. *Cleopatra: Histories, Dreams and Distortions*. New York: Harper, 1990.

Jiménez, Ramon. "Shakespeare in Stratford and London: Five More Eyewitnesses Who Saw Nothing." *Shakespeare Oxford Newsletter* 41.1 (Winter 2005): 3-7.

Julius Caesar. The Riverside Shakespeare. 2nd ed. Boston: Houghton, 1997. 1151-1181.

King Lear. The Riverside Shakespeare. 2nd ed. Boston: Houghton, 1997. 1303-1354.

Marcus, Leah S. "Shakespeare's Comic Heroines, Elizabeth I, and the Political Uses of Androgyny." *Women in the Middle Ages and the Renaissance: Literary and Historical Perspectives*. Ed. Mary Beth Rose. Syracuse: Syracuse UP, 1986. 135-153.

Moore, Natanya. In-class correspondence. 4 April 2005.

Morris, Helen. "Queen Elizabeth I 'Shadowed' in Cleopatra." *Huntington Library Quarterly* 32 (1969): 271-278.

Muir, Kenneth. "Elizabeth I, Jodelle, and Cleopatra." *Renaissance Drama 2* (1969): 197-206.

Nelson, Alan H. *Monstrous Adversary*. Liverpool: Liverpool UP, 2003.

Ogburn, Charlton. *The Mysterious William Shakespeare: The Myth & The Reality*. 2nd ed. McLean: EPM, 1992.

Ogburn, Dorothy and Charlton Ogburn. *This Star of England*. Westport: Greenwood, 1952.

Plutarch. *The Life of Marcus Antonius*. Trans. Thomas North. 1579. *Antony and Cleopatra: A New Variorum Edition of Shakespeare*. Ed. Marvin Spevack. New York: MLA, 1990. 397-455.

Rinehart, Keith. "Shakespeare's Cleopatra and England's Elizabeth." *Shakespeare Quarterly* 23 (1972): 81-86.

Sobran, Joseph. *Alias Shakespeare: Solving the Greatest Literary Mystery of All Time*. New York: Free, 1997.

Van Doren, Mark. *Shakespeare*. 1939. New York: New York Review Books Classics, 2005.

Wells, Stanley. *Shakespeare: A Life in Drama*. New York: Norton, 1995.

Whalen, Richard. "The Queen's Worm." *Shakespeare Oxford Newsletter* 34.2 (Summer 1998): 12-13.

Wilson, Violet A. Queen *Elizabeth's Maids of Honor*. New York: Dutton, 1922.

Antony and Cleopatra: The Women's Voices

Ren Draya, Ph.D.
Professor of English, Blackburn College

Cleopatra, Sir Laurence Olivier once proclaimed, "cannot be explained, she can only be felt" (qtd. in Morales 8). The name alone, Cleopatra—echoed or shouted or whispered—evokes images of woman supreme, a woman of sensuality and excitement and beguilement. Shakespeare's sprawling tragedy, *Antony and Cleopatra*, opens and closes in Alexandria; it is Cleopatra's passionate presence with which Oxford fills and determines the drama.

Most of us can immediately call to mind Enobarbus' description (via Plutarch and North):

> . . . she did lie
> In her pavilion—cloth-of-gold of tissue—
> O'erpicturing that Venus where we see
> The fancy outwork nature.
> (2.2.208-211)

> . . . and Antony,
> Enthroned i' th' marketplace, did sit alone,
> Whistling to the air, which, but for vacancy,
> Had gone to gaze on Cleopatra too.
> (2.2.224-227)

"Overpicturing" means a magnificence greater than the most elaborate of portraits or statues. Cleopatra "overpictures" even Venus. Rare Egyptian, indeed! All creation has stopped to admire her, and the great Mark Antony simply waits and whistles to the air. The first act of this play is Cleopatra's: the first speeches of the play are about her—she is called a "tawny front," a "gypsy," and a "strumpet." All of which make Antony, of course, "a strumpet's fool." In her first appearance, we see Cleopatra

as fiery, extravagant, convincing, cajoling. Next to her, Antony seems a patient Walter Mitty. Thus, from the start, in both language and dramatic presence, the dualities of this great play are laid down: the flamboyant, sensual East vs. the restrained West. Egypt vs. Rome. Love vs. duty. Woman vs. man.

Cleopatra's first line is a request: "If it be love indeed, tell me how much" (1. 1. 14). This seems the dare of a young, very egotistical child: "How much do you love me?" Tactfully, Antony replies: "There's beggary in the love that can be reckoned" (15). Implication: because you are bigger than life, my love for you is boundless—don't ask me to quantify it. This scene, part comic/part romantic, sets a pattern that continues throughout the play. Many of Cleopatra's conversations involve a crescendo of "one-ups-manship" exchanges: a statement or question is offered; it provokes a response; in the next exchange there is increasing exaggeration and expanding hyberbole. Note the progression:

> CLEOPATRA. If it be love indeed, tell me how much.
> ANTONY. There's beggary in the love that can be reckoned.
> CLEOPATRA. I'll set a bourn how far to be beloved.
> ANTONY. Then must thou need find out new heaven, new earth.
> (1. 1. 14-17)

Traversi nicely labels the "superb emotional expansiveness" (81) of the play, and critics have long commented on the richness of the language. Cleopatra's imperious hyperbole stands out. For example, yelling at the messenger who brings news of Antony's marriage to Octavius, Caesar's sister, Cleopatra shrieks: "Thou shalt be whipped with wire and stewed in brine, Smarting in ling'ring pickle!" (2. 5. 66-67). She addresses Antony, at one point, as "Lord of lords, O infinite virtue" (4. 8. 16-17). I could fill pages quoting Cleopatra's extravagant diction, so I offer just one more. It is her response to Antony when he wonders if she has grown coldhearted toward him:

> Ah, dear, if I be so,
> From my cold heart let heaven en-
> gender hail,
> And poison it in the source, and the
> first stone
> Drop in my neck; as it determines,
> so
> Dissolve my life! (3. 13. 161-165)

Her heart could indeed "engender hail"—she is, in her language as in her passions, larger than life.

In addition to Cleopatra's bantering, love-making and commiserating with Antony, we also hear her with her personal satellites— the fluttering women and eunuchs who attend her. She whines, confides, cajoles, rants, bemoans. And we hear those women's voices, too. For example, when a soothsayer tries to assure Charmian and Iras that their fortunes are alike, the following exchange occurs:

> IRAS. But how [alike], but how?
> Give me particulars.
> SOOTHSAYER. I have said.
> IRAS. Am I not an inch of fortune
> better than she?
> CHARMIAN. Well, if you were but
> an inch of fortune better than I,
> where would you choose it?
> IRAS. Not in my husband's nose.
> (1. 2. 58-63)

The sexual quips emphasize Egypt as a place of fruitfulness and fulfillment. Cleopatra's amorous triumphs have created a pervasive atmosphere of sensuality and excess.

Yes, the play opens in a mood of comedy and melodrama. But the realities of Rome quickly intervene: there are political strains as the triumvirate totters and its leaders become foes; there is frequent talk of strate-

gies and battles; there is the news of Fulvia's death (Antony's wife). Perhaps opposition to the eroticism and excess of Antony and Cleopatra—that is, to the world of Egypt—is best exemplified by Octavia, sister to Octavius Caesar. She is a mere pawn, summarily married off to Antony in hopes that the political union will be thus preserved. Caesar advises Antony:

> Most noble Antony,
> Let not the piece of virtue which
> is set
> Betwixt us as the cement of our
> love
> To keep it builded be the ram to
> batter
> The fortress of it . . . (3. 2. 27-31)

Octavius calls her "my dearest sister" (39) and "a great part of myself" (24); Antony addresses her as "Gentle Octavia" (3. 4. 20). Octavia recognizes herself as "most weak, most weak, your reconciler" (29-30), but she cannot reconcile Antony and Caesar, for Antony cannot leave Cleopatra. We see Octavia only twice with Antony, saying very little and lamenting her own unhappiness:

> A more unhappy lady,
> If this division chance, ne'er should
> between,
> Praying for both parts.
> The good gods will mock me pres-
> ently
> When I shall pray, "Oh, bless my
> lord and husband!"
> Undo that prayer by crying out as
> loud,
> "Oh, bless my brother!"
> (3. 4. 12-18)

When Octavia returns modestly to Rome, it is her brother who breaks the news of Antony's decision. In this noisy play, Octavia's restrained voice provides contrast to the shrill, the martial, the exaggerated.

It is certainly a busy play, far ranging in time and place, filled with messengers and meetings, with confrontations and shifting alliances. Egos are easily bruised—pride is perhaps the unifying feature of this large cast. The stage is almost always crowded. Certainly, everything about Cleopatra is public. We never see her alone.

Let's consider this crowded stage from a dramatic and thematic standpoint: Hamlet broods, Macbeth hallucinates, Lear rants, Iago schemes, Juliet pines. At some point, all speak soliloquies: Shakespeare's plays are replete with characters who give us interesting moments of self realization, self confession, self delusion. But this play, *Antony and Cleopatra*, has precious few soliloquies! Cleopatra has none. I've tried to make an accurate count—in some forty-five scenes, I think I've found seven soliloquies. Anthony has four, Enobarbus two; and Scarus one (see the Appendix). Of course, a director can always pull the actress playing Cleopatra to one side of the stage during a seemingly public scene, or have her clearly not speaking to anyone, thereby creating a soliloquy. One example might be at the close of the play, when she is imprisoned. A guard announces that "a rural fellow" has come to deliver figs, and she says, "Let him come in" (5. 2. 236). It is for her next words that I suggest the soliloquy mode. Cleopatra could turn away from Charmian, Iras, and the other women as she plans her own death:

> What poor an instrument
> May do a noble deed! He brings
> me liberty.
> My resolution's placed, and I have
> nothing
> Of woman in me. Now from head
> to foot
> I am marble-constant; now the fleet-
> ing moon
> No planet is of mine. (5. 2. 241)

Such a fine irony. At the play's end, the extravagant Egyptian has taken on the stance and logic of the most stoic Roman. Her Antony is dead. No more can the lovers seek to fill each moment with pleasure. She throws off her sensuality and she recasts herself in marble.

Oxfordians, of course, ask about the possible correspondences. Is Queen Elizabeth I to be equated with Cleopatra? From the sheer length of her lines, from her dominance—on and off the stage—we know that Cleopatra stands for power. Keith Rinehart, writing in *Shakespeare Quarterly* more than thirty years ago, found a number of similarities between the English monarch and the "serpent of the Nile":

> . . . both were queens regnant, both used courtship as a mainstay of their statecraft, and both attained apotheosis of a sort as female deities . . . Both treated courtiers and maids of honor roughly; both affected illness or other shams to give false impressions; both were marvelously facile in foreign languages; both governed their kingdoms with skill; both desired amusement and revelry; both wore gorgeous apparel; both were witty . . . (81)

Rinehart believes that Elizabeth is clearly the model for one scene—a scene that is not mentioned in Plutarch (83). Cleopatra grills her messenger, who has just returned from Rome, about Antony's new wife, Octavia, wanting to know everything about this potential rival: "Is she as tall as me…Didst thou hear her speak? Is she shrill-tongued or low?…What majesty is her gait?…Guess at her years…Bear'st thou her face in mind? Is't long or round?" (3. 3. 9-32). Similarly, as reported by Scotland's ambassador to England, Sir James Melville, Queen Elizabeth asked many of the same questions about Mary, Queen of Scots (during negotiations for a possible marriage of Mary to Sir Robert Dudley). When Cleopatra asks, "Is she as tall as me?" the messenger responds, "She is not, madam" (11), and Cleopatra concludes triumphantly, "Then she is dwarfish"—similarly, when Elizabeth heard that Mary was the taller, Elizabeth noted, "she is too high; for I myself am neither too high nor too low" (qtd. in Rinehart 83).

Today, we can laugh at the vanity and

humor in this womanly spite. As for the comparison between Shakespeare's Cleopatra and England's Elizabeth, I see both pros and cons: Elizabeth was fair, Cleopatra quite dark; Cleopatra is labeled a strumpet; for any author to call Elizabeth a whore would surely be courting danger. In terms of strategy, both women gambled on a sea victory; but Cleopatra fled from the Battle of Actium, and Elizabeth's naval forces proved victorious over the Spanish Armada. Both women seem well aware of the burdens that are borne by public figures:

> CLEOPATRA. Be it known that we,
>   the greatest, are misthought
> For things that others do; and when
>   we fall,
> We answer others' merits in our
>   name,
> Are therefore to be pitied.
>   (5. 2. 176-179)

> ELIZABETH. For we Princes are set
>   as it were upon the stages,
> in the sight and view of the world.
>   The least spot
> is soon spied in our garments, a
>   blemish quickly
> noted in our doings. It behoveth us
>   therefore to be
> careful that our proceedings be just
>   and honourable.
>   (qtd. in Chamberlin 242)

Keith Rinehart calls attention to similarities in their temperaments, particularly in their quickness to anger. Cleopatra's outburst to her messenger—which included striking him roughly—can be matched by Elizabeth's slapping her maids of honor, once handling a maid so roughly ("liberall bothe with bloes and yevell words") that she broke the maid's finger (Wilson 107). And, like Iras and Charmian in the scene quoted above, one of Elizabeth's chief gentlewomen "loved to dabble in the dark mysteries of the occult" (7-8). Rinehart also sees similar ambiguities in the theme of love. He compares Elizabeth's

vacillations about marriage reflected in considerations of whether Cleopatra's love is for Antony or for his imperial power.

I remain on the fence: yes, both Cleopatra and Elizabeth employed feminine wiles to gain political advantage; yes, both were highly dramatic and flamboyant—but these are general and, most likely, necessary traits for any powerful queen, no matter how many hundreds of years apart they lived.

By the utterly public nature of their love and by the power of their language, Cleopatra and Antony are, I believe, among the writer's finest achievements. Audiences and readers cannot fail to be moved by their love. After the shame of Actium, Antony asks, "Oh, whither hast thou led me, Egypt?" (3. 11. 50) and Cleopatra replies, simply, "Oh, my lord, my lord, Forgive my fearful sails! I little thought you would have followed" (53-55). Any doubt we may have held about his love for her is now dispelled:

> Egypt, thou knew'st too well
> My heart was to thy rudder tied by
>   th' strings,
> And thou shouldst tow me after.
>   O'er my spirit
> Thy full supremacy thou knew'st,
>   and that
> Thy beck might from the bidding
>   of the gods
> Command me. (55-60)

She begs his pardon; she cries. And one of her tears, he exclaims, is worth "[a]ll that is won and lost" (69). But at Alexandria, Antony doubts, again, and impulsively rails: "All is lost! This foul Egyptian has betrayed me" (4. 12. 9-10); "O, this false soul of Egypt!" (25). Confused by his rage, Cleopatra rushes to her monument and follows the advice of Charmian to send Antony word that Cleopatra has died. And, again, Antony reacts impulsively, falling on his own sword. Brought to the monument, he is hoisted up and dies in her arms. Her words remind us of the youthful Juliet:

> Yet come a little,
> Wishers were ever fools. O, come,
>   come, come!
> And welcome, welcome! Die when
>   thou hast lived;
> Quicken with kissing. Had I my lips
>   that power
> Thus would I wear them out.
>   (4. 15. 37-41)

And her grief must be expressed publicly:
>   Oh, see my women,
> The crown of the earth doth melt.
>   My lord!
> Oh, withered is the garland of the
>   war . . . (64-66)
> And there is nothing left remark-
>   able
> Beneath the visiting moon.
>   (69-70)

At the close of the play, Cleopatra's voice has gained lyricism. True, she can return to the familiar hyperbole—ranting, for example, that she has no intention of being paraded about as a trophy in Rome: "Rather a ditch in Egypt be gentle grave unto me! Rather on Nilus' mud lay me stark nak'd . . . " (5. 2. 56-58). We see that she is driven by two thoughts: first, her determination not to be shown as an "Egyptian puppet" (5, 2, 208); and, second, her intense desire to join the dead Antony. Her words reflect her complete love and admiration for Antony:

> His legs bestrid the ocean; his reared
>   arm
> Crested the world; his voice was
>   propertied
> As all the tuned spheres . . .
>   (80-82)

Still the performer, still the powerful queen, Cleopatra is even at the end surrounded by people. She deals with her women, with the clown who brings her "figs," and Caesar himself. I believe that she finally achieves nobility.

> Give me my robe. Put on my crown.
>   I have
> Immortal longings in me . . . me-
>   thinks I hear
> Antony call; I see him rouse him-
>   self
> To praise my noble act . . . . Hus-
>   band, I come!
> Now to that name my courage prove
>   my title!
> I am fire and air . . .
>   (280-81; 283-84; 287-89)

Appendix

Soliloquy lines in *Antony and Cleopatra*

1. Antony (2. 3. 33-44). "I will to Egypt; And though I make this marriage for my peace, In the East my pleasure lies." Reference to Octavia.
2. Enobarbus (4. 6. 12-20; 31-40). "I have done ill . . . I will go seek some ditch wherein to die."
3. Enobarbus (4. 9. 6; 9-12; 15-26). "Forgive me. . . ." His suicide.
4. Scarus (4. 12. 3-9). On omens.
5. Antony (4. 12. 18-30; 39-49). "Fortune and Antony part here . . . . The witch shall die. To the young Roman boy she hath sold me. . . ."
6. Antony (4. 14. 44-54). "I will o'ertake thee. . . . the torch is out." Believes Cleopatra to be dead.
7. Antony (4. 14. 95-104). "I will be a bridegroom in my death." Response to death of Eros; Antony falls on his own sword.

Works Cited

Chamberlin, Frederick. *The Sayings of Queen Elizabeth.* London: Dodd, 1923.

Morales, Helen. "Egypt's Influence." *Times Literary Supplement.* 27 January 2008: 8.

Rinehart, Keith. "Shakespeare's Cleopatra and England's Elizabeth." *Shakespeare Quarterly* 23. (1972): 81-86.

Shakespeare, William. *Antony and Cleopatra. The Necessary Shakespeare.* Ed. David Bevington. 2nd ed. New York: Pearson, 2005.

Traversi, Derek. *Shakespeare's Roman Plays.* Stanford: Stanford UP, 1963.

Wilson, Violet A. *Queen Elizabeth's Maids of Honour.* New York: Dutton, 1922.

Bisexuality and Bastardy:
The Reasons for the Shakespeare Cover-up

John Hamill

The Shakespeare authorship debate has been rumbling for about two centuries with no resolution. This paper focuses on an accumulation of evidence which points to two identifying characteristics. First, the realization that the author was interested in bisexual themes and scenarios, thus pointing to a bisexual author. It may be clearly demonstrated that the subject of bisexuality is present in almost every play and poem of Shakespeare's. Now that resistance to this issue of the presence of bisexuality in "Shakespeare" has been largely overcome in academia, we can take a new look for an author who reflects this interest. Second, it is clear that the author was also interested in bastardy. References to bastards and legitimacy are common in the plays, and even the *Sonnets* mention a bastard. As far as we know, Mr. Shakspere of Stratford (as he spelled his name) had no known issues with bastards. Neither did the other two major contenders for authorship of the works of Shakespeare, Christopher Marlowe and Francis Bacon. Can we find a possible author who was both bisexual and himself accused of being a bastard? The only candidate that fits this scenario is Edward de Vere, the 17th Earl of Oxford—and not coincidentally, for anti-Stratfordians, Oxford is already the leading contender for the authorship of the "Shakespeare" canon. This paper presents how these two themes are crucial of the author's need to have created and maintained an alias, a need that only Oxford's biography supports. I propose that the scandal of the bisexual love triangle, and its bastard issue, reflected in *Shake-speares Sonnets*, may be the reason for the motivation for an alias in 1593.

Joseph Sobran, in his *Alias Shakespeare* (1997), was not the first to point out Shake-speare's homoeroticism, but he was the first to connect it to apparent bisexual behavior in the biography of the Earl of Oxford. Yet, despite Sobran, few Oxfordians seem to understand either its importance or how it supports Oxford's case for the authorship. Orthodox Shakespeare scholars are just as hesitant. As Maurice Charney states, "The issues of the homoerotic in Shakespeare are hopelessly entwined in academic controversy. Everything seems to come back to the unanswerable question of Shakespeare's own sexual orientation" (159). With Oxford as Shakespeare, the question is no longer unanswerable.

Perhaps it is not a coincidence that, of the three current rivals with the strongest claims to the authorship, two are widely accepted to have been homosexuals: Sir Francis Bacon and Christopher Marlowe. The third candidate, Edward de Vere, the 17th earl of Oxford, appears to have been bisexual—he married twice, had children, and also had mistresses, but he was also accused of buggering boys. Of the sexuality of Shakspere of Stratford-upon-Avon, all we know is that he was married and had three children.

It has also been noted by Shakespeare scholars such as Professor Daniel Wright that a central theme of the author was the subject of bastardy. Why? With Oxford, at least, the issue is clear. At age thirteen, his half-sister accused him of being a bastard; for years, he refused to acknowledge paternity of his first wife's daughter, Elizabeth; and it seems that his second wife's son, Henry, may have been a bastard. In the social status of the time, there was nothing lower than a sodomite and a bastard.

I. Homosexuality in the Renaissance English Theater

Maurice Charney states that "[t]here has been a flurry of interest in the whole subject of the homoerotic in Shakespeare . . . . None of these books attempt to prove that Shakespeare was a practicing homosexual, but by calling attention to the large amount of homoerotic material, they raise serious questions about the nature of love in his works" (3). Although "it is surprising how much same-sex love there is in Shakespeare," unlike in Marlowe or Barnfield, it is not limited to a particular response, but shows "a dramatic expression of a whole variety of sexual impulses" (6). As Stanley Wells observes, "From the beginnings of Shakespeare's career... to the end of it... his plays are full of close, loving, even passionate male friendships" (9).

Despite anti-sodomy laws, the English theater in the sixteenth century had a strong cross-dressing tradition and was an especially important arena for the expression of various lewd and erotic desires (Thompson 7; Summers 4). The Elizabethan and Jacobean theater acquired a reputation for homosexuality (Bray 54).

Homoeroticism on the English stage was inescapable because plays in England were performed solely by boy companies or by youths and men in the adult companies. Women did not act on the stage, so the love scenes between Romeo and Juliet, Kate and Petruchio, and Antony and Cleopatra were played, not by a man and a woman, but by two males.

Indeed, seductive boy actors had the reputation of sexually arousing men (Greenblatt 186). These were referred to in sermons and Puritan pamphlets as ganymedes, minions, catamites or ingles—Elizabethan slang terms for youths used for sexual purposes (Bray 33-38; DiGangi 67-70).

II. Bisexuality in Shakespeare's Plays

It appears that bisexuality occurs as an important motive and plot device in many of Shakespeare's plays: *Troilus and Cressida,*

Twelfth Night, The Merchant of Venice, Two Gentlemen of Verona, The Two Noble Kinsmen and *As You Like It* are well-known examples. Intimate male friendships are portrayed, such as Lucius' passion for Fidele in *Cymbeline*, but also in more covert forms in *All's Well that Ends Well, Romeo and Juliet, Much Ado About Nothing* and *A Winter's Tale.* In *Othello*, in particular, the vagaries of sexual jealousy are combined with bisexual desire (Garber 14-15; Wells 83).

Shakespeare's own bisexual feelings seem to come through even in situations where no such desires would normally be present, a possible biographical revelation. For instance, in *King Lear*, the Fool nonchalantly reveals bisexuality by including a "boy's love" in the list of what should not be trusted: "He's mad that trusts in the tameness of a wolf, a / horse's health, a boy's love, or a whore's oath" (3. 6.18-19). In *Henry IV, Part Two*, the Hostess, in her sly commentary on Falstaff, says:

> In good faith, 'a cares not what the
> mischief he doth,
> If his weapon be out: he will foin
> like any devil;
> He will spare neither man, woman,
> nor child. (2. 1.15-18)

According to Stanley Wells, the character who has "surely the most homoerotically charged lines in Shakespeare is Iago, when attempting to substantiate his imputation of Cassio's adultery with Desdemona, he tells Othello what happened when he shared Cassio's bed"... "The straightforward description of one man making love to another is anaesthetized by its presentation as a heterosexual dream fantasy... " (84-86).

In *The Two Noble Kinsmen*, Palamon and Arcite's exchange is full of terms expressing their love and devotion to each other, as when Arcite says:

> And here being thus together,
> We are an endless mine to one
> another;
> We are one another's wife, ever
> begetting

New births of love. (2. 2. 78-81)

A little later, Palamon asks: "Is there any record of any two that loved / Better than we do, Arcite?" Arcite replies: "Sure there cannot" (2. 2. 112- 114). Yet these sentiments do not appear to conflict in any way with their interest in the opposite sex. This situation is presented time and time again in the plays.

III. Bisexuality in the Poetry
Venus and Adonis

Shakespeare's long narrative poem shares a homoerotic focus with other examples of the genre like Marlowe's *Hero and Leander* (printed in 1598) and Francis Beaumont's *Salmacis and Hermaphroditus* (printed in 1602). Dedicated to Henry Wriothesley, Earl of Southampton, this interest shows up not in the plot situation in which the aggressive goddess, Venus, falls in love with the passive adolescent Adonis, but in the perspective that the readers are invited to take toward that situation. Erotic desire in the poem is all on Venus's side. The center of erotic attention is not her body, but that of Adonis.

Finally, the goring of Adonis by a wild boar is portrayed as an act of rape or seduction:

> 'Tis true, 'tis true; thus was Adonis slain:
> He ran upon the boar with his sharp spear,
> Who did not whet his teeth at him again,
> But by a kiss thought to persuade him there;
> And, nuzzling in his flank, the loving swine
> Sheathed unaware the tusk in his soft groin. (1111-1116)

Failure to recognize the homosexual imagery here reflects the inability to notice Shakespeare's sexual allusions if those allusions are not heterosexual.

The Rape of Lucrece

Also dedicated to Southampton, *The Rape of Lucrece*, published in 1594, focuses on the familiar theme of two male allies set apart by a woman (Smith *Homosexual Desire* 66). However, it is not this that has attracted the most attention, but the remarkable tone of the dedication: "The love I dedicate to your lordship is without end;... What I have done is yours; what I have to do is yours; being part in all I have, devoted yours..." Speaking of the overflowing affection in these lines, Nichol Smith declared, "There is no other dedication like this in Elizabethan literature'" (qtd. in Akrigg 198). What Smith actually is saying is that there is no other dedication of Shakespeare or anyone else with such homoerotic overtones. "This was not, as might have been expected, an exercise in praise..., this was a public declaration of fervent, boundless love" (Greenblatt 246).

IV. Sonnets
The Sexuality in the Sonnets

The *Sonnets* are different from other sonnet sequences because "like some of Richard Barnfield's, but none, so far as I know," declares Stanley Wells, "by any other sonneteer of the period, many of Shakespeare's sonnets are explicitly addressed to, or concern, a man" (53). Sonnet cycles were the established format to express one's most intimate and passionate feelings for an idealized loved one, but in all but these two instances the loved object is a female. The majority of the poems—126 of 154—are concerned with the author's obsession with a fair-complexioned young nobleman of surpassing physical beauty, who, though idealized, is of questionable character and is considerably younger than the speaker. Looney, while he avoids the subject of homosexuality, admitted that the Sonnets "express a tenderness, which is probably without parallel in the recorded expressions of emotional attachment of one man to another" (100).

The first seventeen sonnets are the so-called marriage sonnets, in which the poet urges the Fair Youth to procreate, to make a copy of himself for posterity. According to Bruce R. Smith, by Sonnet 16 ("But wherefore do not you a mightier way / Make war upon the bloody tyrant, time") "the author has begun... to insinuate his own designs on the young man, first by promising to preserve the young man's beauty in the medium of verse, then by speaking more and more openly about his own desires" ("William Shakespeare" 609).

"He was but one hour mine"

In his commentary on the Sonnets, Martin Seymour-Smith surmises that "[i]t is likely that at least on one occasion Shakespeare did have some kind of physical relationship with the Friend. The sonnets addressed to him, particularly 33-36, are difficult to explain under any other hypothesis"; this seems to be the result of an intimacy, however brief: "[H]e was but one hour mine" (Sonnet 33); it is a view that has been expressed by Samuel Butler, Martin Smith and others.

The homosexual consciousness of the first 126 sonnets is seen not merely in the celebrations of the young man's beauty, in the obsessiveness of the author's love, or even in his repeated attempts to define his relationship with the young man in terms of marriage ("So I shall live, supposing thou art true, like a deceived husband" (Sonnet 93.1-2); and "Let me not to the marriage of true minds admit impediments") (Sonnet 116.1-2); but also in the author's profound sense of being different. "None of Shakespeare's poems are as explicitly homoerotic as any of Barnfield's. Yet, says Wells, "Shakespeare's are more intense in their expression of love—perhaps simply because Shakespeare was the greater poet" (65).

This sense of difference is expressed in the startling and angry Sonnet 121, in which the author declares "I am that I am," defiantly defending a sexuality that is socially abhorred; Giroux interprets it "as Shakespeare's response to the 'reproach' of being homosexual" (30). For Summers (3) and Pequigny (99), the sonnets that give "Shake-speare's" sequence its distinctive aura of embattlement, despair

and melancholy, correspond particularly well to a homosexual theme, one of forbidden and frustrated love.

Many of the poems are immersed in expressions of obsessive desire and of grief in the boy's absence. The author speaks of emotions that typically affect the lovesick: of sleepless nights when the poet's thoughts make a pilgrimage to the beloved (27 and 61); of the poet as a slave to his friend's desire (57); of being deceived (93); and of sexual dependency (75). Paul Ramsey concedes that the clause: "'Thy self thou gav'st' at 87.9 if said of a woman, would certainly suggest consummation" (qtd in Pequigney 50). Why should the identical clause take another meaning if the recipient is a man?

Of these expressions, G.P.V. Akrigg writes, "The love which he (the author) felt for Southampton may well have been the most intense emotion of his life" (237). Stanley Wells knowingly concludes: "It would be a naive young man who, addressed in these terms, did not regard himself as the object of desire. If Shakespeare himself did not, in the fullest sense of the word, love a man, he certainly understood the feelings of those who do" (65). While the sexuality of the sonnets addressed to the Dark Lady is quite explicit and is not questioned, "the notion that such a relationship is implicit in the earlier group was for a long time anathema to admirers of Shakespeare" (Wells 60).

The history of *Sonnets* criticism in the nineteenth and twentieth centuries has been a history of tortured logic, among which criticism is Michael Wood's in his recently-published *Shakespeare*, wherein he suggests that Shakespeare was addressing his eleven-year-old son Hamnet in the Sonnets (166)! The *Sonnets*—filled as they are with sexual puns that express sexual desire and reflect consummation, replete with bitter sexual jealousy—do not, however, reflect the language or emotions in which one would address one's own son. Marjorie Garber observes: "Amid all of these ingenious and enlightening critical maneuverings no one wants to comment on the obvious—that the sonnets describe a bisexual triangle" (514-515).

The evidence of homoeroticism in the plays, narrative poems, and autobiographical sonnets clearly point to an author who experienced sexual desire for men as well as women. This strongly suggests that bisexuality was a theme that ran through the author's own life, one that we might expect would leave traces in his biography.

V. The Sexuality of the Author

As to the sexuality of William Shakspere of Stratford, we have next to nothing with which to make a determination. We have no personal letters from him or to him, and no one else makes any reference to his personal life.

Thus, solid evidence that Oxford was bisexual should certainly add to his status as a candidate for the authorship of the Shakespeare canon. It is clear that Oxford had sexual relations with women. He married twice, fathering legitimate children. Also, he had at least two mistresses, one of whom gave him a son.

And yet, the 25-year old Oxford spent approximately eleven months, from May 1575 to March 1576, in Italy, and there met a Venetian choirboy named Orazio Coquo (Nelson 215). Oxford brought Orazio back to London to live with him as his page during the period that Oxford was separated from his wife, Anne.

Oxford's confrontation with Henry Howard and Charles Arundel in 1581-84 also resulted in the traitor lords' accusation of Oxford of having "buggered" several boys of his household. In view of Oxford's known reputation for wild behavior, it may be that Howard and Arundel were aware that their allegations would be thought credible. Indeed, we do have a picture of Oxford that could support their accusations. Over a period of years, Gabriel Harvey made consistently disparaging remarks about Oxford and about John Lyly, his secretary who also ran his company of boy actors. In June 1580, just prior to the Howard and Arundel libels, Harvey, in his *Speculum Tuscanismi*, described Oxford as "vain," "no man, but minion," "womanish" and "frivolous" (qtd in Nelson 225-27). In 1589, Harvey again attacked Oxford with not very subtle puns, accusing his amanuensis, John Lyly, of being "Oxford's minion secretary" and "once the foil (mirror) of Oxford, now the stale (prostitute) of London" (qtd in Ogburn 627; qtd in Williams 36, 123) Again, in 1593, Harvey called Lyly "sometime the fiddlestick (penis) of Oxford, now the very bauble (penis) of London" (qtd in Ogburn 627; qtd in Williams 36, 123). To Harvey, the flamboyant Oxford seems to have been the Oscar Wilde of the 16th century.

In relation to Oxford's writings, it should be noted that Oxford published at least one homoerotic poem: "The Lyvely Larke stretch forth her wynge" (qtd. in Nelson 161). Thus, an extant poem, written under his own name, testifies to bisexual interests.

Although Oxford's recorded involvement in the theater from 1583-1604 does not give evidence of homosexual behavior, it does put him squarely in the environment that was giving most concern of this behavior to the city fathers, due to the erotic content of the plays and the initiation of the boy actors into cross-dressing and erotic role-playing.

VI. The Earl of Southampton

Southampton, born in 1573, turned seventeen in 1590, an appropriate age for the Fair Youth. He was considered "fair" as is the "lovely boy" of the *Sonnets*. He was a nobleman, as many of the *Sonnets* (2, 4, 13, 26, 37, 57, 58) imply. Southampton's father was dead while his mother was living, as is indicated of the Fair youth in the *Sonnets* (3, 13,14) ("you had a Father, let your Son say so" [13]). Most significant is the fact that, at this same time, Southampton's guardian, Lord Burghley (Oxford's father-in-law), was pressuring Southampton to marry; this urging is the very theme of the first seventeen sonnets. Although there is no document directly connecting Oxford and Southampton, the facts that (1) both were royal wards under Cecil's care, (2) the young woman who Burghley was urging Southampton to marry was Oxford's daughter, and (3) all this was taking place at the same time that the Marriage Sonnets were being written demonstrates a likely intimate connection between these two noblemen.

In his teen years, Southampton was considered so cold to the female sex that he had to be encouraged to marry by homoerotic terms in the sonnets of Shakespeare and Clapham's *Narcissus*. Moreover, there is also William Burton's translation of *The most delectable and Pleasant History of Clitiphon and Leucippe*, dedicated to Southampton in 1597, which contained a striking defense of "Greek love" (Akrigg 54-55).

There also exists a contemporary report of Southampton's homosexual activities that took place after Southampton's marriage while the earl was in Ireland with Robert Devereaux, the 2nd earl of Essex. A letter from William Reynolds to Robert Cecil (Oxford's brother-in-law) in February 1601 reveals that Southampton (and also Essex) had a sexual interest in a male attendant: this involved a subaltern of Essex's, one Piers Edmonds, who, we are told, "ate & drank at his [Southampton's] table and lay in his tent. The Earl of Southampton gave him a horse.... The Earl of Southampton would cull and hug him in his arms and play wantonly with him" (Akrigg 182; Rowse, *Southampton* 161-162). Essex, too, provided Edmonds with gifts. Thus, the nature of the books dedicated to Southampton, as well as the testimony of at least one eye-witness, suggest that Southampton was, according to Katherine Duncan-Jones, "viewed as receptive to same-sex amours" (79).

VII. Earl of Essex

Both G.P.V. Akrigg and A.L. Rowse believe that Southampton was sexually attracted to the handsome, virile earl of Essex, seven years his senior. The evidence also suggests that it was a mutual infatuation. Essex kept Southampton by his side constantly, even in his military campaigns, to the point of mak-

ing him his second in command in Ireland in 1599 over the Queen's furious objections.

Southampton was deeply involved in the 1601 Essex rebellion to overthrow the government, on the eve of which he attended Shakespeare's *Richard II*, a play that focuses on the deposition of a king, which was financed by Essex's supporters to stir up the populace (Rowse, *Shakespeare's Southampton* 156). Southampton was the only one who remained loyal to Essex following his downfall and refused to denounce him at the trial for treason where they were tried and sentenced together. The beginning of the trial started dramatically when they publicly demonstrated their affection by kissing each other's hands and embracing (Akrigg 121-2; Rowse *Shakespeare's Southampton* 158).

If Southampton was the Fair Youth of the *Sonnets*, the Rival Poet must have been Essex. Essex was Queen Elizabeth's Master of the Horse, an Admiral and a Privy Councilor, but, like most young men at Elizabeth's Court, he also wrote poetry (May 250-64). As Peter Moore explains,

> Sonnets 78 to 86 describe a man who was Shakespeare's rival for the affections of Southampton during the 1590s. . . . The man who is known to have had Southampton's affection during that period was the heroic and charismatic Earl of Essex. . . . Essex was rated a gifted poet by his contemporaries. Essex wrote poems for specific occasions rather than out of dedication to poetry, he penned his verses only for his own circle and the Queen, and very little of his poetry survives. . . . It may be protested that Essex's talent was so slender that Shakespeare could not possibly have regarded him as a rival. But this objection ignores the fact that the rivalry lay in the eyes of Southampton and not in the views of literary critics. Any poetic praise from Essex was bound to make Southampton ecstatic, given his

idolization of Essex. . . . The rival was of "tall building and goodly pride. . . ." (8-12)

This is a description that fits Essex.

Moore continues: "Finally, comes the following passage on the Rival: 'He lends thee virtue, and he stole that word from thy behavior'" (79); Essex's mottoes were *Virtutis Com Invidia* (literally "envy accompanies manly virtue") and *Basis Virtutum Constantia* ("loyalty is the basis of manly virtue").

VIII. The "Dark Lady"

A leading candidate today for the Dark Lady, first suggested by A. L. Rowse and accepted by some Oxfordians, is Emilia Bassano Lanier. For some Oxfordians, the best candidate for the Dark Lady is the dark-haired and dark-eyed Anne Vavasour. She and Edward de Vere had a scandalous affair, and in March 1581 she bore his illegitimate child, also named Edward.

However, Oxford's marriage in December 1591 to the wealthy Elizabeth Trentham, one of the Queen's Maids of Honor, undermines the case for either Bassano or Vavasour as the Dark Lady. Is it possible that Oxford could have had a relationship with Emilia Bassano, the mistress of Henry Hunsdon and the wife of Alphonse Lanier, or with Anne Vavasour, the wife of a sea captain and mistress of Sir Henry Lee, while he was courting Elizabeth Trentham, and at the same time having a homosexual affair with the Fair Youth, Southampton?

Could the Dark Lady have been Elizabeth Trentham, the woman Oxford married? We have almost no information about her personality and no description of her looks— only that in 1582 she is described as "fair" (qtd. in Ogburn 722). The few additional facts we can glean from the *Sonnets* conform with what little we know of Elizabeth Trentham: she was significantly younger than the author (Sonnet 138) and as a Lady in Waiting, she would have been trained in music (Sonnet 128). Of course, these qualities are also true

of the other two candidates, Emilia Bassano and Anne Vavasour, and all three seem to have been very independent women.

Two distinctive qualities separate these candidates, however. The author describes the woman as "fair" in Sonnet 131, even though she is referred to by commentators as the Dark Lady because she is mentioned as "black" or "dark" in four sonnets (127, 131, 132, 147). The author also repeatedly states that she is not a beauty (see Sonnet 130's "My mistress' eyes are nothing like the sun," as this is the most famous example). Of the three, only Elizabeth Trentham was "fair" but probably not a beauty, which, combined with a strong and demanding personality, might explain why a wealthy Maid of Honor would remain unmarried for ten years: "In nothing art thou black save in thy deeds, / And thence this slander, as I think, proceeds" (131. 13-14).

The author of the *Sonnets* makes it clear that she is physically "fair"; only her deeds are black, and this is how he and others slander her—by making everything about her black. She is continuously, morally, black. In Sonnet 147, Shakespeare makes it clear that it is her character that is infernally "black": "For I have sworn thee faire, and thought thee bright, / Who art as black as hell, as darke as night" (147. 13-14). She is also "black" because he contrasts her with the Fair Youth, who, unlike her, is beautiful.

What is the sexual treachery that caused such a deep irreparable wound? Sonnets 40-42 and 133-144 speak of how the Dark Lady created the sexual triangle among them all by seducing his "man right fair." Henry Wriothesley, the 3rd Earl of Southampton, was nineteen in 1593. Elizabeth Trentham had a son in February 24, 1593, who, curiously, was named Henry. In the first sonnet to the Dark Lady (127), the poet accuses her of having a bastard: "And beauty slandered with a bastard shame"; and in Sonnet 143 he calls her a wife who has a child.

Thus, the circumstances of Henry de Vere's birth in 1593 and the language of the *Sonnets* suggest that this boy was not the son of Edward de Vere but none other than the spawn of Elizabeth Trentham and Henry Wriothesley.

Willobie his Avisa

Supporting evidence for identifying Henry de Vere as the son of Trentham and Wriothesley can be found in the accusations made in *Willobie his Avisa*, an anonymous narrative poem published in 1594. *Willobie* tells a story coded in double meanings about a chaste "Lady" who is pursued by several suitors, two of whom are identified as W.S. and H.W.

One critical clue is that *Willobie his Avisa* contains the first published mention of Shakespeare: "Yet *Tarquyne* pluckt his glistering grape, / And *Shake-speare*, paints poor Lucrece rape," and thus hints that the poem was written as a parody of *The Rape of Lucrece*, published four months earlier in 1594 (Sams 96-97). The initials W.S. and H.W. in *Willobie* would bring to mind the uniquely amorous dedication of *Lucrece* by Shakespeare to Southampton (Akrigg 198).

The cuckold's horns decorating *Willobie's* frontispiece, the subtitle ("The True Picture of a Modest Maid, and a Chaste and Constant Wife"), and the lampooning tone of the poem leave little doubt that this poem is a tale of adultery committed by an important woman. Pauline K. Angell, in her intriguing 1937 article, "Light on the Dark Lady: A Study of some Elizabethan Libels," asserts that the identity of the deceived husband is revealed in *Willobie's* frontispiece by the crescent over the animal's head—the crescent being

> the distinguishing mark of the Oxford crest... a boar set apart from all other armorial boars by the fact that a crescent is emblazoned upon it. Crescents are also emblazoned on the stars of the Oxford standard. In fact, these crescents were so thoroughly identified with Oxford that the Queen called him her Turk. And so the horned ass [or stag] embellished with a crescent .

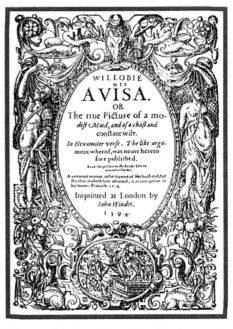

Title page of the first edition of "Willobie his Avisa" (1594)

. . was as good as a name-plate in 1594. (653-654)

In *"Shakespeare" Identified*, J.T. Looney disclosed the same information: "Several families had the Boar as their crest; but the distinguishing mark of this one is the crescent upon the left shoulder of the animal. This is peculiar to the De Vere Crest..." (455).

According to Angell, the following additional clues in the poem identify Avisa as Elizabeth (Eliza) Trenham:

1. Her name—Avisa—is a made up name, and is similar to "Eliza," a common nickname for Elizabeth. This rules out Anne Vavasour (whose nickname was not Elizabeth but Bessie [Amphlett 116]);

2. She was a Maid of Honor. This would rule out both Emilia Bassano and the Queen;

3. She was born in the west of England. Elizabeth Trentham was born in Staffordshire, north*west* of London.

4. The poem mentions an eagle-eyed

Banner of Sir John de Vere, 16th Earl of Oxford, from an Elizabethan manuscript in the College of Arms.

bird; there is a bird—a griffin—on the Trentham coat of arms;

5. Her father was a mayor of a town but not of noble stock; Trentham's father was not a nobleman, and he was twice the sheriff of Stafford-shire—a similar, minor office.

6. She was about 30 years old and had been a Maid of Honor for ten years before she married; Elizabeth Trentham married at about the age of thirty, after having served ten years as a Maid of Honor.

7. She lived "in public eye"; *Willobie* contains numerous details about the theater neighborhood where Tren-tham and Oxford lived, a district surely near to the "public eye."

In addition, Avisa is described as having "modest lookes and a filed tongue." In their aggregate, these clues point to Elizabeth Tren-tham. They assuredly do not point to Queen Elizabeth, as Akrigg (217-219) and De Luna (5) claim in their interpretation, nor to Emilia Bassano, Anne Vavasour, nor to a common innkeeper's wife from the city of Oxford, as others have claimed.

But more significantly, several scholars have pointed out that the affair described in the Sonnets between the poet, the Fair Youth and the Dark Lady might be the motivating source for both *The Rape of Lucrece* and *Wil-lobie his Avisa*. A.L. Rowse asserts that "it has often been observed that *The Rape of Lucrece* parallels the Dark Lady sonnets, as *Venus and Adonis* does the earlier Southampton ones" (*The Annotated Shakespeare* 710). *Willobie* is also seen by many scholars as providing

a clue to the relationship of the Fair Youth, the Dark Lady and the poet of the Sonnets. Could this be why the author dedicated a poem in 1594 to Southampton about that man raping his wife?

Angell argues that *Willobie* implies that both Southampton and Shakespeare suc-ceeded in their seductions of Avisa/Elizabeth. Angell notes the passages in the H.W. sec-tion of *Willobie* that describe "a woman who brought forth a man child, a woman who was with child by whoredom, and a man who stole his neighbor's wife" (667). H. W. is presented as receiving W. S.'s endorsement of the seduction of his own mistress (his wife?). *Willobie* even has W. S. play the role of procurer, actually encouraging H. W. Angell's interpretation (developed independently from the *Sonnets*) that suggests an arrangement in which W.S. serves as a willing cuckold in favor of Southampton, who might be the father, if the cuckholded husband/poet were Oxford, of Henry de Vere, who was born in 1593.

Is the author cynically referring to his newborn heir, Henry de Vere, in the 1593 *Venus and Adonis* dedication to Southamp-ton? Consider: "But if the first heir of my invention prove deformed, I shall be sorry it had so noble a god-father, and never after ear so barren a land, for fear it yield me still so bad a harvest"? Could *Venus and Adonis* be about Elizabeth Trentham's attempt to seduce Southampton?

IX. The Two Noble Henries

It is curious that even though Henry Wriothesley's father was also named Henry, and Southampton had two sons (one born in 1605 and another in 1608), neither was named Henry. It may well be that the Henry in Southampton's life was Henry de Vere. The two earls—Henry, the 3rd earl of South-ampton and Henry de Vere, the 18th earl of Oxford, developed a deep personal relation-ship and became close political allies. It is arguable that portraits of Henry de Vere show a closer likeness to Henry Wriothesley than to Edward de Vere. In fact, the only portrait of

At left, an engraving (c 1636) by Robert Vaughn of a portrait of Henry de Vere, 18th Earl of Oxford. At right, detail from a portrait of Henry Wriothesley, 3rd Earl of Southampton, by an unknown artist (c 1600).

Engraving of "the two most noble Henries" by Thomas Jenner (c 1620s).

either with anyone else is of the two of them together—the "Two Noble Henries"—and I would also add that, to me, *neither Henry looks like Oxford.*

Henry de Vere, Henry Wriothesley, Elizabeth Trentham, and their families—a strong closely-knit group allied by blood, marriage and politics—had much to lose should Oxford be exposed as the author "Shakespeare." But they were in a unique position to safeguard the pseudonym and prevent the scandal that could have destroyed the de Veres and Wriothesleys. The pseudonym also protected the legitimacy of Henry de Vere as the hereditary Lord Great Chamberlain of England and the 18th earl of Oxford, the most prestigious earldom in the kingdom.

This is reminiscent, too, of the successful royal cover-up of the Anthony Bacon conviction (in Navarre) for sodomy in1587, a conviction that, if exposed in England, would have destroyed the Bacon and Cecil families and seriously embarrassed Queen Elizabeth. If Anthony Bacon's international sex scandal could be suppressed so effec-

tively, the fact that an eccentric lord might be scripting plays under an alias could be even more easily hidden—especially if his father-in-law's political power were second only to the Queen's. During King James' reign, we can assert that James also would not want the revelation of a homosexual relationship among his inner circle, especially since this might draw attention to his own affair with the Duke of Buckingham and other males. Thus, the maintenance of the pseudonym benefited both rival political groups, and it seems that in this endeavor they were entirely successful.

Conclusion

In the new Oxford Dictionary of National Biography (2004), Peter Holland acknowledges that the "explicit homoeroticism [of the Sonnets] suggests that Shakespeare's sexuality was consciously bisexual in its desires" (952).

In his landmark *Shakespeare: The Invention of the Human*, Harold Bloom confidently asserts: "The human endowment Shakespeare keeps intimating, is bisexual" (714). Scholars increasingly acknowledge that the author expresses bisexual desire in the plays, poems and Sonnets, but they are reluctant to discuss this fact or how it should be reflected in his biography. Bruce Smith affirms: "The author of the Shakespeare canon speaks about both heterosexual and homoerotic desire in a variety of modes: across the broad expanse of public theater, among the coterie readership of *Venus and Adonis* and *The Rape of Lucrece*, within the circle of friends who read his sonnets in manuscript." He continues: "In the Sonnets, as in the plays, it is both/and, not either/or, that makes better sense of the textual evidence" ("William Shakespeare" 614). One usually writes about what one is personally interested in. "Shake-speare" was certainly interested in the complexities of bisexuality.

Of the leading candidates for authorship, Will Shakspere, Francis Bacon, Christopher Marlowe and Edward de Vere, Oxford alone shows evidence of being bisexual, and only de Vere matches the bisexual and biographical scenario presented in the *Sonnets* and plays. This is another of the many coincidences that connect deVere with the author of the Shakespeare canon. Keevak observes that Baconians, Marlovians and Oxfordians have all failed to use their claimant's homosexuality or bisexuality as a powerful argument for authorship. Keevak faults the Oxfordian movement for failing, since the beginning, to discuss Oxford's "attitude toward either sex," despite Looney's claim that this "may indeed afford an explanation for the very existence of the Shakespeare mystery" (119).

The libel in *Willobie his Avisa* is the key to the hypothesis that Elizabeth Trentham was the Dark Lady of the *Sonnets* and Henry Wriothesley was the Fair Youth and the father of Henry de Vere. This reveals an extraordinary bisexual triangle and the bastard of an illicit union that finally explain the conflicted and abiding anguish of the poet expressed in *Shake-speare's Sonnets*. This bisexual triangle also explains the 1593 and 1594 dedications to Southampton of *Venus and Adonis* and *Lucrece*, in which the alias first appeared, and it offers the reason for the subject matter of each poem. Surprisingly, it also explains the close, lifetime relationship between Henry Wriothesley and Henry de Vere: they were, in fact, father and son!

Bisexuality and bastardy are the elephants in the closet of the Shakespeare authorship debate. Many scholars have made the point that we would better understand Shakespeare's works if we knew more about the author's sexual and family situation. With Oxford as the author, the connections between the canon and the author become clear.

Note

This article is a condensation and revision of two articles previously published as "The Dark Lady and Her Bastard: An Alternative Scenario" in the *Shakespeare Oxford Newsletter* 41.3 (Summer 2005): 1, 4-11; and "Shakespeare's Sexuality and How it Affects the Authorship Issue" in *The Oxfordian* 8 (October 2005): 25-59.

Works Cited

Akrigg, G.P.V. *Shakespeare and the Earl of Southampton.* Cambridge: Harvard, 1968.

Amphlett, Hilda, *Who Was Shakespeare?* London: Heinemann, 1955.

Angell, Pauline. "Light on the Dark Lady: A Study of Some Elizabethan Libels," *PMLA* 52 (1937): 652-74.

Bloom, Harold. *Shakespeare: The Invention of the Human.* New York: Riverhead, 1998.

Bray, Alan. *Homosexuality in Renaissance England.* London: Columbia, 1982.

Charney, Maurice. *Shakespeare on Love and Lust.* New York: Columbia, 2000.

De Luna, B. N. *The Queen Declined.* Oxford: Oxford UP, 1970.

Di Gangi, Mario. *The Homoerotics of Early Modern Drama.* Cambridge: Cambridge UP, 1997.

Duncan-Jones, Katherine. *Ungentle Shakespeare: Scenes from His Life.* London: Arden, 2001.

Garber, Marjorie. *Vice Versa: Bisexuality and the Eroticism of Everyday Life.* New York: Simon & Schuster, 1995.

Giroux, Robert. *The Book Known as Q: A Consideration of Shakespeare's Sonnets.* New York: Vintage, 1983.

Greenblatt, Stephen. *Will in the World.* New York: Norton, 2004.

Holland, Peter. "Shakespeare, William (1564-1616)".

Oxford Dictionary of National Biography, Ed. Lawrence Goldman. Oxford University Press, 2004: 952.

Keevak, Michael. *Sexual Shakespeare*. Detroit: Wayne UP, 2001.

Looney, J. Thomas. *Shakespeare Identified*. London: Palmer, 1920.

May, Steven W. *The Elizabethan Courtier Poets*. Ashville, NC: Pegasus, 1999.

Moore, Peter. "The Rival Poet of Shakespeare's Sonnets." *Shakespeare Oxford Society Newsletter* 25.4 (1989): 8-12.

Nelson, Alan. *Monstrous Adversary*. Liverpool: Liverpool UP, 2003.

Ogburn, Jr., Charlton. *The Mysterious William Shakespeare*, McLean VA: EPM, 1984.

Pequigney, Joseph. *Such is My Love: A Study of Shakespeare's Sonnets*. Chicago: Chicago UP, 1985.

Rowse, A.L. *Shakespeare's Southampton*. London: Macmillan, 1965.

—. *The Annotated Shakespeare*. London: Orbis, 1978.

Sams, Eric. *The Real Shakespeare*. New London: Yale University Press, 1995.

Seymour-Smith, Martin. *Shakespeare's Sonnets*. London: Heinemann, 1963.

Smith, Bruce R. *Homosexual Desire in Shakespeare's England: A Cultural Poetics*. Chicago: UCP, 1991.

—. "William Shakespeare" *The Gay and Lesbian Literary Heritage*. Ed. Claude J. Summers. New York: Henry Holt, 1995. 608-615.

Sobran, Joseph. *Alias Shakespeare*. New York: Free Press, 1997.

Summers, Claude J. "Homosexuality in Renaissance and Enlightenment England': *Literary Representations in Historical Context*. Ed. Claude J. Summers. Boston: New England, 1992. 1-8.

Thompson, Anne. "Shakespeare and Sexuality." *Shakespeare and Sexuality*. Ed. Stanley Wells. Cambridge: CUP, 2001. 1-13.

Wells, Stanley. *Looking for Sex in Shakespeare*. Cambridge: CUP, 2004.

Williams, Gordon. *A Glossary of Shakespeare's Sexual Language*, London: Athlone Press, 1997.

Wood, Michael. *In Search of Shakespeare*. London: BBC, 2003.

Wright, Daniel L. "An Obsession with Succession: Shakespeare, Bastards and the Ubiquity of Crises of Legitimacy in the Canon." The 9th Annual Shakespeare Authorship Studies Conference. Concordia University, Portland, OR. 10 April 2005.

Some Aspects of the Monument Theory

Hank Whittemore

The Monument, my edition of the Shakespeare sonnets, published in 2005, sets forth and demonstrates a comprehensive, fully-integrated theory to explain the form and content of the entire sonnet sequence. This paper describes aspects of the Monument Theory related to its thesis that the Sonnets contain a 100-sonnet central sequence focusing on events in the final years (1601-1603) of the Elizabethan reign. A major theme developed in the paper is that this "century" of sonnets is based on the structure of *The Hekatompathia or Passionate Century of Love* (1582) as by Thomas Watson, who dedicated this earlier sequence of 100-consecutively numbered "passions" or sonnets to his patron, Edward de Vere, 17th Earl of Oxford (1550-1604), the man I and many others believe to be the real author of the Sonnets and other works attributed to William Shakespeare.

Shake-Speares Sonnets—154 verses published in 1609—is the most intensely sustained poetical sequence the English literary world has known. The Monument Theory identifies this string of consecutively numbered sonnets by Shakespeare as a work of nonfiction dressed as fiction.[1] It reveals the Sonnets to be a single, unified masterwork of verses all related to each other within the narrative as a whole. To put it another way, the Shakespeare sequence is akin to a living organism whose various parts harmoniously function within the whole creation; and furthermore, according to this theory, the Sonnets contain a politically explosive account of contemporary history during the final years in the life and reign of Queen Elizabeth I (1533-1603), leading inexorably to the nation's inevitable date with succession and, as it happened, to the triumph of King James VI of Scotland—proclaimed as King James I of England in 1603, which, as a consequence, resulted in the collapse of the House of Tudor and the establishment of the House of Stuart as England's royal house.

The subject matter of the Sonnets is viewed as so dangerous that the author would be arrested for treason if the verses fell into the wrong hands; and because, by his own admission, he was "tongue-tied by authority" (Sonnet 66) or silenced by the government—he used an "invention" to make ostensible fiction reveal genuine historical truth. In this construct, the true story unfolds within the fabric of the conventional poetry of love by means of special language working in conjunction with a deliberate and elegant design that produces, accordingly, a double image—one epistolary and revelatory and one poetic and obscure. On the surface, what appears is the story of a "love triangle" in which passionate sexual affairs are carried out first by a poet and his mistress, then by the poet and his younger male friend and, finally, by this so-called Dark Lady and this so-called Fair Youth in an act of betrayal the author calls a "trespass" and "crime" and "fault" and an "offense." This double infidelity causes him nearly bottomless grief and leads him to bitterly condemn his tyrannical, deceitful mistress while forgiving the younger man his fault and even pledging to build a "monument" of verse that will give him immortality.

The view offered here, however, is that this superficial story—the "surface" story—is a fiction, a protective cover for a more dangerous-to-be-openly-disclosed truth. The same lines can be read consistently, however, and with more specific revelatory power, not as a sexual soap opera but as the record of a real-life story of a *family* triangle, made up of father, son and mother, in which the central drama is less sexual than *political*. Within this framework, most traditional critics have correctly identified just one member, the beloved Fair Youth of the Sonnets—as Henry Wriothesley, the third earl of Southampton (1573-1624), the charismatic young nobleman to whom "William Shakespeare" had dedicated his first publications, *Venus and Adonis*, in 1593, and *The Rape of Lucrece* in 1594; by the same token, most orthodox commentators, I would suggest, have incorrectly identified the other two family members, and it is to the correction of this error that the Monument Theory is dedicated.

The Monument Theory shares the view with many sceptics that the greatest writer in the history of the English language was not the businessman-player, William Shakspere of Stratford-upon-Avon (1564-1616), but, rather, the Hamlet-like nobleman, Edward de Vere, the seventeenth earl of Oxford (1550-1604), the hereditary Lord Great Chamberlain of England and Queen Elizabeth's chief poet-playwright.

Oxford was the foremost poet as well as patron of literature and drama in the fifteen years prior to the sudden, seemingly miraculous arrival of "Shakespeare" in the 1590s. In the same year he attained his majority at twenty-one, in 1571, and taken his place in the House of Lords, Oxford succumbed to an arranged marriage with the Ophelia-like, fifteen-year-old daughter of the Queen's chief minister, William Cecil, the newly-ennobled Lord Burghley. Up to the date of Southampton's recorded birth on October 6, 1573, Oxford enjoyed the most intimate royal favor at Court, to a point, indeed, that reports suggested he and Elizabeth were lovers:[2] The young Court observer, Gilbert Talbot, wrote to his father, the Earl of Shrewsbury, on May 11, 1573:

> My Lord of Oxford is lately grown into great credit . . . , for the Queen's Majesty delighteth more in his personage and his dancing and his valiantness than any other... My Lady Burghley [wife of Lord

Burghley and Oxford's mother-in-law] unwisely hath declared herself, as it were, jealous [angry], which is come to the Queen's ear: whereat she hath been not a little offended with her, but now she is reconciled again. At all these love matters my Lord Treasurer [Burghley] winketh, and will not meddle in any way." (Ward 78)

The Monument Theory agrees with the conclusion of many scholars that, as a consequence of this relationship, Southampton was Oxford's son by Elizabeth, the dark, tyrannical and deceitful *sovereign* mistress who, trapped in the prison of her own politically expedient and carefully-manufactured image as the childless Virgin Queen, refused to acknowledge this "natural issue of her Majesty's body" as her own heir. In the real story, narrated beneath the surface platitudes of the Sonnets, Henry Wriothesley as the Fair Youth is "fair"—a near-homonym of Vere—not because he's handsome or pretty but principally because of his stature, in the author's eyes, as the only rightful royal prince and heir; just as Elizabeth Tudor, as the Dark Lady of the Sonnets, is "dark" not because of her hair or eyes or skin but because of her imperial frown, which casts its silent shadow over their unrecognized son. Furthermore, the "crime" each committed was, first, Southampton's treasonous attempt to overthrow the government and, second, Elizabeth's equally treasonous imprisonment of their royal son despite his "true rights" to the throne. In Oxford's eyes the crime committed by Southampton and the punishment delivered by Elizabeth are joined together in one heinous betrayal of "love" or royal blood.

According to the Monument Theory, the two different and even opposite images of the "story" preserved within the Sonnets—the false "love" triangle and the true "family" triangle—have always overlapped; but the power of deeply ingrained, traditional perception has allowed most readers to see only a strained, convoluted and fantastic fiction while the biographical drama is recorded parallel to and beneath the fictional story as the poet reacts to authentic circumstances and actual events as they unfold in real time, measured by the calendar. As might be expected, given the subject matter of the true story, the sequence is driven by the single, powerful undercurrent that constantly moves toward confrontation with the issue of the the royal succession; and the result, which has been visible for centuries to discerning eyes while remaining unseen to those given to conventional assessments of the Sonnets, is a "dynastic diary" that corrects and supplements the official version of England's history at the time of this epochal drama. The poet, in effect, in this Sonnets sequence, has created a true and living record of Elizabeth's unacknowledged heir—a Tudor prince—and has sealed this account of his blood and its fate within a carefully erected "monument" for future generations—as though inserting a message in a bottle and setting it adrift on the sea of time, hoping it will reach the distant shores of posterity,[3] to tell the truth of an age that will not be recorded in the official documents and sanitized history of the State.

The most important structural element postulated by the Monument Theory is a self-contained sequence of exactly one hundred chronological verses (Sonnets 27-126) at the center, flanked by two smaller series (1-26 and 127-152) of precisely twenty-six sonnets apiece—resulting in a simple and elegant numerical description of 26-100-26, with the epilogue of Sonnets 153-154 coupled to the end. The recorded story within this crucial sequence—referred to here as the 100-Sonnet Center—is suggested not only as the centerpiece of the numerical structure, but also as the sole reason *Shake-Speares Sonnets* of 1609 came into existence in the first place; that is, the hundred verses proceed to the moment of the succession and finally to the Queen's funeral and the official end of her dynasty, when the real-life story is over. But the 100-Sonnet Center within the sonnet cycle itself contains a multi-faceted numerical de-

sign with each component having a definite, specific purpose. For example, the string is divided in half, fifty-fifty, with the two verses at the center (Sonnets 76-77) serving as the "entrance" to the monument and containing the explanation of how the reader is rightly to comprehend the story. Sonnet 76, for example, announces that "my verse" is being written with an "invention"—or revelatory language—woven within a "noted weed," i.e., the familiar garb of poetry, so that "every word" conceals, yet simultaneously reveals, the author's "name" or identity along with the ongoing recorded story.

> Why write I still all one, ever the same,
> And keep invention in a noted weed,
> That every word doth almost tell my name,
> Showing their birth, and where they did proceed? (ll. 5-8)

Sonnet 77, in turn, dedicates "this book" to the younger man, Southampton—declaring it to be "thy book"—and indirectly refers back to the cryptic Dedication of the Sonnets, which begins: *To the onlie begetter of these ensuing sonnets, Mr. W. H.*, reversing the stature and initials of Lord Southampton to "Mr. Wriothesley, Henry," in reflection of his commoner status as an attainted prisoner in the Tower of London while yet and comparing him to another Prince—*the onlie begotten Son*[4] of the New Testament. That Southampton is also *the onlie begetter* or sole inspirer of the Sonnets—the one who gave birth to them—is confirmed when the author, addressing him in Sonnet 77, refers to the verses as "those children nursed, delivered from thy brain," an identification repeated in the very next verse, Sonnet 78, when Oxford tells the young prince: "Yet be most proud of that which I compile, whose influence is thine, and born of thee."

The 100-sonnet sequence also consists of ten "chapters" of ten sonnets: Sonnets 27-36; 47-56; 57-66; 67-76; 77-86; 97-106;

Discovering Shakespeare: A Festschrift in Honour of Isabel Holden

107-116; 117-126, each "chapter" taking up a new subject and theme. One result of this perfect mathematical arrangement is that the traditionally-perceived Rival Poet series now can be seen as actually comprising the ten-verse "chapter" of Sonnets 77-86. Here, therefore, is an example of how the Monument Theory has led to a "discovery" that unexpectedly validates the existence of a traditional concept involving the Sonnets—in this case, verifying readers' perception of a specific segment that scholars long have recognized without, however, being able consistently to identify with regard to the so-called "rival poet"—much less comprehend the situation involving him.

One of the most dramatic aspects of the theory is a shift in our detection of the sonnets' compositional time frame that leads us to recognize that the composition of the narrative of this middle sequence occurred not during the 1590's, as most scholars conventionally have assumed, but during the radically different and politically-volatile years of 1601-1603, the bleak ending of the Elizabethan reign leading to the Queen's death in her seventieth year after four and a half decades of rule as an absolute monarch. As a result, we can now unambiguously discern that the poet begins with Sonnet 27 in reaction to the Essex Rebellion on February 8, 1601 (a failed attempt by Robert Devereux, the 2nd earl of Essex [1566-1601] to storm Whitehall Palace and physically remove Robert Cecil [1563-1612], the little hunchbacked Principal Secretary, from his pernicious influence over an aging Elizabeth and deprive him of his power to determine the succession upon her death). Imprisoned with Essex in the Tower on the night of the abortive palace coup was its co-leader, Southampton, the military-minded lord to whom "Shakespeare" had publicly and exclusively dedicated his work, thereby uniquely linking the popular earl to his name and writings—and particularly to his royal English history plays that, as Professor Daniel Wright has addressed in detail, helped raise public awareness of current issues

regarding the succession while confronting crucial questions about what constitutes rightful qualification for monarchy in order that its government might be affirmed as well and truly legitimate.

Within the context of contemporary history suggested by the Monument Theory, Edward de Vere applied the Shakespeare pen name to poems and, ultimately, to revised versions of plays he had written much earlier for Elizabeth and the Court as a way, at the end of the century, of lending public support to Southampton amidst growing political struggles for power behind the throne after the Queen turned sixty in 1593. However, in February of 1601, with all hope for any linear continuance of the Tudor line obliterated by the Queen's steadfast refusal, despite pleas from her Government, to name a successor, and with Southampton having lost any possible royal claim (and, in all likelihood, apparently about to lose his life) as a consequence of the failure of the Rebellion, the power struggle for the succession was over; with the fall of Essex and Southampton, the cunning Cecil had emerged as victor and supreme commander of the government, with the ability to guide the State toward his vision of the future. As soon as the trials and executions had run their pre-ordained course, the triumphant Secretary would begin a secret correspondence with King James to prepare for the transfer of power to the Scottish monarch upon the death of Elizabeth—a ploy by which the politic Cecil knew he could gain effective, lasting control of the State by manipulating the easily-influenced and docile King and thereby assure himself the ability to maintain his recently-won and long fought-for power behind the throne long after the death of what he has determined would be its last Tudor occupant.

In the midst of this calamitous turn of events, what the Sonnets reveal is a heartbroken and exhausted earl of Oxford who had returned (perhaps from Whitehall Palace) on the night of the failed rebellion to his Hackney home, a few miles on horseback's ride from the Tower, from which prison Southampton was spending his first night as an accused traitor. There he writes a sonnet. This first entry of the 100-sonnet sequence is not the loud cry of pain we might expect. Instead, Oxford pictures himself finally lying on his bed, past midnight, in the darkness of his room—a darkness that reflects the bleakness of his spirit.

The Monument Theory contends that only within such an historical and biographical context can we realize the immense sadness, even horror, permeating the lines of the opening verse, the poem which he will number, eventually, as Sonnet 27 and upon which he will build his 100-sonnet monument to Southampton and his (and England's) lost hopes.

In the second line of that Sonnet, the word *travail* refers to "work," but the usual interpretation by editors is that it concomitantly means "travel"; that is, most have viewed the poet as literally traveling far away from the younger man—but how, we ask, could any such separation account for the terrible grief expressed in this verse? For this, however, the Monument Theory provides an answer: after what must have been a physically taxing day, Edward de Vere attempts to send his own thoughts on a *zealous pilgrimage* to the imprisoned Southampton, whose shadow appears to his inner eye as *a jewel hung in ghastly night* ; in this context we can begin to perceive the emotions being held in check by the artist's restraint:

Sonnet 27
Weary with toil, I haste me to my
    bed,
The dear repose for limbs with
    travail tired,
But then begins a journey in my
    head
To work my mind, when body's
    work's expired.
For then my thoughts (from far
    where I abide)
Intend a zealous pilgrimage to
    thee,

And keep my drooping eyelids open
    wide,
Looking on darkness which the
    blind do see.
Save that my soul's imaginary sight
Presents thy shadow to my sight-
    less view,
Which like a jewel (hung in ghastly
    night)
Makes black night beauteous, and
    her old face new.
Lo thus by day my limbs, by night
    my mind,
For thee, and for my self, no quiet
    find.

Now Oxford begins to write the equivalent of *one sonnet per day* to preserve the truth of his royal son, who will be summarily tried by his peers, found guilty of treason and sentenced to die. From here on he is compiling these "prayers" or "hymns" that ordinarily would be recited or sung at a funeral—in this case, in anticipation of the interment of royal blood. "This is the first of a series of five sonnets" as Katherine Duncan-Jones writes of Sonnet 27 (164), and, indeed, the likelihood is that Oxford would have poured out his anguish in five verses during the same sitting:

When day's *oppression* is not eased
    by *night*, but day by *night* and
    night by day *oppressed* . . . to
    torture me . . . *clouds* do *blot* the
    heaven . . . the *swart*-complex-
    ioned *night* . . . But day doth
    daily draw *my sorrows* longer,
    and *night* doth *nightly* make
    grief's length seem stronger (28)
    . . . (emphasis added)

When *in disgrace* with Fortune and
    men's eyes, I all alone *beweep
    my outcast state*, and trouble
    deaf heaven with *my bootless
    cries*, and look upon myself and
    curse my fate (29) . . . (emphasis
    added)

Then can I *drown an eye* (un-used to flow) for precious friends *hid in death's dateless night* (30) . . . (emphasis added)

How many a *holy and obsequious tear* hath dear religious love stolen from mine eye, as interest of *the dead*, which now appear but things *removed* that *hidden in thee* lie. Thou art *the grave* where *buried* love doth live (31) . . . (emphasis added)

If thou survive . . . (32) . . . (emphasis added)

In Sonnet 32, the poet continues with thoughts of his own death (Oxford is now in his fifty-first year) amidst unbearable regret over having been unable to give his son *a dearer birth* than this—a birth that should have allowed him *to march in ranks of better equipage* as a prince. Instead, now that all has come down to this calamity, he recalls the birth of *my Sunne* who was *masked* by *the region cloud* or Elizabeth Regina's imperial frown:

> Even so my Sunne one early morn
> did shine
> With all triumphant splendor on
> my brow,
> But out alack, he was but one hour
> mine,
> The region cloud hath masked him
> from me now.
> (Sonnet 33.5-8)

Oxford will continue constructing a "tomb" to conceal Southampton, but he will also build a "womb" to give him rebirth and growth within a chronological diary of his life until the succession is decided.[6] Meanwhile, he has been summoned by Secretary Cecil and the Privy Council to *the Sessions* or treason trial of Essex and Southampton, the leaders of the Rebellion who will be tried together on February 19, 1601 in Westminster Hall; and

he now records this specific "summons to the Sessions" in the universal language of poetry: "When to the Sessions of sweet silent thought / I summon up remembrance of things past . . ." (Sonnet 30.1-2).

Suddenly, we see that Edward de Vere is not merely reacting to events but also entering the stage as an active participant, to serve as the highest-ranking earl on the tribunal of peers who will sit in judgment at the carefully orchestrated trial, a travesty of justice whose unanimous conferral of a guilty verdict and sentence of execution are a foregone conclusion.[7] His reaction to the prospect of having to condemn his own son to death (a son who, from his point of view, should become Henry IX of England) is to feel the emotional burden of Christ on the way to his crucifixion:

> Nor can thy shame give physic to
> my grief;
> Though thou repent, yet I have still
> the loss;
> Th'offender's sorrow lends but
> weak
> To him that bears the strong offense's
> cross. (Sonnet 34.9-12)[8]

The younger earl had joined forces in the 1590s with Essex, the war hero whose popularity exceeded even that of his sovereign, and Southampton had served with Essex on two military ventures—the Islands Voyage of 1597 and the Irish Campaign of 1599. When both expeditions proved failures, Elizabeth was inflamed by Cecil's whisperings and turned against the two swashbuckling earls.[9]

In response to that royal opposition, Southampton himself led secret meetings at Danvers House in which plans for the Rebellion were finalized; and upon the request of the conspirators, and presumably with "Shakespeare's" consent, the Chamberlain's Men gave a special staging on February 7, 1601 at the Globe of the politically-charged *Richard II* to help rouse support for a bloodless deposition. Cecil, however, who had agents like Sir Henry Neville penetrate the conspiracy, was not fooled. The sleuth-like

Cecil countered by sending an emissary to Essex House and incited the earls into acting hastily and without due preparation. The Rebellion was doomed even as it began the next morning.

Although several of the company's actors were questioned after the Rebellion's collapse, "Shakespeare," curiously, was never called to answer for his play; but Oxford, the author, clearly privately blamed himself for contributing to his son's downfall by having "authorized" the "trespass" or treason of his son in writing the play wherein an English monarch is deposed—the very play used by the Essex-Southampton faction to encourage an overthrow of the Cecil-run government. (Indeed, the comparison was not lost on the Queen either; six months later she will exclaim in anger to her antiquarian: "*I am Richard II, know ye not that?*" [qtd. in Shewring 191].) So it was that Edward de Vere took on his share of the blame while promising to purify, incense-like ["in sense"] his son's sin as well as balance his son's irrational act by bringing "in sense" or rationality. And although he would be forced to act as his "adversary" by voting guilty at the trial, he will continue to work behind the scenes as Southampton's "Advocate" or counsel and defender:

> All men make faults, and even I
>   in this,
> Authorizing thy trespass with com-
>   pare,
> Myself corrupting salving thy
>   amiss,
> Excusing thy sins more than thy
>   sins are:
> For to thy sensual fault I bring in
>   sense,
>   Thy adverse party is thy Advocate
>   (Sonnet 35.5-10)

Oxford knew that to save Southampton's life (and gain the promise of his possible release from prison) he would have to deal with Robert Cecil, his former brother-in-law, and make an infamous bargain. The price to be paid was as steep as possible in his view,

for it would require that his son give up any royal claim forever, and would require both of them to refrain from any public relationship to avoid the suggestion that they might be father and son:

> Let me confess that we two must
>   be twain,
> Although our undivided loves are
>   one . . .
> I may not ever-more acknowledge
>   thee,
> Lest my bewailed guilt should do
>   thee shame,
> Nor thou with public kindness
>   honor me,
> Unless thou take that honor from
>   thy name;
> But do not so: I love thee in such
>   sort
> As thou being mine, mine is thy
>   good report.
>   (Sonnet 36.1-2, 9-14)

These sorrowful lines, addressed by a father to a son who is in danger of losing his life, conclude the first chapter of ten verses (Sonnets 27-36) of what ultimately will amount to ten such chapters of ten sonnets apiece—a sequence of one hundred verses that will become an extended meditation on loss of kingship, loss of paternity and loss of truth by a proud lord whose personal motto is *Vero Nihil Veritas* (or *Nothing Truer Than Truth*) and who will strive to preserve the truth in his "monument" of verse for "eyes not yet created" to behold, in future, that which official "Cecilized" history will attempt forever to conceal.

At the end of a day-long trial, both Essex and Southampton are unanimously (and predictably) found guilty of high treason and sentenced to death. Essex is executed six days later; four of the five remaining condemned are executed shortly thereafter—Southampton, notably, excepted—and, though spectators prepared daily for the earl's death, it is not until the final week of March that it becomes clear he actually is not going to be executed and, in fact, unaccountably has been spared. No record exists of Southampton's death sentence being commuted to life imprisonment; but the Monument thesis perceives Edward de Vere recording in the Sonnets that he acted to save the younger earl by making an infamous bargain with the all-powerful Robert Cecil, whose own survival depended upon his success in bringing James to the throne without opposition. If the Secretary fails, he knows he will lose not just his power but his life; and Oxford, Cecil knows, still has the power to put him in mortal jeopardy by alerting Elizabeth or, worse, by publicly revealing the big lie of the "Virgin Queen" and Southampton's true parentage. Therefore, Cecil will keep Southampton alive in the Tower, not out of sympathy or mercy, but precisely to be able to silence Oxford and yet hold out the threat that the death sentence can be carried out at any time should Oxford talk. In this way, Oxford was blackmailed into the terribly ironic position of having to support Cecil's secret effort to ensure the fall of the House of Tudor and help launch the dynasty of the Stuarts in order to save his son's life.

The hundred-sonnet chronicle at the center of the "monument" uses exactly eighty consecutive verses (or eight chapters) to cover the two years and two months of Southampton's continuous confinement. The eighty-verse "prison section" begins, as noted earlier, with Sonnet 27 and Southampton's arrest and confinement on the night of the Rebellion on February 8, 1601; it nears its end with Sonnet 105 upon the death of Elizabeth on March 24, 1603, when members of the nobility (including Oxford), in accord with Cecil's contrivances, proclaimed James her successor. This was the single most important political event in England in nearly half a century— the transfer of power from one sovereign to another, and in this case, as historians note, it was engineered by Secretary Cecil so swiftly that the expected civil war for the throne had no time to develop.

The long-planned-for events to raise James of Scotland to the throne unfolded rapidly and according to script. And what did those plans include? Among his most immediate acts was the issuance—and one might conclude (absent the evidence of the Sonnets) the *amazing* issuance—of an order to release the rebel, Southampton, from the Tower. Indeed, James was still in Edinburgh when he sent ahead orders on April 5, 1603 for Southampton's release—thereby ending the long, dark night of Southampton's internment that brings, too, the prison sequence to its end with Sonnet 106 discoursing upon Southampton's final night in the royal fortress.

"When in the Chronicle of wasted time," Oxford begins this poignant verse, referring not only to the "wasted" time spent by Southampton in the Tower, but also to the fact that "wasted time" (the unproductive—having provided the kingdom with no acknowledged heir—life of the Queen) has ended; he concludes by stating that the astonishing public events of "these present days" are unfolding while he and his royal son can only stand by in silence: "For we which now behold these present days, / Have eyes to wonder, but lack tongues to praise" (Sonnet 106.13-14).

The final twenty verses (two chapters) begin with Sonnet 107 and focus upon the glorious (but bittersweet) morning of April 10, 1603, when Southampton walks from the Tower as a free man after, for so long, having been "supposed as forfeit to a confined doom." This moment is the dramatic climax of the previously recorded events, and Oxford begins with "a single sentence, one marvelous breath" that "could only have been written by a poet in the fullness of his powers" (Giroux 194):

> Not mine own fears nor the pro-
> phetic soul
> Of the wide world dreaming on
> things to come
> Can yet the lease of my true love
> control,
> Supposed as forfeit to a confined
> doom. (Sonnet 107.1-4)

"This is what Shakespeare had to say to Southampton upon his release from imprisonment," G. P. V. Akrigg writes, trumpeting "the mass of evidence which has firmly established the dating of this sonnet" as having been composed in the spring of 1603 (254). "We may rest assured that Shakespeare was one of the first to greet his 'dear boy,'" Gerald Massey perceptively wrote in 1866. "He had loved him as a father loves a son . . ." (79) and firmly declared that

> [t]here can be no mistake, doubt, or misgiving here! This sonnet [107] contains evidence beyond question—proof positive and unimpeachable—that the man addressed by Shakespeare in his *personal* sonnets has been condemned in the first instance to death, and afterwards to imprisonment for life, and escaped his doom through the death of the Queen. . . . In this sonnet we have his written congratulation of the Earl on his release. It proves his sympathy with him in misfortune, and it proves also that he had been writing about the Earl. (79, 312, 314)

The fifth and next line of Sonnet 107, of course, is famous for its reference to Queen Elizabeth as Cynthia or Diana, the chaste goddess of the Moon, with most commentators agreeing that the poet is unambiguously referring to her recent death in declaring that "[t]he mortal Moon hath her eclipse endured . . ." (Sonnet 107.5), succumbing to the mortality of her natural body, yet overcoming that "eclipse" of her mortal life by virtue of the immortality in which she participates as the bearer of a divine charism that belongs to monarchy (for more on the doctrine of the sovereign's immortality and its medieval foundation in the conviction that the monarch's divine, or "twin," self never dies, see Wright, *The Anglican Shakespeare* 85-86ff). Oxford begins the concluding couplet of this sonnet by addressing Southampton directly and promising once again to keep him and his story alive in these sonnets: "And thou in this shalt find thy monument" (Sonnet 107.13). In the final line, he castigates Elizabeth as a "tyrant" ("When tyrants' crests and tombs of brass are spent" [Sonnet 107.13-14]) for having allowed all that has come to such an unfortunate pass by selfishly permitting the Tudor lineage to die with her. "This sonnet could not have been written before 24 March 1603, the date of Queen Elizabeth's death," Giroux observantly writes, because "the word 'tyrant' was risky to put on paper at any time during [Elizabeth's] reign, and mortally dangerous if coupled with a reference to her" (192).

The chronicle now marches to its end with nineteen verses matching *each of the nineteen days from Southampton's liberation to the solemn funeral procession for Queen Elizabeth* on April 28, 1603, when four noblemen bore the Canopy of State over her effigy and coffin through the London streets on the way to Westminster: "Were't ought to me I bore the canopy, / With my extern the outward honoring . . ." (Sonnet 125.1-2).

So far it remains unknown whether Edward de Vere, now fifty-three, was one of the four noblemen bearing the canopy on this occasion, although it does appear that he had done so during the Queen's life and helped to bear it over the Queen in November 1588 during the public celebration of England's victory over the Spanish Armada. The point of the opening lines of Sonnet 125, however, other than to mark the occasion in relation to the timeline of the diary, is, of course, the poet's declaration that he no longer cares about honoring her. He had spent all his adult life in Her Majesty's service, but she had gone to her death without ever acknowledging their son, regardless of any previous oaths or vows made.[10] With the Tudor dynasty officially dead, he abruptly concludes with the "envoy" of farewell from father to son: "O Thou my lovely Boy who in thy power / Dost hold time's fickle glass, his sickle hour, / Who hast by waning grown . . ." (Sonnet 126.1-3).

Southampton, naturally, has continually "grown" (in life and in these sonnets) in direct contrast to the "waning" of the Moon goddess, Elizabeth. In the Sonnets, one of the metaphors for the Queen used by the poet has been "nature"—now transformed into the universal "nature, sovereign mistress over wrack," of whom Oxford writes to Southampton, in conclusion: "Her *Audit* (though delayed) answered must be, / And her *Quietus* is to render thee" (Sonnet 126.11-12).

The final accounting of the younger earl, the revelation of his real identity, will be preserved in these sonnets, which are "pyramids" belonging to time.[11]

The Power of Context

The consequences of this shift forward in the perceived dates of the central story are far-reaching. Any given framework of time and circumstance will allow for the presence of a certain set of real-life participants, while another context may well rule out some or all of the same individuals. The value of knowing the chronological framework of the verses was predicted by editor Hyder Edward Rollins in 1944:

The question when the sonnets were written is in many respects the most important of all the unanswerable questions they pose. If it could be answered definitely and finally, there might be some chance of establishing to general satisfaction the identity of the friend, the dark woman, the rival poet (supposing that all were real individuals), of deciding what contemporary English sources Shakespeare did or did not use, and even of determining whether the order of *Q* is the author's or not. In the past and at present such a solution has been and remains an idle dream. (53)

The 1601-1603 timeframe, however, precludes all candidates suggested as the Fair Youth of the Sonnets other than Southampton,[12] who, if the Monument Theory is cor-

rect, can now be identified as the Fair Youth beyond a reasonable doubt. He alone, facing execution, can be the object of the poet's deep, urgent, paternal concern. Accordingly, as we might expect, the torrent of legal terms, along with copious expressions of fear that the younger man's life will be cut short, can be seen as much more than a poet's regret that a pretty boy will grow old and wrinkled. Instead, emotions are mediated in these verses into what can only be properly understood as the personal, direct reactions of a father responding to a specific, dire situation faced by his son and sovereign prince:

"To *guard the lawful reasons* on thy part (49) . . . Whilst I, *my sovereign, watch the clock for you* (57) . . . The *imprisoned absence of your liberty* . . . To you it doth belong yourself to *pardon* of self-doing *crime* (58) . . . To play *the watchman ever for thy sake* (61) . . ." (emphasis added)

The effect achieved is that of a double image, with concern over "age" and "beauty" the apparent subject matter, while simultaneously the poet braces himself for the "cruel knife" or executioner's axe that literally will "cut" or sever Southampton's head from his body and end his "life" on the scaffold:

For such a time do I now fortify
Against confounding age's *cruel knife*,
That he shall never *cut* from memory
My sweet love's beauty, though my lover's *life*.
(Sonnet 63.9-12; emphasis added)

The indeterminate stay of execution for Southampton that prolongs the poet's agony is recorded by Sonnet 66—a virtual suicide note in which a despairing Oxford can be seen listing all the reasons he now is tempted to release himself from his protracted anxiety and die. Among these provocations are his laments for "purest faith unhappily foresworn" (accusing the Queen of having broken her promises and betrayed him); "right perfection wrongly

50

disgraced" (referring to his royal son who is being made to suffer like a traitor); "strength by limping sway disabled" (a conjuration of limping Robert Cecil holding "sway" or power over the imprisoned earl) and "captive-good [Southampton the captive in prison] attending Captain ill [Cecil now running the government]," with Oxford concluding: "Tired with all these, from these would I be gone, / Save that to die, I leave my love alone" (Sonnet 66.13-14).

He would choose to depart from this world because of the fact that Southampton, to have any chance of remaining alive and gaining his freedom, must give up any royal claim; but he will not succumb and kill himself, because by doing so he would leave his son "alone"—in the Tower, at the mercy of Cecil—serving a "term of life," as Oxford will later phrase it in Sonnet 92. And this litany of sorrow is followed, in the opening quatrain of Sonnet 67, by Oxford wondering why his son—a royal heir—should have to continue to abide with, and be debased by, true criminals in prison:

> Ah wherefore with infection should
>   he live,
> And with his presence grace im-
>   piety,
> That sin by him advantage should
>   achieve,
> And lace itself with his society?
> (1-4)

The succeeding sonnets can be seen as reflecting the author's strenuous efforts to gain the promise of the younger earl's liberation with a royal "pardon" (which can only be granted by the reigning monarch) for having led the "purposed overthrow" or "revolt" of the Rebellion:

> "Thou truly fair wert truly sympa-
> thized by thy true-telling friend"
> (82) . . . "Such is my love, to thee I
> so belong, that for thy right my self
> will bear all wrong (88) . . . To linger
> out a purposed overthrow (90) . .
> . For term of life thou art assured

mine . . . since that my life on thy revolt doth lie . . . (92)

Here are his most urgent reactions to a life-or-death personal and political situation in which the poet's beloved is playing a lead role; here is a real-life drama of the poet's personal (and that which also is the nation's unspoken) history, unfolding verse-by-verse within a diary by which he is recording so much which has been lost that in Sonnet 106 he will refer to it as "the Chronicle of wasted time."

The later compositional framework dates also confirm that the Dark Lady cannot be anyone but the monarch herself, since she ultimately is responsible for Southampton's fate. All other candidates, accordingly, must be removed from a pitch that, over the years, has become crowded with a rather large field of candidates; and now, rather than seeing these intensely wrought poems as a confusing sexual escapade or romp in forbidden fields of affection wherein some treacherous mistress steals away a younger man from her husband or his older lover, the story is revealed, at last, as a real-life drama in which we discover the background to what dispassionate history affirms: that the sovereign mistress of England has confined Southampton in prison—first, to face the prospect of execution but later to escape execution with the unaccountable receipt of a life sentence that itself, upon the Queen's death, will be voided by a royal pardon from England's new King.

It might seem incredible, to we who see the common sense of the Monument Theory, to comprehend that more than two centuries went by after 1609 before anyone even suggested Southampton as the younger man of the Sonnets, since, after all, "Shakespeare" had introduced himself in print in the dedications to Southampton, who, though still in his teens in 1593 and 1594, was rising to unprecedented and ostensibly inexplicable heights of royal favor, replete with the attainment of astonishing honours, at the Elizabethan court. In the latter public epistle, "Shakespeare" pledged to him:

"The love I dedicate to your Lordship is without end . . . What I have done is yours, what I have to do is yours, being part in all I have, devoted yours. Were my worth greater, my duty would show greater; meantime, as it is, it is bound to your Lordship . . . "

"There is no other dedication like this in Elizabethan literature," D. Nichol Smith wrote in 1916, referring to the public display of love and affection coupled with open-ended devotion, adding that as

> . . . *The Rape of Lucrece* was the last book that Shakespeare published [personally brought to the publisher], he did not again have occasion to speak of Southampton by name, and further proofs of their friendship must be sought in the Sonnets. (201)

One of Drake's important observations, which might seem all too evident, was that the *Lucrece* dedication to Southampton is mirrored by Sonnet 26:

> Lord of my love, to whom in vassalage
> Thy merit hath my duty strongly knit,
> To thee I send this written ambassage
> To witness duty, not to show my wit.
> Duty so great, which wit so poor as mine
> May make seem bare . . . (1-6)

In making his pronouncement about Southampton as the younger man, Drake was pointing out what should have been obvious to scholars of Shakespeare's works all along. So why had it taken until 1817 for someone to recognize Southampton as the Fair Youth? One clear answer is that, given his inferior social status, the Stratford player never could be credibly imagined as writing such intimate sonnets to this powerful

young lord nor, for example, arrogantly and egocentrically demanding (as in Sonnet 10) that, to satisfy his commoner's desire for some kind of reflected glory, Southampton should "make thee another self for love of me." The opening seventeen sonnets, a sequence lecturing—almost badgering—seventeen-year-old Southampton to hurriedly marry and procreate, have never made sense in the context of considering their composition by the butcher's apprentice-cum-poet that is the traditional author; and it has defied logic to think such a person could or would promise to be the one who would or could create immortality for a supremely confident, youthful and lofty young aristocrat. Operating on the assumption that "William Shakespeare" was in fact William Shakspere from the market town of Stratford-Upon-Avon in Warwickshire, scholars obviously, until Drake, could not bring themselves to name Henry Wriothesley as the Fair Youth for whom the poet wrote these deeply personal and intensely autobiographical sonnets. Indeed, the fact that, in Shakespeare's 1593 and 1594 poems, this young lord had been linked, unaccountably, to Shakespeare, and who, necessarily, had to be the younger man of the two in the Sonnets, had proved enough, by itself, to trigger an "authorship question" in the nineteenth century. If the Sonnets were written to and/or about Southampton, then Shakspere as "Shakespeare" had to be a myth.

One of the most eloquent and persuasive "heretics" with respect to challenging who it was who penned those poetic works in the early 20th century was Sir George Greenwood; Greenwood wrote in 1908 that

> [i]nfinite labor and time without end has been bestowed upon the Sonnets, but no Shakespearean critic has yet succeeded in explaining them satisfactorily, and I venture to say that such success will never be obtained on the assumption that they were written by Shakspere of Stratford. . . . The real problem of the Sonnets is to find out who

"Shake-speare" was. That done, it might be possible to make the crooked straight and the rough places plane—but not till then. That he would be found among cultured Elizabethan courtiers of high position, I can entertain no doubt. (83)

The context of the Monument Theory, obviously, severely narrows the field of replacements for the Stratford man. For one thing, the new historical framework leads to an inescapable conclusion that not only was the writer of the Sonnets no common jack but a formidable lord of the realm who sat on the tribunal of peers for the treason trial of Essex and Southampton held on February 19, 1601 at Westminster Hall. And of course the highest-ranking earl on the tribunal was fifty-year-old Edward de Vere, Earl of Oxford, the Hamlet-like nobleman first suggested as Shakespeare by British schoolmaster J. Thomas Looney in 1920, a dozen years after Greenwood's prediction that the real Shakespeare would be found "among cultured Elizabethan courtiers of high position" (83).

A Century of Sonnets

Returning to consideration of the structure that Oxford/Shakespeare utilized in crafting the story of the Sonnets, it is vital to note the central one-hundred-sonnet sequence and its division into unequal parts of eighty and twenty sonnets are essential structural aspects of the Monument Theory. Some months after my edition of the Sonnets had been published in 2005, evidence came to my attention for the first time that led me to realize *The Hekatompathia or Passionate Century of Love* by Thomas Watson, published in 1582 and dedicated to Edward de Vere, appears to have served as the model for both structural features of Shakespeare's central sequence. Watson's cycle, I learned, contains a century of "passions" or "sonnets" (he uses the two words interchangeably), arranged and numbered in consecutive order

from No.1 to No. 100. In *The Monument*, I had suggested that both the book entitled *A Hundredth Sundry Flowres* of 1573, containing a hundred lyrical verses within its prose sections (and with which Oxford appears to have been involved as writer, editor and even publisher),[14] and Watson's *Hekatompathia* of 1582 (which Watson dedicated to Oxford, his patron) had undoubtedly served as precedents for Edward de Vere's creation of a hundred-verse sequence at the center of *Shake-Speares Sonnets*. When my edition was completed, however, I had yet to become aware that Edgar I. Fripp, an orthodox scholar of Shakespeare, had put forth the same view of the important influence of the Watson work in the first volume of *Shakespeare, Man and Artist* that he published in 1938.

In a section of the first volume—a section entitled "A Century of Sonnets"—Fripp suggested that Watson's sequence may have inspired Shakespeare's "century" of sonnets, which he identified as the same "century" set forth by *The Monument*—that is, the string of centrally-positioned verses from Sonnet 27 to Sonnet 126:

> Centuries or "hundreds" of literary pieces were in fashion—of Songs, Sonnets, Prayers, Sermons, Hymns, Sentences, "Flowers," "Points of Husbandry," Emblems, Medical Observations, or what not . . . *The Hekatompathia or Passionate Century of Love* by Thomas Watson, otherwise a *Century of Passions*, may have served as a model for Shakespeare's Century of Sonnets. . . . *Shakespeare's Sonnets 27-126 are a Century* . . . (322-325; emphasis added)

The Hekatompathia or Passionate Centurie of Love states on its title page: "Divided into two parts: whereof the first expresseth the Authours sufferance in Love: the latter, his long farewell to Love and all his tyrannie." More specifically, however, the sequence was *also divided into two unequal parts of eighty (1-80) and twenty sonnets (81-100)*, just

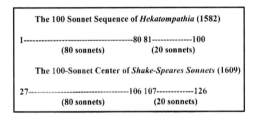

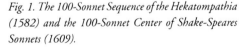

Fig. 1. The 100-Sonnet Sequence of the Hekatompathia (1582) and the 100-Sonnet Center of Shake-Speares Sonnets (1609).

as Shakespeare's hundred-sonnet sequence is divided. And Watson drew the reader's attention within this scheme to No. 81 as the "pillar" or high point of the overall sequence, which is exactly where the dramatic climax of *Shake-Speares Sonnets* is located. In other words, within the 100-Sonnet Center of Shakespeare's sequence, the eighty-first verse is Sonnet 107, coinciding with Southampton's release from the Tower of London on 10 April 1603 (see fig. 1). The evidence shows, I believe, that this exact correlation between the sequences by Watson and Shakespeare cannot be accidental; and that *the two are similar because, in fact, both were written and constructed by Edward de Vere, Earl of Oxford.* It appears that Oxford drew upon his own hundred-sonnet design for the *Hekatompathia* of 1582, along with its eighty-twenty division, as the model or blueprint for his later construction of the hundred-verse sequence within the Sonnets of 1609; therefore, if Shakespeare was borrowing from Watson, as now seems more clear than ever, then he was borrowing from himself; and in that case, Shakespeare could only have been Edward de Vere.

So important is No. 81 within Watson's scheme that he sets it up with the previous entry, No. 80, which is a long prose introduction of the verse immediately to follow as printed in "the form of a pillar":

> All such as are but of indifferent capacity, and have some skill in *Arithmetic*, by viewing this Sonnet following compiled by rule and number, into the form of a pillar, may soon judge how much art and

study the Author hath bestowed in the same. Wherein as there are placed many pretty observations, so these which I will set down, may be marked for the principal, if any man have such idle leisure to look it over, as the Author had, when he framed it. First therefore it is to be noted that the whole pillar (except the basis or foot thereof) is by relation of either half to the other *Antithetical or Antisyllabical* . . . .

The description of No. 81 becomes increasingly complex until: "And lastly, this observation is not to be neglected, that when all the foresaid particulars as performed, the whole pillar is but just 18 verses [lines]. . ."

No. 81 of the *Hekatompathia* is indeed a "pillar," printed according to a special design roughly in the shape of Aladdin's Lamp (see fig. 2). The verse is also an acrostic, with letters and numbers down the left side and more letters on the right side; and No. 82 presents the same pillar or acrostic in the normal eighteen lines. Each verse of Nos. 81-100 is

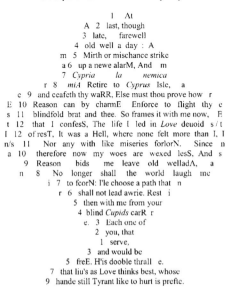

Fig. 2. Thomas Watson. Hekatompathia. Sonnet 81.

given the title LOVE IS PAST, emphasizing that these twenty poems comprise the second (and separate) sequence of the hundred "passions" or sonnets.

Noting that this work attributed to Watson, and dedicated to Oxford, "was in 1582 the first published Elizabethan sequence," Carol Thomas Neely, in the prestigious journal, *English Literary History*, observes that the act of dividing the hundred sonnets into two strings of eighty and twenty "could easily apply to Dante's or to Petrarch's sequences." And she adds: "In Watson's *Centurie* of eighteen-line passions, as in the Italian sequences, the second half is shorter than the first. The division [in Watson's sequence] is flamboyantly marked—by Sonnet 81, a shaped, acronymic and syllabic . . . poem" (371).

Watson's dedication begins with the heading: "To the Right Honorable *my very good Lord* Edward de Vere, *Earle* of Oxenford, Viscount Bulbecke, Lord *of Escales, and Badlesmere, and Lord High Chamberlain of England, all happinesse*"—and then he launches into it:

> Alexander the Great, passing on a time by the workshop of Apelles, curiously surveyed some of his doings, whose long stay in viewing them brought all the people into so great a good liking of the painter's workmanship, that immediately after they bought up all his pictures, what price soever he set them at.

He compares Oxford's influence upon the popular English taste in literature to the power of Alexander the Great to create a huge demand for the paintings of Apelles. He then reports that the earl, his patron, has generated a clamor for "my love passions" by letting it be known that he has "willingly vouchsafed the acceptance of this work," which he had "favorably perused" while it was "as yet but in written hand":

> And the like good hap (Right Honorable) befell unto me lately concerning these my Love Passions, which then chanced to Apelles for

his Portraits. For since the world hath understood (I know not how) that your Honor had willing vouchsafed the acceptance of this work, and at convenient leisures favorably perused it, being as yet but in written hand, many have oftentimes and earnestly called upon me to put it to the press, that for their money they might but see what your Lordship with some like had already perused.

Publication of the *Hekatompathia* in 1582 occurred a year after Oxford had been sent to prison in the Tower of London with one of Queen Elizabeth's maids of honor, Anne Vavasour, who had given birth to Oxford's illegitimate son.[15] This scandal erupted amidst slanders being made against him by his erstwhile Catholic associates, many of whom he had accused of having plotted treason against the Crown. Her Majesty had banished Oxford from Court; but by December 1581, under pressure from his father-in-law, Lord Burghley, he had resumed living with his wife, Anne Cecil. Then, in March 1582, he was attacked by a Vavasour relative, Thomas Knyvet, who injured him during a sword fight and apparently caused him, by infliction of a severe wound, to limp for the rest of his life.

Despite all this turmoil, however, Oxford was engaged in a whirlwind of activity at the center of the English renaissance of literature and drama that would continue through the 1580s before reaching a new plateau with the 1593 arrival of "William Shakespeare" as the signature printed, for the first time ever, at the close of the dedication to Southampton of *Venus and Adonis*. Oxford himself had already received some fourteen dedications by 1582, such tributes having been made to him by Anthony Munday and Geoffrey Gates in 1579 and by his private secretary John Lyly, who had dedicated to him the novel, *Euphues and His England*, in 1580. (Munday, dedicating his *Zelauto* of 1580 to Oxford, appeared to identify him as the real Euphues in the flesh.)

Over the next dozen years, public acknowledgments would come from not only Thomas Watson but also from John Southern, Robert Greene, Angel Day, Edmund Spenser, John Farmer (the musician) and even apparently Thomas Nashe, who dedicated his *Strange News* of 1593 to "the most copious Carminist [poet] of our time . . . Master Apis Lapis," who was also "an infinite Maecenas" to scholars and who many scholars maintain is a near-indisputable reference to Oxford.

In other words, Oxford was regarded by England's young writers (those known to us as the University Wits who also were the immediate "forerunners" or "predecessors" of Shakespeare) not only as their most intensely committed patron and guiding literary light, but as the literary figure who stood tallest amongst them all; indeed, as William Webbe wrote in *A Discourse of English Poetry* in 1586:

> I may not omit the deserved commendations of many honourable and noble Lords and Gentlemen in Her Majesty's Court, which, in the rare devices of poetry, have been and yet are most skillful; among whom the right honourable Earl of Oxford may challenge to himself the title of most excellent among the rest. (qtd in Ward 146)

And the anonymous author (probably George Puttenham)[16] of *The Arte of English Poesie* of 1589 would write in that landmark publication:

> And in her Majesty's time that now is are sprung up another crew of Courtly makers [i.e. poets], Noblemen and Gentlemen of Her Majesty's own servants, who have written excellently well as it would appear if their doings could be found out and made public with the rest, of which number is first that noble gentleman Edward Earl of Oxford. (qtd in Ward 299)

Orthodox Shakespeare scholar Wendy Phillips noted in 1989 that "Watson, like his friend John Lyly, has a markedly euphuistic style" (77) in the *Hekatompathia or Passionate Century of Love*, which is "remarkable not only in displaying the erudition of its author, but in the meticulous acknowledgment of his sources, which are entirely drawn from classical and continental literature" (71). But "perhaps the most distinctive feature" of Watson's sequence is "the presence of prose head notes prefacing each poem, pointing out the poet's devices and listing his sources . . . ." (78), wherein the writer of these notes "not only cites primary sources but is sufficiently familiar to be able to play with them. . . ." (78). "His treatment of his sources is far from slavish imitation" (78), Phillips observes about the writer of the head notes (who she presumes is Watson). "One of his greatest strengths" is the ability to bring about "a valid and convincing synthesis of quite eclectic elements," she writes, noting, also, that Watson took "obvious delight in transmitting the cream of foreign learning into his native language" (78). The *Hekatompathia* of 1582 "was sufficiently influential to start the trend of sonnet sequences and petrarchian imitation that flourished in the 1590s," she continues, adding: "Contemporary references to his wit, his jests, and his work as a playwright serve only to tantalize posterity, *for as yet none of his dramatic works has come to light*" (80; emphases added).

All aspects of this description of Thomas Watson apply directly to Edward de Vere, who was cited in 1586 (along with the late Richard Edwards) as "best for comedy" in the Elizabethan reign (and much later, in 1598, by Francis Meres, who would cite him amongst the foremost writers of comedies for the stage). As in the case of Watson's plays, none of Oxford's dramatic works have come to light (unless, of course, they have survived as part of the Shakespeare canon).

Oxfordian researchers Eric Lewin Altschuler and William Jansen have been pursuing the thesis (1) that Watson "may have been Oxford's primary pseudonym" prior to the use of "Shakespeare" in 1593, and they are continuing to find "connections between Watson's works and the works of Shakespeare." The breadth and depth of the work attributed to Watson is "remarkably Shakespearean," they write, adding that his opus "established him in his day and today as the greatest modern Latin poet and the finest English translator of Latin and Greek," while his intellectual interests included not only music but also "a remarkable knowledge and interest in astronomy and astrophysics" (13). Meanwhile, they note—importantly for us—that the *Hekatompathia* "can be seen as the godhead of the English Renaissance," and its 100 sonnets "have always been highly regarded, indeed, they are considered a model and forerunner for *Shake-Speares Sonnets*" (13). Indeed, among the similarities one finds are

> "My gentle bird, that sang so sweet of late"—*The Hekatompathia* (Sonnet 16.1)

> "Bare ruin'd choirs, where late the sweet birds sang"—(Shakespeare's Sonnet 73.4)

According to Phillips, Watson's knowledge of Continental literature "came from seven and a half years spent in Italy and France," but Altschuler and Jansen argue that scholars "can find no evidence that Watson had either the educational qualifications he claims in frontis material to some of his works, or that he visited the Continent as claimed." They add that "precious little is known about Watson, not even his year of birth" (13), while not letting it escape attention that his death in 1592 "comes just before Shake-speare's public entrance the next year" (13).

The usual biographical sketch of Watson, based on the information supplied in his published works, reads like a list of activities during Oxford's first twenty-five years. In 1872, Edward Arber noted, for example, that the material about Watson to be found in his

publications "tells us, in one way or another, that he was of gentle blood" and also "educated at Oxford: a student at law, probably a member of one of the Inns of Court; and that before 1581 he sojourned some while at Paris" (4)—all of which could have been said, of course, as well, of Edward de Vere.

"Whoever reads this remarkable work will wonder how it could have fallen into such oblivion," Arber wrote of the *Hekatompathia*, adding:

> On the poems themselves we shall here say nothing. They reveal themselves. Each of them is headed with an 'annotation.' To these short introductions we would call attention. They are most skillfully written. Who wrote them? Who was the Annotator? *May he have been the Earl of Oxford?* Was he the friend, whom Watson addresses in No. 71 as 'Deere *Titus* mine, my ancient friend'? Or was he the author himself, writing in the third person? We cannot say. *Whoever he were, he was perfectly informed*—certainly by the Poet himself—as to every allusion made, every Author imitated or referred to … The object of these annotations [was] to bring Watson's erudite verse to the appreciation [of the masses] … Though they failed in their attempt to popularize the book, *these annotations show us the vast learning of our Author* . . . (9; emphasis added)

Wendy Phillips writes that the annotations or head notes for the *Hekatompathia* as by Watson are "somewhat analogous to, though not as detailed as, E.K's glosses to Spenser's *Shepheardes Calender*" (78) which had appeared just a few years before, in 1579. Oxfordian researcher Nina Green has speculated that the unidentified "E. K." and Edward de Vere were "one and the same individual" who "understood exactly what Spenser was attempting to do, and who facilitated the introduction of Spenser's fledgling work by serving as an interpreter between the poet and his readers" (8, 24)—a description that would apply to the unidentified annotator of Watson's work as well.

Oxfordian scholar Barboura Flues has been making comparative tests of words and phrases used in various Elizabethan literary works—including Oxford's—as well as tests of the words and phrases used in the poems, plays and sonnets attributed to Shakespeare. "It's hard to work with Watson because most of his major work is in Latin," Flues says, "but what I am *sure* of is that the comments or annotations in the *Hekatompathia* are by Oxford. Those pass the word test with flying colors."[17]

A further link between Oxford and Watson is *The Tears of Fancie or Love Disdained*, which was published anonymously in 1593; it concluded with "*Finis. T. W.*"[18] This poetical sequence contains sixty consecutively-numbered sonnets in the same fourteen-line form used in the Shakespeare sonnets. Parts of a poem under the pen name "*Spraeta tamen vivunt*" (identified as Oxford by B. M. Ward) in *A Hundredth Sundry Flowres* of 1573 reappear almost verbatim two decades later in *Tears of Fancy*, as in the following, cited on page 91 in Ward and Miller:

> The lustie *Ver* which whillome
>   might exchange
> My griefe to joy, and then my joyes
>   encrease *Flowres*, 1573

> The lustie ver that whillome might
>   exchange
> My griefe to joy, and my delight in-
>   crease *Tears* Sonnet 47, 1593

Even more noteworthy is that Oxford's youthful poem, "Love Thy Choice," written in the 1570s (the first recorded sonnet of the Elizabethan reign to be composed in the fourteen-line form that eventually would become known as the Shakespearean Sonnet form [!] and expressing Oxford's devotion to the Queen) shows up again in *Tears of Fancy*

of 1593 as Sonnet 60, the final verse of the sequence. Observe the opening two lines of each:

> Who taught thee first to sigh, alas,
>   my heart?
> Who taught thy tongue the woeful
>   words of plaint?
> "Love Thy Choice," *circa* 1573

> Who taught thee first to sigh, alas,
>   sweet heart? Love.
> Who taught thy tongue to marshal
>   words of plaint? Love.
> Sonnet 60 of *Tears of Fancy*, 1593

The lines of Oxford's early sonnet contain rhetorical questions that he puts to himself, and the unspoken answer to each query is *Queen Elizabeth*, such as: "Above the rest in Court who gave thee grace?"

"Who in Elizabeth's Court could have given the 17th Earl of Oxford grace?" Charlton Ogburn Jr. asked, "or who would he have said had done so? I can hardly imagine anyone but Elizabeth" (513). Two decades later, in *Tears of Fancy*, the same line is altered so it no longer refers so obviously to the Queen: "Who forc'd thee unto wanton love give place? Love"[19]

Oxfordian researchers have been uncovering an increasing number of links between "Shakespeare" and the work of Thomas Watson—because, many of us believe, it is becoming all-too-undeniably apparent that Oxford and "Watson" are virtually indistinguishable. One notable example of the Watson-Shakespeare link is demonstrated when Sonnet No. 7 of the *Hekatompathia or Passionate Century of Love* seems to show up again in Shakespeare's Sonnet 130 of the Dark Lady series—but with its theme turned inside-out; what appears to have been a flattering homage to Queen Elizabeth in 1582, beginning, "Hark you that list to hear what saint I serve," is now an angry slander against her: "Her sparkling eyes in heaven a place deserve," Watson writes. "My Mistress' eyes are nothing like the Sunne," Shakespeare counters. Other examples include these comparisons:

Watson: "Her lips more red than any *Coral* stone."

Shakespeare: "Coral is far more red than her lips' red."

Watson: "Her neck more white than aged *Swans* that moan; Her breast transparent is, like Crystal rock."

Shakespeare: "If snow be white, why then her breasts are dun."

Watson: "Her yellow locks exceed the beaten gold."

Shakespeare: "If hairs be wires, black wires grow on her head."

Watson: "On either cheek a *Rose and Lily* lies."

Shakespeare: "I have seen Roses damasked, red and white, But no such Roses see I in her cheeks."

Watson: "Her breath is sweet perfume or holy flame."

Shakespeare: "And in some perfumes is there more delight Than in the breath that from my Mistress reeks."

Watson: "Her words are music all of silver sound"

Shakespeare: "I love to hear her speak, yet well I know That Music hath a far more pleasing sound."

Given that Watson displays an obvious interest in acrostics, particularly in No. 81 of the *Hekatompathia*, with which Oxford is so intimately connected, it becomes entirely possible that the suggestion of an acrostic in the Shakespeare sequence may be correct. Altschuler and Jansen (crediting John Baker of Centralia, Washington) note that in Sonnet 76 (at the middle of the 100-Sonnet Center),

the name **T. WATSOAND** appears when the first letters of several lines are spelled downward:

Why is my verse so barren of new pride?

So far from variation or quick change?

Why with the time do I not glance aside

To new-found methods, and to compounds strange?

Why write I still *all one, ever the same,*

And keep invention in a noted weed,

That *every word doth almost tell my name,*

Showing their birth, and where they did proceed?

O know, sweet love, I always write of you,

AND you and love are still my argument,

So all my best is dressing old worlds new,

Spending again what is already spent.

For as the Sun is daily new and old,

So is my love still telling what is told. (emphases added)

"We associate the ending of 'and'—rather than simply 'n'—as correlating perfectly with the phrase in line seven that "every word doth *almost* tell my name," Altschuler and Jansen write, adding that "we think that 'Watso-and' sounds essentially the same as 'Watson,' while also only *almost* telling the name of the author of the Sonnets" (16).

Edward de Vere, in youthful work composed under his own name, played upon his own name as *ever* or *never* and *every*. Might it be that in writing *every word doth almost tell my name*, he is pointing as well to Thomas Watson and leading us to the 100-sonnet sequence of the *Hekatompathia*? If so, it would seem he also is indicating that a "century" exists within Shakespeare's sonnet sequence—of which the eighty-first verse, Sonnet 107, reflects the acrostic-laden Sonnet 81 of Watson's sequence. In effect, if he is doing this, Oxford is leading us directly into to the heart of the structure and interpretive context of the Shakespeare sonnets, culminating in the dramatic climax of Sonnet 107 upon the death of Elizabeth, the accession of James and the liberation of Southampton in the spring of 1603. These similarities between the *Hekatompathia* (1582) and *Shake-Speares Sonnets* (1609) not only support the Monument Theory but lend new weight to research pointing to Oxford as the link between Watson and Shakespeare, indicating Watson = Oxford = Shakespeare.

Notes

[1] The publisher, Thomas Thorpe, registered the book on 20 May 1609; earlier versions of two sonnets (138 and 144 in the so-called Dark Lady series) had appeared in *The Passionate Pilgrim* of 1599; printed immediately following the 154 sonnets was a newly printed narrative poem, *A Lover's Complaint*, as by William Shakespeare. The printer, George Eld, had printed two editions of *Trolius and Cressida* by Shakespeare in 1608, the first with an enigmatic epistle declaring the missive to be from "*A never writer, to an ever reader*" [an E.Ver(e) writer to an E.Ver(e) reader (?)]. Amazingly, despite the popularity of Shakespeare's earlier poems, *Venus and Adonis* and *The Rape of Lucrece*, there is no evidence that anyone bought or read the Sonnets in 1609; instead, the little book simply vanished and went underground for more than a century—until 1711, when a surviving copy was reproduced.

[2] Oxford was seventeen years younger than Elizabeth but two years older than the Duke of Alencon of France, who, in her typically shrewd and self-preservationist manner, she led the world to believe she was going to marry.

[3] "'Gainst death and all oblivious enmity / Shall you pace forth! Your praise shall still find room / Even in the eyes of all posterity / That wear this world out to the ending doom" (Sonnet 55. 9-12).

[4] John 1:14; also 1:18: "No man hath seen God at any time; the only begotten Son, which is in the bosom of the Father..."

[5] In his notes for Sonnet 27, Booth defines "ghastly" as "terrifying, horrible" but "with the suggestion of apparition-like or ghost-like," which, we would argue, is appropriate to Oxford reflecting on the circumstances of Southampton in the Tower.

[6] "Though heaven knows it [my verse] is but as a tomb / Which hides your life and shows not half your parts" (Sonnet 17.3-4); "That did my ripe thoughts in my brain inhearse, / Making their tomb the womb wherein they grew" (Sonnet 86.3-4).

[7] "He [Oxford] was summoned from his retirement to act as the senior of the twenty-five noblemen who unanimously declared Essex and Southampton guilty, after the veriest travesty of a trial on February 19th." (Ward 336; emphasis added).

[8] The emendation from "loss" to "cross" is usual, Booth notes.

[9] During that time, I and others believe, Oxford was revising his plays of English royal history to be performed by the Lord Chamberlain's Men (known, colloquially, in the future as "Shakespeare's company") to raise public awareness about moral, legal and practical issues surrounding the succession and

addressing the question of who should or should not be allowed to govern with absolute power.

[10] The traditional perception of the Dark Lady is that she is married and has broken her "bed-vow" by some adulterous liason, but the Monument Theory views this vow as one made to Oxford with regard to her duty to their son. "In act thy bed-vow broke and new faith torn / In vowing new hate after new love bearing" (Sonnet 152)—by which we take the phrase "new love bearing" to refer to the Dark Lady's birth of a son with "love" or royal blood.

[11] "No! Time, thou shalt not boast that I do change! / Thy pyramids built up with newer might / To me are nothing novel, nothing strange, / They are but dressings of a former sight" (Sonnet 123.1-4).

[12] After Nathan Drake, in 1817, first suggested Southampton as the Fair Youth in *Shakespeare and His Times*, more than two hundred years after the 1609 printing of the quarto, many other scholars, perhaps the majority, have concluded the same. William Herbert, the 3rd Earl of Pembroke (1580-1630) has been favored by those who feel Southampton at age twenty-nine in 1603 was too old to be called "my lovely Boy" in Sonnet 126, but these critics preclude consideration that this is not the address of an old man carnally fawning on a young boy but an expression of tender affection that is characteristic of any father's loving salutation to his son.

[13] Candidates have included Emelia Bassano Lanier, Lucy Negro and Mary Fitton. Even Oxford's second wife, Elizabeth Trentham, has been suggested; Mark Anderson does so in *Shakespeare by Another Name*. Anderson writes that Southampton, as the Fair Youth, pursued a sexual relationship with Oxford's wife, Elizabeth Trentham (Anderson's Dark Lady), whereupon she gave birth to a son, conceived by Southampton, who became Henry de Vere, 18th Earl of Oxford (283)—a scenario that, to us, appears more convoluted, fantastic and insupportable than even the traditional fictions spawned by the candidacy of the Stratford man.

[14] See Ogburn Jr., on his thought that *Flowres* was "chiefly Oxford's handiwork" (625). "It will be found that if we include the thirteen lyrics signed F. I. in the *Adventures of Master F. I.*, there are exactly a hundred lyrics and poems in the book, excluding the two plays," B. M. Ward wrote in his co-edited (with Ruth Miller) publication of *A Hundredth Sundry*

Flowres. "I cannot think that this is just a coincidence … I only discovered that there were exactly a hundred poems while compiling the index" (378).

[15] Oxford's illegitimate son by Anne Vavasour, Sir Edward Vere, born in 1581, has been suggested by some Oxfordians as the younger man of the Sonnets; but here again, no one has set forth any coherent explanation of the Sonnets according to that perspective.

[16] While *The Arte of Poesie* is generally attributed to George Puttenham, some have suggested Lord Lumley.

[17] Barboura Flues, e-mail to the author, 16 October 2006.

[18] In my view, *Tears of Fancy* contains sonnets written much earlier than its publication date of 1593—probably from the early 1570s—around the same time Oxford wrote his sonnet, "Love Thy Choice" (which appears slightly altered as Sonnet 60), the last of the consecutively numbered verses of *Tears of Fancy*.

[19] The original line may have been changed to remove Oxford's direct reference to Her Majesty's royal court so general readers would not suspect that the author of *Tears of Fancy* was a nobleman-courtier.

Works Cited

Akrigg, G. P. V. *Shakespeare and the Earl of Southampton*. Cambridge: Harvard, 1968.

Altschuler, Eric Lewin and William Jansen. "Was Thomas Watson Shakespeare's Precursor?" *The Shakespeare Oxford Newsletter* 40.4 (Fall 2004): 1, 13-16, 24.

Anderson, Mark. *"Shakespeare" by Another Name*. New York: Penguin, 2005.

Arber, Edward, ed. *Thomas Watson: Poems*. London, 1870.

Booth, Stephen. *Shakespeare's Sonnets*. New Haven: Yale, 1977.

Drake, Nathan. *Shakespeare and His Times*. London: Cadwell, 1817.

Duncan-Jones, Katherine. *Shakespeare's Sonnets*. London: Nelson, 1997.

Fripp, Edgar I. *Shakespeare, Man and Artist*. Vol. 1. London: Oxford, 1938. 2 vols.

Flues, Barboura. E-mail to the author. 16 October 2006.

Giroux, Robert. *The Book Known as Q*. New York: Atheneum, 1982.

Green, Nina. "Who Was Spenser's E. K.? Was He the Seventeenth Earl of Oxford?" *The Oxfordian* 1 (October 1998): 5-25.

Greenwood, Sir George. *The Shakespeare Problem Restated*. London: Lane, 1908.

Looney, J. Thomas. *"Shakespeare" Identified in Edward de Vere, The Seventeenth Earl of Oxford*. 1920. Ed. Ruth Loyd Miller. Jennings, LA: Minos Publishing, 1975.

Massey, Gerald. *The Secret Drama of Shakspeare's Sonnets Unfolded, With the Characters Identified*. 1872. New York: AMS P, 1973.

Nashe, Thomas. *"Strange News*. 1592." Trans. Barboura Flues. Ed. Robert Brazil. < www.elizabethanauthors.com/snewsOrig101.htm>.

Neely, Carol Thomas. "The Structure of English Renaissance Sonnet Sequences." *English Literary History* 45.3 (Autumn 1978): 359-389.

Ogburn Jr., Charlton. *The Mysterious William Shakespeare*. McLean, VA: EPM, 1992.

Phillips, Wendy. "No More Tears: Thomas Watson Absolved." *Comitatus: A Journal of Medieval and Renaissance Studies* 20 (October 1989): 71-84.

Rollins, Hyder Edward, ed. *A New Variorum Edition of Shakespeare: The Sonnets*. By William Shakespeare. Philadelphia: Lippincott, 1944.

Shewring, Margaret, *King Richard II*. Manchester: Manchester UP, 1996.

Smith, D. Nichol. *Shakespeare's England*. Vol. 2. Oxford: Clarendon, 1916. 2 vols.

A Hundredth Sundry Flowres, From the Original Edition of 1573. Bernard M. Ward and Ruth Loyd Miller, eds. Port Washington, NY: Kennikat, 1975.

Ward, Bernard M. *The Seventeenth Earl of Oxford, 1550-1604*. London: Murray, 1928.

Watson, Thomas. "*Hekatompathia 1582*." Trans. Barboura Flues. Ed. Robert Brazil. <www.elizabethanauthors.com/hek05.htm>.

Watson, Thomas. *The Hekatompathia or Passionate Centurie of Love*. London, 1582.

Whittemore, Hank. *The Monument*. Marshfield Hills, MA: Meadow Geese, 2005.

Wright, Daniel L. *The Anglican Shakespeare: Elizabethan Orthodoxy in the Great Histories*. Vancouver, WA: Pacific-Columbia, 1993.

— . "'Fine word, "legitimate!"!' Legitimizing Illegitimacy in Shakespeare." The 12th Annual Shakespeare Authorship Studies Conference. Concordia University, Portland, OR. 4 April 2008.

Unveiling the Sonnets

William E. Boyle

The following paper is based on preparations for a panel discussion on Shakespeare's Sonnets at the 2006 Shakespeare Authorship Studies Conference at Concordia University in Portland, Oregon. I appeared there with author Hank Whittemore to present and defend Whittemore's "Monument Theory" on the meaning and purpose of the Sonnets. As a friend and colleague of Whittemore for 20 years, and as an editor of his work in the *Shakespeare Oxford Newsletter* and *Shakespeare Matters*, this was not the first time we had worked together or participated in joint presentations on the Monument Theory. Whittemore's article, elsewhere in this tribute to Elizabeth Holden, explains the Monument Theory in much more detail than I will attempt in this paper. My purpose here is to provide a perspective on how a *bonafide* historical context influences the interpretation of certain words in several of the sonnets, thereby transforming interpretation of the sonnets themselves from mere speculation or guessing into sound theorizing.

In an article in *Modern Language Notes* in 1917, Henry David Gray neatly captured the dilemma of all commentators who dare take on the infamous sonnet enigma; his words ring as true today as they did 89 years ago:

> [One might do well to introduce himself thus] . . . "I am a Southamptonite, dating the Sonnets with Sarrazin from 1592 to 1596, accepting with Dowden the quarto order of the first 125 as chronological, with Massey identifying the Dark Lady as Elizabeth Vernon, and with Wyndham proclaiming the Rival Poet to be Drayton." Or, "I am a Pembrokist, dating the Sonnets with Mackail from 1598 to 1603, with Tyler identifying the Dark Lady as Mary Fitton, and holding with Minto that the Rival Poet is Chapman." Or, "I agree with Sir Sidney Lee that the Sonnets are literary exercises which do not record the poet's own experiences; I believe with Alden that it is impertinent to try to identify the Dark Lady; I think with Fleay that W.H. is not the youth to whom the First Series is addressed at all but Thorpe's 'only procurer' of them; I am confident, with Walsh, that the order is wholly haphazard and must be completely readjusted to make the Sonnets intelligible; I haven't the faintest idea who the Rival Poet could have been, for I hold with Rolfe, that many of the First Series may have been addressed to a woman." Or finally: "I am a free lance among the Sonnets' critics with a special set of conjectures all my own; though I do agree with Butler that W.H. is William Hughes, with Acheson that the Dark Lady is Mistress Davenant, and with Montgomery that the Rival Poet is Spenser; I realize, with Beeching, that Sonnet 107 must refer to the death of Elizabeth, though the majority, as McClumpha shows, are contemporary with *Romeo and Juliet* and *Love's Labour's Lost*." Having thus, or by some similar formula, presented his credentials, the new

champion may enter the lists and proceed to break his spear against the Veiled Knight who guards the Mystery of the Sonnets. (17-18)

Little has changed since Gray's time, even with the subsequent identification, by J.T. Looney, of Edward de Vere, the 17th earl of Oxford, as Shakespeare, for Oxfordians have battled each other just as furiously over these same points as have any groupings of Stratfordians or anti-Stratfordians. But identifying who's who in the Sonnets is just half the task of the Sonnet Mystery; the other half is resolving the question of "Just what *is* the story?" Indeed, one might ask (and many have): "Is there any story at all?" Theories that suggest a story range from speculations on love trysts to love triangles to peculiar forms of adultery, to suggestions that the Sonnets are all about man-on-man love, most often referred to as homosexual love. The only point on which most can agree is that the poet exhibits deep passion and deep anguish over *something*.

More recently, writing on Sonnet 29 in the *Durham University Journal*, David Thatcher covers some of this "what is the story" ground in what he describes—quoting Harold Bloom—as engagements in "strong misreading" that only complicate and add to already "weak and repetitious ones [i.e., other interpretive scenarios] still at large" (59-60). Thatcher offers (echoing Sonnet 66, while still talking about readings and misreadings), that he, too, is "tired, especially with biographical interpretations." Yet Thatcher, peeling away successive layers of Sonnet 29 to prompt questions like "What is this?" and "Why is that?" seems to contradict the basis for his exasperation, for, in posing such questions to us, he surely must recognize that, in the end, such questions, of course, can only be answered by knowing *who* is writing to *whom* and about *what*. For example, Thatcher notes that

[a] crucial ambivalence the poem [Sonnet 29] never resolves is whether the disgrace is real or illusory, deserved or undeserved,

making it difficult for the reader to know if sympathy towards the speaker (the conventional reaction) is really an appropriate and justified response. Theoretically, only an historical human narratee, if there had been one, might have been in a position to know what precisely the narrator was referring to in this opening line. . . . But such knowledge is irrecoverable. (61)

There we have the sonnet dilemma in a nutshell: "Such knowledge is irrecoverable." *But what if such knowledge were not irrecoverable?* What if there were a correct answer to the entire Sonnet Mystery, and all that one needed to achieve it were the proper set of interpretive tools?

Sonnet commentary background

These essays by Gray and Thatcher are just two of the thousands of writings to have been published over the past two centuries on *Shakespeare's Sonnets*. In a recent book of critical essays on the Sonnets,[1] James Schiffer introduces the collection with an excellent sixty-eight page essay that surveys the history of sonnet commentary, making several interesting points along the way.

Perhaps most helpful in Schiffer's survey is its presentation of a history that has ebbed and flowed more than once over the "biographical vs. fictive" schools of interpretation, and, as part of the larger sonnet debate, advances the notion that appreciating the Sonnets' themes does not require knowing the particular events in the author's life that may have inspired any particular verse. This notion is summed up in a 1907 quote from commentator Walter Raleigh:

It would help us but little to know the names of the beautiful youth and the dark woman; no public records could reflect even faintly those vicissitudes of experience, exultations and abysses of feeling which have their sole and sufficient record in the Sonnets. . . . Poetry is not biography; and the value of the Sonnets to the modern reader is independent of all knowledge of their occasion. That they were made from the material of experience is certain: Shakespeare was no puny imitative rhymster. But the processes of art have changed the tear to a pearl, which remains to decorate new sorrows. The Sonnets speak to all who have known the chances and changes of human life. Their occasion is a thing of the past; their time is eternal. (qtd. in Schiffer 32)

Schiffer then comments that "such attention to theme divorced from . . . biography, while not exactly new, would become a dominant note as sonnets criticism moved into the twentieth century" (33). But it is this "divorce" of theme from biography that really is at the heart of the Sonnets' mystery, and demonstrates—even if unknowingly—the overriding importance of the authorship debate in *any* commentary on *Shakespeares Sonnets*. Without having "real" known biographical facts with which to buttress any biographical interpretation, all interpretations become thematic musings, with any biographical implications being nothing more than attempts to recover the "irrecoverable knowledge," the absence of which Thatcher laments but which Raleigh says is irrelevant anyway.

So the traditional critical approach to the Sonnets that has evolved from this situation is that all that needs to be done is to identify a Fair Youth and a Dark Lady, and then proceed to *hypothesize* unknown events into a story of some sort—or else, as Raleigh wrote, ignore the story of the Poet, the Youth and the Dark Lady altogether and just enjoy the eternal pearl of the poems' lyrical beauty. For Stratfordians, of course, this approach can never be tempered with the idea that it is Shakespeare himself (the Poet) who needs to be "correctly"

identified before any progress can be made, but *this is where the authorship debate and anti-Stratfordian Sonnet commentary become factors in our hopes of achieving as full an understanding of the Sonnets as possible.*

Yet for all Sonnet commentators (Stratfordian and anti-Stratfordian) the equally important task of identifying an *actual* history involving the parties (Poet, Fair Youth, Dark Lady) about which the Poet was writing has presented a seemingly insurmountable obstacle. And it has been attempts to overcome this obstacle that have resulted in an abundance of commentary that "hypothesizes" what this actual history "must" have been based *only* on what any given Sonnet "seems" to be about to the interpreter of those Sonnets.

All this highly subjective, impressionistic criticism has led to the current state of the traditional sonnet debate. For example, Joseph Pequigney's *Such is My Love* (1985), with its homoerotic reading of the Sonnets, has won many converts. Yet Pequigney's reading coexists with those of Booth (1977), Kerrigan (1986), Vendler (1997) and Duncan-Jones (1998), all of which steer clear of going down the autobiographical road in interpreting the Sonnets.

One of the gems in Schiffer's essay is the story of an early round of sonnet commentary in which Edmund Malone responded to George Steevens' moral revulsion over Shakespeare's declaration to his addressee in Sonnet 20 that he is "the master-mistress of my passion." In his 1783 edition of Shakespeare, Steevens had written that "[i]t is impossible to read this fulsome panegyrick, addressed to a male object, without an equal mixture of disgust and indignation." Malone responded in 1790 that "[s]ome part of this indignation might perhaps have been abated if it had been considered that such addresses to men, however indelicate, were customary in our author's time, and neither imported criminality, nor were esteemed indecorous . . ." He added that "Master-mistress" does not mean "man-mistress," but [rather] "Sovereign mistress" (the same two words are used together in Sonnet 126, line 5). Little did he know (as we shall see) the import of what he was saying, because while he was certainly not promoting the youth as really "sovereign" in any sense, he nonetheless introduced into the equation a thesis that has resonated for the past 150 years among many anti-Stratfordian commentators (notably Oxfordians, but before them, Baconians). In rejecting possibly homosexual allusions, Malone found *royal* allusions (qtd in Schiffer 21-23).

That initial showdown over interpreting a single line in one sonnet set the stage for the next 200 years, with the central point of contention always being whether to accept the words as literally true and autobiographical (and hence, as some commentators maintain, "diminish" Shakespeare since the perceived man-to-man love could, to them, only be homosexual) or adopt more benign interpretations that are not autobiographical and thereby "protect" Shakespeare from any suggestion that he was gay or bisexual (Schiffer 27-31). This "true/diminishing" vs. "benign/protecting" dichotomy has also bedeviled anti-Stratfordian commentary, for the suggestion that the Poet was being "real" when he calls the Youth "my sovereign" in Sonnet 57 (one of many royal allusions throughout the sonnets[2]) has been every bit as contentious for some anti-Stratfordians as the homosexual thesis has been for Stratfordians.

The notion of the royal allusions being real was introduced into the Oxfordian movement in the 1930s by B. M. Ward and Percy Allen.[3] Their theory was that the Poet/Fair Youth relationship was not one of an older lover and a younger lover but rather one of father and son—and that the son was a prince, seen by the father as the rightful heir to Elizabeth (the Dark Lady). This theory—generally referred to among contemporary Oxfordians as the "Prince Tudor" theory (Whittemore xxxv-xxxvi)—has divided the Oxfordian movement ever since it was first proposed, not least because there seems to be no independent historical evidence for it, but also because it seems, to many, so outrageously

"over the top," or "hopelessly romantic," or —worst of all—conspiratorial.

This theory of the *Sonnets* was aptly summed up by Charlton Ogburn, Jr.:

> We are left with a compelling question raised by the *Sonnets*. It is a question that is inescapable and one that traditional scholarship is resolved upon escaping at all costs … How is it that the Poet of the *Sonnets* can—as he unmistakably does—address the fair youth as an adoring and deeply concerned father would address his son and as a subject would his liege-lord? (75)

The "royal" theory has been the source of much contention among Oxfordians over the past seventy years. The exact details of who may have slept with whom to create such a scenario we will leave to another day,[4] but the import of demonstrating the "royal" theory, if it can be demonstrated, is crucial to the resolution of the Shakespeare Mystery, as this is the one issue that divides Oxfordian scholars more than any other contested issue within the Oxfordian community.

A proposed solution

Writing in support of Hank Whittemore's "Monument Theory" of the Sonnets' meaning and purpose in the Summer 2004 *Shakespeare Matters* (in an article titled "With the Sonnets Now Solved…"), I chose a headline that boldly declared the Sonnets Mystery solved. In response, Lynne Kositsky and Roger Stritmatter submitted an article, "Critique of the Monument Theory," for publication in the Fall 2004 issue of *Shakespeare Matters*. In the years since the publication of that article, the debate has raged, with opponents of the Monument Theory (with its royalist "Prince Tudor" implications) contending that one cannot claim the Sonnets are "solved," or that there is no answer to the sonnet enigma.

Therefore, let me justify the above headline by restating it: I think the sonnets *can be solved* if one has the right elements in place, and I submit that, in Whittemore's work, *they have been solved.* By "solved" let me be clear about what I mean, for it goes back to Thatcher's contention that "only an historical human narratee 'might' . . . know what was being referred to . . . but that knowledge is irrecoverable." I believe that knowledge is indeed "recoverable," and that several particular words within the sonnets, when read in the light of their actual historical context —as opposed to the subjective guesses of de-historicized impressionistic readers—reveal the true story. The key to recovering this true story lies in correctly identifying the narrator (Poet), the narratee (Fair Youth), the Dark Lady, *and* the historical circumstances. *All* these elements must be identified before anyone can dare declare, "Sonnets solved."

Unlike all previous sonnet theories, the Monument Theory accomplishes this. It hypothesizes "Poet" identity (Edward de Vere, 17th earl of Oxford), "Fair Youth" identity (Henry Wriothesley, 3rd earl of Southampton), "Dark Lady" identity (Queen Elizabeth I) and *documented* historical circumstances that are applicable to the *entire* sonnet sequence while bringing to the foreground *key*

words that appear in the sonnets but have never been understood in *contextual terms,* i.e., a *bona fide* historical context. Briefly, I believe that the key to the solution lies in *both* the primary historical context identified by Whittemore—the Essex Rebellion of 1601—and in the relationship of the Poet to the Fair Youth as one of father to royal son. Further, it is important to note that both father and son were involved in the Rebellion and that both suffered its consequences.

In my 2004 article supporting the Monument Theory, I focused on three sonnets (35, 87, 120), and I wish to revisit them in this essay in more detail to make the point that the answer to the mystery of the sonnets has been embedded in the sonnets the whole time, hiding in plain sight, waiting to be found. When one places the royal allusions (Hotson Ch. 2-3, Whittemore 773-777) and the abundance of legal language (Whittemore xlvii) in the sonnets side-by-side with the royal succession agenda and the subsequent treason trials of the Essex Rebellion, the meaning of the Sonnets comes into focus.

Essex Rebellion background

Before delving into these three sonnets, let's first look at some of the history surrounding the Essex Rebellion, since it is posited as being central to the Monument Theory. As I wrote in 2004, one important question that seldom has been asked (let alone answered) about the Essex Rebellion is why the life of its co-leader, the 3rd earl of Southampton, was spared (he was tried with Essex, convicted of treason and sentenced to die). A second question is why the author, Shakespeare, was not rounded up, tried and punished—or even interrogated—when his play *Richard II*, depicting the deposition of a monarch, was used to *set the stage for the Rebellion.* A third question focuses on just what the conspirators' goals were that day (i.e., were they, in fact, advancing James's claim as Elizabeth's successor?). And a final question asks what Essex had been up to in the years leading up to the rebellion, a period during which he was often perceived as a contemporary Bolingbroke to Elizabeth's Richard II. Much of this history has been written about in Essex biographies and other histories of the period, but always from a conventional viewpoint in which neither Shakespeare nor Southampton is seen as having any stake in the succession debate.

A recent article by Chris Fitter in *Early Modern Literary Studies* sheds some light on this last question (about Essex), and, of special significance, Fritter attempts to comprehend what Shakespeare was up to as he wrote and rewrote *Richard II* over a period of five years leading up to the Rebellion (Fitter never considers that Shakespeare could have been revising work written before 1596).

After the Rebellion's failure, it was recorded at the rebels' trial that Prosecutor Edward Coke said Essex had designs on becoming King Robert the First (Camden par. 18) and that Robert Cecil had stated that Essex wished to set himself up as King (Harrison 151). In fact, some of Cecil's words seem remarkable, considering that Essex had no blood claim to the throne whatsoever (Bolingbroke, at least, was Richard II's cousin, the son of one of his uncles):

> And had I not seen your [Essex's] ambitious affections inclined to usurpation, I could have gone on my knees to her Majesty to have done you good ... You, my good lords, counselors of state, have had many conferences, and I do confess I have said the King of Scots is a competitor, and the King of Spain is a competitor, and you [i.e. Essex] I have said are a competitor: you would depose the Queen, you would be king of England, and call a Parliament. (qtd in Keeton 55-56)

Here is Cecil mentioning Essex right in the company of the two most powerful claimants angling to succeed Elizabeth. How could this perception of Essex as a "would be king of England" have developed in the

years leading up to 1601 without Essex ever having faced any *serious* rebuke? Neither the Privy Council hearing in the Fall of 1599 nor the quasi-official "commission" hearing in June 1600—both of which did begin to take action in response to these perceptions, precipitated by the dedication to Essex in Dr. John Hayward's 1599 *History of Henry the Fourth*—seem sufficiently serious forums for consideration of the risks allied to a potential usurper. And consider further that Essex's almost year-long house arrest during this period was just that—house arrest, *not* the Tower (which is where Hayward was sent and remained until Elizabeth died). Moreover, it was just six months after his release from house arrest that the Rebellion took place. It is even recorded that Robert Cecil had seen *Richard II* in 1597 and that, upon learning of this fact, Essex was "wonderful merry" at Cecil's reaction to the play (we have no direct evidence of what Cecil's reaction was, just that Essex commented upon it). Chris Fitter's take on this (Fitter pars. 31-32, 36-37)—the main point of his essay, in fact—is that Shakespeare actually is sabotaging the overreaching earl more than seriously promoting his Bolingbroke-like ambitions, so perhaps Cecil is enjoying a laugh at Essex's expense. If so, he must have overlooked the depose-and-kill-the-monarch ending of the play, or perhaps—in the *realpolitik* world of Elizabethan statecraft—he had a different ending in mind.

Fitter's article makes clear what dangerous times these were with the politics of succession so unsettled, and how risky it was for anyone to speak out. Yet speak out is exactly what some (including Shakespeare) did. Robert Parson's *Conference About the Next Succession to the Crowne of England* (1594/1595) contained a dedication to Essex that Fitter describes as "treasonably suggesting him to be Elizabeth's next heir" (Fitter par. 7). As noted above, the dedication to Essex in Hayward's 1599 *History of Henry the Fourth* had landed the author in the Tower for his daring. Yet, even as Fitter makes the case for Shakespeare's active involvement in such dangerous politics with his *Richard II*, he never asks how Shakespeare could have—or why he would have—dared to do so. At one point, Fitter cites a letter from Rowland Whyte to Robert Sidney in which Whyte says, "To wryte of these Things are [sic] dangerous in so perillous a Tyme." And in the next sentence Fitter writes, "And this is precisely what Shakespeare now did" (Fitter pars. 39-40).

One final note on Fitter's intriguing examination of the period: he never mentions the earl of Southampton. Considering that he is explicating Shakespeare's political agenda on the succession, the Queen, and the Earl of Essex, and given the sudden appearance of Shakespeare on the literary scene in 1593-1594 (coincident with the rise of Essex) with two long poems dedicated to Southampton, Fitter's omission seems strange. It does seem to reflect the larger problem that Oxfordians have frequently noted over the years—namely, that if one has the wrong Shakespeare, then any history involving him cannot be fully, nor correctly, understood. Southampton was definitely involved with Essex throughout this period, and was, in fact, a co-leader and co-conspirator in the Rebellion. If, as Fitter speculates, Shakespeare was actually sabotaging Essex during this critical period when Essex was openly seen as a Bolingbroke-like challenger in the succession sweepstakes, how can Fitter not wonder how Southampton (publicly linked to Shakespeare through the popular *Venus and Adonis* and *Lucrece* poems) factors into all of this?

The unanswered question here—if Fitter is right in his speculation about Shakespeare and Essex—is, then, what was Shakespeare up to? Just what are his concerns in *Richard II* about the succession crisis of the 1590s? His play does seem to suggest approval of the notion of Bolingbroke usurping a monarch such as Richard, but if Shakespeare didn't approve of Essex as an Elizabethan Bolingbroke, did he have another Bolingbroke in mind? After all, the future of the Elizabethan state was at stake in these years; would there be a peaceful

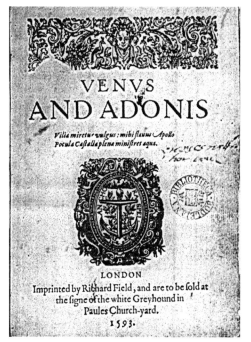

succession or civil war if the Tudor Dynasty were to disappear without an heir having been named before the Queen's death?

Why was Southampton spared?

To return to the Southampton side of the equation in the Essex Rebellion, we must ask how, in the *quid pro quo* world of Elizabethan justice, Southampton's life was spared without any record of something having been done, either by him or by someone acting for him. For all the other conspirators there is a record of their swift executions following their trials (Essex, Blount, Meyrick, Danvers and Cuffe), or of staggering fines being assessed and—for the most part—paid (e.g., by Rutland, Bedford, Neville, and many others), or, in the interesting case of Sir John Davis, of full cooperation with the state that secured the death penalty for himself and the four others tried with him (Blount, Meyrick, Danvers, and Cuffe), yet as these other four went to their deaths within weeks of their trial, he (Davis) was spared and eventually granted a pardon by the Queen in 1602 (Devereux 198); was this a *quid pro quo* for his cooperation? And was it the only one exacted following the Rebellion? After all, what was it that saved the co-leader of the Rebellion itself: Henry Wriothesley, 3rd earl of Southampton?

Charlotte Stopes, in her biography of Southampton, mentions this *quid pro quo* system:

> . . . As soon as the Privy Council felt safe by the apprehension of the chief offender, they turned their attention towards possible mercy, in order to ingratiate themselves with the people. This rarely meant politic mercy, as in the case of Mountjoy, who was needed where he was; or even compassionate mercy, as in the case of the Earl of Southampton. It in general expressed itself as mercantile mercy, measured in proportion, not to the degree of the offender's guilt, but of his capacity to pay. (233; emphasis added)

Although Stopes notes the "mercantile" nature of the system, in the absence of any record of a *quid pro quo* for Southampton, she concludes that it was "compassion" alone that spared him. In the face of the enormity of Southampton's crime, however, is such a sentimental conclusion credible?

A closer examination of the extant records involving Southampton tells a different story than that offered by Stopes. The primary records are Southampton's letters to the Privy Council in February and March of 1601. While these letters (in which "her Majestie" and "mercy" are mentioned often) are reproduced in their entirety by Stopes (225-231), they are curiously absent in both Rowse's and Akrigg's biographies (perhaps—however difficult it is to imagine—because neither saw Southampton's reprieve as a story worth reviewing in detail). The story that these letters tell is of a man who seems to have a defense counsel (his "advocate" [Sonnet 35]) hovering over his shoulder, telling him exactly what to say and how to say it. The letters, even

as they beg for mercy for his "fawte" [fault], reflect a perfect understanding of the legal difference between "treason" and the lesser charge of "misprision of treason" as it was used at this time. When Southampton writes that he had no idea what Essex was up to, and no idea that events were headed toward treason, he sets himself up to be plea-bargained from treason and death to "misprision of treason" and life in prison ("supposed as forfeit to a confined doom" [Sonnet 107]). That precise legal mechanism had been perfected throughout the 120-year Tudor dynasty, whereby treason charges could be, at the discretion of the Crown, reduced to "misprision of treason" (Bellamy 30; Rastell 153).

Finally, while the phrase "misprision of treason" cannot be directly linked to a reduction in sentence to account for the failure of the State to execute Southampton with the other conspirators sentenced to die, it has been used to refer to the fate of one of his fellow conspirators: Sir Henry Neville. In a 1978 article by Clayton Roberts and Owen Duncan about the English parliament circa 1614, Neville is mentioned, and a reference is made by the authors to his having been accused of "misprision of treason" in the Essex Rebellion and thereby imprisoned. The article does not cite any contemporary source for using this phrase, but it does state that although he knew of the plot, he did not inform Cecil, and that Neville, "for this was accused of misprision of treason and sent to the Tower" (494).[6] Southampton, in his pleading letters to the Privy Council, not only acknowledged not informing anyone, but even claimed that he really didn't know where the events for which he had been convicted were headed— almost as if he were asking *how* he could have informed anyone. And Neville, though he was released on the same day as Southampton (10 April 1603), had his lands restored and also was pardoned (James and Rubinstein 147), still *had to pay* a substantial portion of his original £10,000 fine (estimated at £3,000 [James and Rubinstein 146]). Further, as Neville's biographers note, Neville was tainted by the Rebellion for the rest of his life and barred from high office. Neville's punitive treatment highlights how Southampton—the co-leader of the rebellion—stood *alone* among all the conspirators as apparently having been required to *perform nothing* and *pay nothing* for his special treatment. In fact, not only was Southampton not punished; he was fully restored, pardoned, *and even honored* upon his release; he even was made a Knight of the Garter.

So, was Southampton as disconnected from intimate association with Essex and the conspirators of the Rebellion as his pleading letters to the Privy Council would indicate? I think not. The historical record seems to belie his words, beginning with his unarguably close association with Essex in the years leading up to the Rebellion. Both of them, after all—and more than once—had been arraigned before and were in frequent trouble with the Queen over their disobedient behavior. There is also an intriguing account from John Nichols about an event in the spring of 1603, shortly after Southampton's release and pardon (Akrigg 136-137; Massey 77-78) that is illuminating. Nichols reports that Southampton told James' wife, Queen Anne, that the Rebellion could have—perhaps would have—succeeded if *only they could have followed through with their plans.* The Nichols report relates how Queen Anne remarked "in amazement" that "so many great men did so little for themselves," a remark to which (in Akrigg's words), "Southampton had a ready reply: they [the Essex Rebellion conspirators] had no choice but to yield, since their sovereign had sided with their enemies" (136).

Lord Grey, an Essex/Southampton opponent in the years leading up to the Rebellion (one of "their enemies"), is then reported to interrupt, saying (in Akrigg's words) that "he and his friends could have done much more than the Essexians" (137). Argument ensued, and Grey and Southampton were sent briefly to the Tower. But consider what this moment in 1603 reveals: Southampton is still fighting the same fight and *justifying* what occurred

in 1601—and this from someone who had claimed in his letters to the Privy Council that he didn't even *know* what was going on! The tone of the exchange (as reported) seems to cast in doubt that the placement of James of Scotland on the throne of England was the goal of the Rebellion; otherwise, what are they arguing over? Why would Queen Anne say that so many great men did so little for *themselves* if they were doing it for James? Southampton's words, uttered just months after his release, are not the same words one finds in his obsequious letters written two-and-one-half years earlier.

Also of interest in this matter of the Essex-Southampton relationship is an attempt by Captain Thomas Lee, just days after the Rebellion, to find a way to get *both* Essex and Southampton out of the Tower and into the presence of the Queen to explain themselves (Lacey 298; Myers 48). Lee, a notorious assassin involved with Essex in Ireland, was caught, and within two days tried, convicted and executed for treason. James P. Myers, writing about Lee in a 1991 article, reports that at his trial[7] he said his only intention was "with the aid of a half dozen resolute men [to] step unto the queen, and kneel before her, and never rise till she had signed a warrant . . . and never stir till the earls of Essex and Southampton were brought to the queen's presence" (qtd. in Myers 48). Myers comments that Lee's true intentions may never be known and that he was reported to have died "still [denying] the treason for which he was executed" (48). Myers further notes that Lee's trial also does not make apparent that Lee "until the Essex Rebellion, had enjoyed repute as the Crown's creature, a successful mercenary and assassin . . . Evidence in the state papers suggests that someone [other than his brother Sir Henry], possibly the Cecils or the queen or even all three, had for almost twenty years protected him . . . " (48). Myers then notes:

> Given, moreover, the residual popularity of Essex and the lingering potential for further disturbances, Lee's treason could conveniently

be made to pressure the vacillating monarch into authorizing Essex's death. The ploy succeeded: Cecil, writing of Essex's execution to the lord deputy of Ireland on 26 February, pointedly observed that the earl's death 'was the more hastened by the bloody practice of 'Thom' Lee'. (49)

Myers' speculation leaves open the possibility that the entire Lee episode was a Cecil ploy from the beginning. If so, it would reinforce and reaffirm how cut-throat and double-dealing were the politics of this era, especially the politics surrounding the Rebellion. Lee's claim that he wished only to bring *both* Essex and Southampton before the Queen is noteworthy, but who it was who put him up to risking and losing his life in this cause to present Essex and Southampton before Elizabeth is unknown.

In both of these instances, we can see that Essex and Southampton were, indeed, co-leaders of the Rebellion. Southampton's protestations to the Privy Council were transparently false, but they were necessary if he were to hope to secure a reprieve from his death sentence. However—and astonishingly—there is no written record in Southampton's case of exactly how or why his sentence alone was commuted when *all* of the other conspirators were punished in severe degree. The upshot of all this history is that Rebellion co-leader Southampton was clearly unique in how his case was handled. History has yet to explain why he received such special and unaccounted-for leniency. If Southampton did not have to pay for his acts with his life, did someone else pay Cecil's, i.e., the State's, price for the young earl's life?

With some of this background in place, let's take a look at how Sonnets 35, 87 and 120 may be concerned with those events and their consequences.

"That which thou has't done"

Sonnet 35 begins, "No more be grieved at that which thou has't done." The word "that" clearly refers to "something done" which, in turn, is the key to the "story." But how can we ever know what "that" is which has been done? Isn't it "irrecoverable knowledge"? Consider, however, that "that" is referenced again in the same sonnet—both as a "trespass" and as a "sensual fault":

> All men make faults, and even I
>   in this
> Authorizing thy trespass with com-
>   pare (ll. 5-6)
>
> For to thy sensual fault I bring in
>   sense
> (Thy adverse party is thy advocate)
>   (9-10)

Consider further that "trespass" is repeated once later in the sequence (Sonnet 120) in which we observe that "trespass" and "crime" are used interchangeably:

> To weigh how once I suffered in
>   your crime (8)
>
> But that your trespass now becomes
>   a fee,
> Mine ransom yours, and yours must
>   ransom me (13-14)

So, using just these two sonnets, one could propose a straightforward formula:

> that = fault = trespass (Sonnet 35)
> = crime = trespass (Sonnet 120)

by this, we can see that "that which thou has't done" refers not to just a minor offense of some sort, but to a crime (and "crime" also appears in Sonnet 58 [12] as the Youth's "self-doing crime"). Is there a Fair Youth candidate who is known to have committed a crime? Yes: Henry Wriothesley, 3rd earl of Southampton, was convicted of treason in the Essex Rebellion and sentenced to death.[8] And considering that the range of Sonnets between 35 and 120 covers almost the entire 100 middle-sonnet sequence (27-126), it seems reasonable to consider that the *only thing* being discussed between the Poet and the Youth throughout this entire sequence is just this one thing: "that which thou hast done," i.e., the crime which you have committed.[9]

The other key word/concept that can be gleaned from these sonnets (35, 120 and also Sonnet 34) is "ransom" as some form of expiation of the Fair Youth's crime. Our chief consideration here is to recall that—with Southampton posited as the Fair Youth—we have a Fair Youth who had been convicted of a crime and sentenced to die but was later reprieved. In a world where "ransom and fines" were almost always paid to obtain commutations by convicts who could afford them, there is no record of any ransom or fine being paid by the youthful Southampton for his commutation. But might a ransom have been paid for him by another? *Is it possible that the Sonnets may provide the missing explanation for Southampton's freedom and what price was paid—and by whom—to obtain it?* We will return to this point later.

Trespass and treason

Kositsky and Stritmatter point out in their article critiquing the Monument Theory that the word "treason" does not appear in Sonnet 35 (11) nor even in the middle century of sonnets (27-126), the sequence postulated by Whittemore to be a chronological diary and record of Shakespeare, Southampton and the Essex Rebellion. Therefore, they contend, there is no reason to gloss the words "trespass" or "fault" as references to Southampton's treason. It should be noted here that Whittemore, however, provides in his book several examples from Shakespeare's plays where Shakespeare treated these words interchangeably (Whittemore 478-479).[10]

However, there is another Shakespearean work which uses "trespass" and "fault," *plus* the words "treason" and "crime," interchangeably: *Rape of Lucrece*. In fact, those four words are used throughout that poem in reference only to the *one event* being discussed: Tar-

quin's acts of bursting into Lucrece's bedroom and raping her (the actual word count is: Treason=6, Trespass=6, fault=12, crime=5) (Furness). Significantly, although those words are used to discuss a single event, their usage actually is differentiated within the poem: "treason" is associated exclusively with Tarquin (in his own words or those of the poet/narrator), while "fault" and "trespass" are used principally—though not exclusively—to describe Lucrece (in her own words or those of the poet/narrator). The usage of "crime" is split evenly between Tarquin and Lucrece, with two instances of Lucrece speaking of "his" crime—i.e., Tarquin's crime—and two instances of her speaking of "my" crime, plus one instance of the poet/narrator saying "Though men can cover crimes with bold stern looks / Poor women's faces are their own faults' books" (1252-53).

This word usage results in a "Rashomon" effect of how two people see the same event. For Tarquin, it clearly was treason to do what he did—as he acknowledges before and after the fact—fully considering (like Hamlet) the consequences of what he wants to do but then (unlike Hamlet) acting anyway ("a disputation / 'Tween frozen conscience and hot-burning will," 246-47). But Lucrece feels complicit and talks of "my trespass," "my fault," and "my crime" in (she thinks) "leading Tarquin on" or "allowing" the rape. The extended diversion within the poem where she views the painting of the Fall of Troy reinforces this point, allowing her to curse Helen for her "trespass" (line 1476) in arousing a passion in Paris that caused him to kidnap her.

These distinctions in *Lucrece* demonstrate that the same words in the Sonnets may show how the several parties actually saw and reacted to the events of "that which thou hast done" and what the nuanced use of these words may suggest about these reactions. Tarquin, having spent the first third of the poem talking "sense" to himself about what he was thinking of doing, then goes and does it (his rational "sense" gives way to his emotional "sensual" act). This, I submit, is his "sensual fault," his "treason" (perhaps anticipating Sonnet 35, "to thy sensual fault I bring sense").[11] I should emphasize, too, that I do not mean here "sensuous," which some erroneously equate with "sensual" ("sensuous" means loving, while "sensual" means willful[12]). This poem recounts, after all, not a love story but a *rape*. Then, as now, rape is not about sex; it is about the tyrannical use of power. Tarquin's soliloquies about it underscore that fact: he wants to possess what someone else has, even at the risk of "dispossessing" himself.[13] In fact, the consequences of Tarquin's treason are political disaster for two families: his own, and Lucrece's (when she commits suicide in defense of her chastity).

Sonnet 87 and "misprision"

With this hypothesis in place, i.e., the "that" over which the youth must "no more be grieved" is his "trespass/sensual fault/ crime" in the Essex Rebellion (referred to by Shakespeare as "thy trespass" and "your trespass" in sonnets 35 and 120), other sonnets in the central century-sonnet sequence (27-126) can be read in a proper light. One of the most important of these sonnets is 87, about which Kositsky and Stritmatter write, "In many ways, the crux of Whittemore's argument can be found in a single word in Sonnet 87 [misprision]" (12). While acknowledging that Southampton's death sentence might have been commuted to "misprision of treason," they note that "of treason" is not in the poem,[14] and they claim that 87 is a sonnet about simple "emotional leave-taking." Further, they note that the sonnet is full of financial metaphors (dear, possessing, estimate, charter, bonds, granting, worth, riches, gift, patent) and therefore conclude:

> If we want to understand "misprision" in its actual, as opposed to hypothetical, context, we should read the word in relation to this financial schema. Stephen Booth notes that one definition of "misprision" is "undervaluation,"

which accords perfectly with the language of the sonnet without recourse to the meaning Boyle and Whittemore depend on to make their thesis . . . The *context of the sonnet* does not support [glossing "misprision" as "misprision of treason"]. Instead, the *preferred meaning* is clearly "undervaluation." To accept the meaning supplied by Boyle and Whittemore requires us to ignore the *obvious* context (with its extensive monetary metaphors) of the sonnet itself in favor of a *hypothetical* context, which the sonnet, without the misconstruction of the word "misprision," entirely fails to support. (12; emphasis added)

This critique illustrates much that has been misdirected in Sonnet scholarship for almost two centuries. Although Kositsky and Stritmatter argue for a supposedly "obvious" context that trumps a "hypothetical" context, they at the same time also postulate that such an obvious context must be understood *only* within this sonnet's internal context, not the larger, external context provided by the other sonnets in the sequence (e.g., by "trespass" equaling "treason" in sonnets 35 and 120) let alone any *genuine historical context* within which the Poet lived, wrote, and—most especially—interacted with the Fair Youth.

Apart from Shakespeare's own parallel usage of these words (trespass and treason),[15] it should be noted here that there is, in fact, an independent contemporaneous linkage of the words "misprision" and "trespass" that should settle any questions about whether the word "trespass" could be used to describe a high crime (rather than a misdemeanor or some other petty offense). In a 1567 legal lexicon there appears a revealing entry for "Misprision of felonie or trespasse" (Rastell 152). The entry states "that in every treason or felonie is included *misprision*, and where any hath committed treason or felonie the

[Queen] may cause the same to be indited and [arraigned] but of *misprision* only if she will" (Rastell 153; emphasis added).[16]

The usage of "misprision," coupled with "trespass," in this entry, is evidence, therefore, that "trespass" was synonymous with "felonie"; and, accordingly, it is not unreasonable to see how Shakespeare could also equate it with "treason," especially in light of his usage of those words in *Lucrece*, as if they described degrees of guilt/culpability over the same offense—similar to determining whether a killing was manslaughter or murder. Although such usage of "trespass" may have been slipping into obscurity by 1567, the timing would be a perfect fit for those, like Oxfordians, who believe that Shakespeare was seventeen years old in 1567 and being trained in the law at that time at Gray's Inn. It also is especially interesting to note, in this context, that the Queen could commute any indictment of treason or felony to misprision *at her will*—an important point for the argument that converting Southampton's conviction for treason to "misprision" is exactly what Southampton was seeking in his letters to the Queen.

Turning to some of the more recent mainstream Sonnet commentaries, we find that Helen Vendler has nothing to say about the word "misprision," while Booth (as previously noted) glosses it as "undervaluation" (291) and Duncan-Jones declares it "a false estimate" (284).[17] It is true that there is nothing within Sonnet 87 alone that would compel a reader to think "misprision of treason" *solely* by the appearance of the word "misprision." But this is where the element of historical context must be considered, together with the context provided by considering *all* of Shakespeare's Sonnets to be in authorial sequence and telling a single story. As noted earlier, the key words "trespass" and "fault," linked with the word "crime," lead us *outside* the Sonnets and into what is an event in history: the Essex Rebellion. For *anyone* who postulates Southampton as the Fair Youth, this event must, in my view, come first and foremost in any consideration of the "that" which the

Fair Youth has done. Let me also suggest that if the words "misprision of treason" had ever been associated with Southampton in the historical record, or by any of his biographers, Sonnet commentary would long ago have picked up on it, and there would be no question about it.

The Southampton mystery

Finally, to get to the heart of Sonnet 87, even, as many commentators have, after identifying Southampton as the Fair Youth of the Sonnets, we need to ask ourselves, "Who is Southampton? What is his relationship to Shakespeare? Why is he allied with Essex, and what is their relationship?" Establishing these contexts mean, therefore, not only recognizing that Southampton was a co-leader of the Essex Rebellion but affirms the need to inquire into the many unanswered questions about the Rebellion and its leaders and explore what Shakespeare's perspectives on these persons and events were.

As we noted earlier, Essex's name had been bandied throughout the 1590s as one who might play a possible late-sixteenth-century Bolingbroke to Elizabeth's Richard II; indeed, he was accused at his trial of seeking to become King Robert I. Shakespeare's Richard II had been performed, on Essex's and Southampton's orders, the night before the attempted coup, seemingly both to justify a monarch's downfall and to rally support for the coming coup, yet the author, Shakespeare, never was mentioned during the post-rebellion trials nor was he ever party to those involved in the play and its production questioned, tried and punished for participating, however indirectly, in the Rebellion. And Southampton, notably, once sentenced to die, was inexplicably spared—a point where the Shakespeare problem, i.e., the Shakespeare *authorship* problem, seems to intersect with this little-noticed Southampton mystery. Historians cannot say for certain why Southampton was spared in 1601 anymore than they can say for certain why Shakespeare was never held to account for his role in the Essex Rebellion.

These curiosities lead us back to the "Prince Tudor" theory, i.e., the thesis that Southampton himself may have harbored his own royal aspirations as the unacknowledged son of the Queen and the poet, Oxford/Shakespeare. In addition to the previously-noted curiosities in the Sonnets' references to the Fair Youth, we are told by Shakespeare that the youth has a "charter of his worth" (87:3), and other sonnets also provide a backdrop to this boy's "charter of worth," such as the Poet's astonishing address to him as "my sovereign" in Sonnet 57. Indeed, as also noted earlier, "royal language" is used *throughout* the sonnet sequence to describe the Youth. Add to this an historical context (the Essex Rebellion) concerned with royal succession and, I believe, we have before us—achieved within a defined historical context—the revelation of what Sonnet 87 is all about.

Kings and a king

Sonnet 87 is not the only instance in the sonnets of a "king" being mentioned in a discussion of value and worth. In Sonnet 29, Shakespeare declares, "For thy sweet love remembered such wealth brings / That then I scorn to change my state with kings" (13-14). So, Shakespeare tells us, there are things in this world more valuable than kingship.

As we noted earlier in looking at the Essex Rebellion, Southampton was convicted of treason and sentenced to death, but was then reprieved from his death sentence. At the trial of Essex and Southampton, Essex was accused of seeking to set himself up as King, yet no record exists of Southampton's motives in the Rebellion—other than his letters to the Privy Council, wherein he pleads for mercy and proclaims that he only was involved out of his "love for Essex" (Stopes 225-231).[18]

With these key elements in place, we can now look at the final lines of Sonnet 87 —"Thus have I had thee as a dream doth flatter, / In sleep a king, but waking no such matter" (13-14)—and ask why these particular verses appear here. Turning to Helen Vendler's comments, we find:

> The deposed-by-daylight king of the last line generates the several puns of the closing: mist-a-king [line 10], m-a-king [line 12], w-a-king [line 14], the "nutshells" hiding the nut, a king, which is phonetically speaking, close to "aching." (381)

In fact, Vendler notes, ten of the sonnet's fourteen lines end in verbs with "-ing." It's as if the whole sonnet could be entitled, "To a King—not." Vendler also remarks on the legal terms used in the sonnet, emphasizing that these terms represent *exchanges* between Poet and Youth, which she calls "the giving-and-recalling, or swerving [line 8], of what was, or seemed to be, a gift" [lines 7, 11]. She calls it a "gift of love," and notes that it is a "key word" in the sonnets, with "gift," "gives," "gav'st," and "gift" again appearing in each quatrain, but then becoming suddenly absent from the couplet (making it, in her overall scheme of sonnet analysis, a "defective key word").

Yet neither Vendler (in noting this "gift of love") nor Kositsky/Stritmatter (in noting what they call the sonnet's "financial schema") consider that a "king" itself is a thing of value (being the *Youth's* own "worth"), and if what is occurring in Sonnet 87 is an "exchange" involving "gifts" or "giving," then we must remember that Shakespeare has already noted, back in Sonnet 29, that "love" (and I would add "life") is more valuable than kingship. The "gift of love" could, in fact, be worth a *king's ransom*.

Let's make a deal

Continuing with Sonnet 87, it is reasonable at this point, I believe, to infer that the word "misprision" ("So thy great gift, upon misprision growing," line 11) alludes to a "deal"—a legal maneuver—that saved Southampton's life, not to a "false estimate" or an "undervaluation" as more traditional glosses would have it. Furthermore, let us consider that this deal may be the financial transaction alluded to in the sonnet. Southampton, after all, had "risked" his life in the Rebellion—"his own worth then not knowing"—and, in fact, had *lost his life* by receiving a death sentence. The Poet, in turn, has given him back his life ("...thy great gift, *upon misprision growing*" in line 11 being not a further reference to something going *from* Youth *to* Poet, but rather from *Poet* to *Youth*; emphases added).[19] However, the consequence of the deal is that, from now on, the youth is a king in (the Poet's and his) dreams only. Kingship has been surrendered in exchange for life, echoing Sonnet 29. Sonnet 87 records a deal concluded ("My bonds in thee are all determinate") and the end of a dynasty ("In sleep a king . . . "). And lest we doubt that the most important word in this sonnet is "king," we can thank Helen Vendler for her insight on the phonetic clues that lead us repeatedly to that word (382-383).

But much as I like what Vendler says about this sonnet, she also has this to say:

> The *universal appeal* of this much-anthologized sonnet springs from its very *lack of particular detail*: there are no sexually precise pronouns, no references to a new sexual or affectional or poetic rival, and (because of the modern persistence of its legal vocabulary) *no estranging historical allusions*. (383; emphasis added)

No "estranging historical allusions?" This comment from one of the leading authorities on the sonnets perfectly illustrates all that is at stake in the authorship debate, and, moreover, it illustrates that to correctly interpret a sonnet (its "universal appeal" notwithstanding), one must have the correct historical context—the "particular detail"—about which the Poet is writing. *Standing alone, the sonnet cannot fully explain itself.* What Vendler says is similar to what the critic Walter Raleigh had written in 1907 when he declared that "the value of the Sonnets to the modern reader is independent of all knowledge of their occasion . . . for [once] the processes of art have changed the

tear to a pearl [echoing Sonnet 34, line 13] . . . their occasion is a thing of the past; their theme is eternal" (qtd. in Schiffer 32). Thus Vendler is being true to her mission to gloss the sonnets independent of any consideration for their having been composed within the context of an external story (the "occasion")[20] by which the authorial intent of the composition might be derived.

Similarly, the Kositsky/Stritmatter assertion that Sonnet 87 has its "own context," and that therefore it is "obvious" what is being talked about by looking at this lone sonnet divorced from its context and its place within the series, is, in effect, to claim to know the occasion that inspired the writing without actually knowing the history. This, however, is just another manifestation of "old paradigm" thinking, i.e., "This is a self-evident love sonnet—and only a love sonnet, period"—and, as such, everything about it is obvious (since everyone knows all about love) and the occasion that inspired it, if we care to know anything about it, can be deduced from the "sonnet pearl" without having any knowledge about the cause of the particular "tears" that became that "pearl."

But how can there be a Sonnet Mystery if everything is obvious? Absent a genuine historical context, *everything* in such an interpretive universe can only be—indeed, *must* be—confined to conjecture and empty speculation. In contrast, the Monument Theory introduces a documented historical context, i.e., the Essex Rebellion—with its genuine "tears" over a known "occasion" that never has been part of any previous sonnet commentary.[21] Raleigh and Vendler may eschew contemplation or investigation of the "occasion" behind the Sonnets, but anyone engaged in the authorship debate cannot.

Finally, let us consider the word "deal" that I've been using. As already noted earlier in this essay, there is no official record of any "deal" to save Southampton. And yet Southampton was spared. Even with the skilled legal advice he must have gotten in order to compose his Privy Council letters, was more done to rescue him from the headsman? If so, what—and by whom? Were ransom and fines paid by anyone for Southampton, as happened for the other surviving conspirators? Again, there is no official record of it, but unless the State was determined simply to release the convicted leader of a rebellion against the Crown without the imposition of *any* penalty or ransom, we have no alternative but to conclude that a ransom of *some* kind was paid, by someone.

Sonnet 120

We now come to the idea that the sonnets can furnish historical information not found in official records. Such a notion is, of course, premised on the Monument Theory's recognition that the middle 100 sonnets (27-126) are a diary of events surrounding the Essex Rebellion. I believe that the depth of analysis contained in *The Monument* makes such a case, with Whittemore's extensive research on the meanings and uses of words in each Sonnet—meanings and uses confirmed not by a reader's subjective or impressionistic appraisal but by comparing the uses of those words *used elsewhere by Shakespeare himself.* Accordingly, Whittemore makes an overwhelmingly persuasive case that these verses are about actual historical, *political* events in the participants' lives that disclose, definitively, the identities of those participants—including the Poet, Shakespeare.

In the Sonnets, the word "ransom" appears twice: in Sonnets 120 and 34 (and Sonnet 87 talks of something of value being exchanged). Sonnet 120 also uses the words "crime" and "trespass" interchangeably. More significant, however, is how Sonnet 120 links the occasion of "trespass" and "ransom" in its couplet: "But that your trespass now becomes a fee; / Mine ransoms yours, and yours must ransom me" (13-14). Here, historical context informs a reading and yields far more intelligible results than commentators, left to historical guessing or purely impressionistic musings, have so far proposed. Of the three most recent commentators on the Sonnets

that I have been citing, only Booth analyzes the couplet in detail. He notes that "trespass" *must* refer to the "crime" mentioned in line 8, and declares that "becomes" likely means "turns into" or "takes on the nature of," although he adds that it also could mean "is suitable to" or "is becoming to." He concludes with a purely literary construct on the whole problem however, noting that Shakespeare has skillfully made two separate but intertwined statements: "I feel your pain because my own pain was once as great," and "I do *not* feel your pain because my own pain was once as great." In other words, the "fee" that the trespass has required is offset by the poet's own trespass, i.e., you offended me, and then I offended you, so we're even (Booth 290-291). This is similar to the glosses of Duncan-Jones ("the speaker's trespass cancels out that of his friend . . ." ([350]) and Vendler ("[my trespass] 'buys back' yours" [510]).

None of them, however, considers that "Mine" in line 14, refers, in fact, to the "fee" to be paid—not to the "trespass"—and that "and yours . . ." in line 14 therefore must be saying "and your fee is to ransom me." But within a context of "trespass=treason=crime= conviction for crime," a fee is exactly what is needed to "ransom" the trespasser and get the convicted off the hook! The Essex Rebellion's context for the composition of this poem makes perfect sense of such a reading, but, even more importantly, it tells us something we *didn't* know: that Southampton didn't receive "compassionate mercy" (as Stopes speculated); rather, we learn that a ransom *was paid*—and paid by the Poet, Oxford/ Shakespeare. Shakespeare, indeed, is telling us in straightforward language that *he* has paid the fee to ransom Southampton's trespass, and now "[your—Southampton's—fee] must ransom me." A ransom has been paid—and it truly was a *king's* ransom.

Ransom "me," not "mine"

So, why did the Poet write, "ransom me"? Is Shakespeare telling us something by using "me" rather than "mine"? He could easily have written the couplet as, "But that your trespass becomes a fine / Mine ransoms yours, and yours must ransom mine." But if written that way, he would be saying that he, too, had committed a trespass. Clearly, *he did not see it that way*. He wrote in Sonnet 35 that "all men make faults, and even I in this, authorizing thy trespass with *compare* . . ." (emphasis mine). In other words, "I may have committed a fault, but not quite the trespass you committed, and certainly not the treason for which you were convicted" (an offense which, I suspect, Oxford/Shakespeare felt was not actually treason). This parsing of words echoes *The Rape of Lucrece*, where Tarquin's rape is called treason, but Lucrece feels complicit and speaks of her "fault" and her "trespass" in describing the same event.

The ransom payment that Oxford/Shakespeare made was not one of money, but himself. Not only was Southampton's claim to the throne surrendered in the deal to save Southampton ("In sleep a king, but waking no such matter" [Sonnet 87]), but also Oxford's claim to the authorship of his anonymous and pseudonymous works ("I, once gone, to all the world must die" [Sonnet 81]). Like Lucrece, seeing himself as complicit in the Essex Rebellion ("authorizing thy trespass with compare" [Sonnet 35]), he commits a form of suicide—literary suicide: he agrees to be consigned, forever, to oblivion. It was done under great duress, with Southampton being held hostage in the Tower and the only acceptable ransom being, in effect, a "hostage swap." But he did it, and that is why he doesn't ask for a ransom for "my trespass [mine]," but rather just for himself ("me"). He knew that a political dynasty—the Tudors—would expire with him. And if Southampton were indeed an unacknowledged Tudor heir, then Elizabeth herself had also played Lucrece, placing her reputation for chastity—her political persona as the Queen married only to her country—above all else, ending her life as a phoenix that *would not* arise from its ashes, "leaving no posterity . . ." (from *The Phoenix and the Turtle*, lines 59-61).[22]

Conclusion

To conclude, I would assert that we, with confidence, now can say, in the words of Henry David Gray—with whose words I opened this essay—that the "Veiled Knight who guards the Mystery of the Sonnets" (18) is, of course, the author himself. Yet even Oxfordians, who identify Shakespeare as Oxford (and most of whom affirm that the Fair Youth is Southampton), still have come up short and been at sixes-and-sevens in attempts to solve the mystery because of their inability unanimously to affirm the need to recognize the historical context of these verses as the means by which their right meaning can be discovered. Fortunately, Hank Whittemore's Monument Theory now has provided the context that completes the unveiling, exposing, in unprecedented detail, the connection between the verses and their historical context, thus resolving the mystery and "solving" the sonnets.

In concentrating on only three sonnets (35, 87, and 120), I hope I have made the point that—absent context—individual words and individual sonnets can be (and have been—and are!) interpreted to mean almost anything. Without a comprehensive context, meaning, indeed, is always going to be utterly subjective and remain solely in the eye of the beholder. With context, however, multiple musings and imaginings can be discarded and replaced with the provision of the author's purpose and the context for the work's correct interpretation, for only with a clearly defined external historical context can anyone hope to "unveil" the author's intent in writing these sonnets.

Of greater significance is that the Monument Theory provides, for the first time, a unified theory of how the Shakespeare authorship problem came into existence, and in so doing provides answers to two outstanding unanswered questions from the history of the Essex Rebellion: why Southampton was spared execution, and why Shakespeare was spared punishment for his supporting role in those events. The simple answer to both these questions—an answer that *only* Oxfordians can provide—is that the true Shakespeare (Edward de Vere, 17th earl of Oxford) was punished—virtually erased from history—and it was his punishment, his sacrifice, that saved Southampton. "Shakespeare" died so that Southampton could live.

Such a simple and elegant solution to the authorship problem is just what Supreme Court Justice John Paul Stevens called for over twenty years ago in Washington, DC at the 1987 Moot Court Trial on the Shakespeare Authorship Question. In his closing statement, Justice Stevens declared that while he suspected a conspiracy involving the Queen and Burghley could be behind this incredible story, Oxfordians had yet to articulate an all-encompassing account:

> I would submit that, if their [Oxfordians'] thesis is sound, . . . one has to assume that the conspiracy—[and] *I would not hesitate to call it a conspiracy*, because there is nothing necessarily invidious about the desire to keep the true authorship secret . . . . [T]he strongest theory of the case requires an assumption, *for some reason we don't understand*, that the Queen and her Prime Minister decided, 'We want this man to be writing under a pseudonym.' . . . Of course *this thesis may be so improbable that it is not worth even thinking about*; but I would think that the Oxfordians really have not yet put together a concise, coherent theory that they are prepared to defend in all respects. (qtd in Boyle, "The 1987 Moot Court Trial" 7-8; emphasis added)

The Monument Theory of the Sonnets provides this "concise, coherent" theory, but because of the still controversial nature of the "Prince Tudor" aspect of the theory—not to mention a general aversion by some to the suggestion that the Shakespeare problem is the result of a (gasp!) conspiracy—the question remains: is it a theory that can be defended? That Justice Stevens himself, even as he postulated a possible conspiracy and called for a "concise, coherent theory," could also suggest that such a theory might be "improbable" confirms just how vexing the Shakespeare authorship debate really is and likely will continue to be.

Meanwhile, with a theory in hand that would seem to solve the Sonnet mystery, and also solve the "how and why of the authorship problem,"[23] I would now submit that it is now up to others to refute—if they can—rather than reactionarily reject what Whittemore has accomplished. I do not think, however, that that is any more likely to happen than we are to see a refutation of Copernicus's heliocentric model of the solar system or a refutation of Watson and Crick's double helix solution to the mysteries of how genes work: the sun is at the center of our solar system and things revolve around it; two complementary strands of chemicals drive the reproduction of life, and that is how genes work. But discovery is discovery, and facts discovered will remain facts to the end of time ("For truth is truth though never so old, and time cannot make that false which was once true," as Edward de Vere once wrote [qtd. in Fowler, *Letters* 771]).

It is time to build on what Whittemore has discovered and defined in his "monumental" study and complete our work in gaining the world's acceptance of Edward de Vere as Shakespeare with attendant appreciation for the reasons this writer wrote what he did and allowed his name to be buried these many centuries, in expectation of a time when "eyes to be" could behold his work and "tongues to be" could salute his noble purpose.

Notes

[1] *Shakespeare's Sonnets: Critical Essays.* Ed. James Schiffer. New York: Garland, 1999. Schiffer notes that Herbert S. Donow's 1981 bibliography on the Sonnets lists 1,898 items, and in a footnote (n.2, p. 57) also mentions that a 1972 book by Ball State

80

University Professor Tetsumaro Hayashi, entitled *Shakespeare's Sonnets: A Record of 20th-Century Criticism*, lists even more—2,503 entries. Such a number of books and articles written on Shake-speares Sonnets testify to readers' and scholars' intense and persistent attraction to these enigmatic verses.

² Leslie Hotson, for example, offers a detailed catalog of these royal allusions in Chapters 2 and 3 of *Mr. W. H.* Of course, being a Statfordian, Hotson had to invent a Fair Youth connection (he proposes William Hatcliffe as W.H.) and a royal context (Hotson imagines Hatcliffe as a "Prince of Purpoole" during Christmas celebrations at Gray's Inn) to which, he suggests, the royal allusions refer. His work is mentioned—dismissively—by Schiffer as demonstrative of "the flaw in evidential logic that Schoenbaum describes is a frequent problem in biographical criticism" (42). Whittemore, however, notes that no less venerable a critic as G. Wilson Knight made extended observations on the royal imagery of the Sonnets, calling the Sonnets the "heart of Shakespeare's royal poetry" (Whittemore 806).

³ These thoughts were first published in a 1937 pamphlet by Percy Allen and B. M. Ward: *An Enquiry into the Relations between Lord Oxford as "Shakespeare," Queen Elizabeth, and the Fair Youth of Shakespeare's Sonnets* (cited in a 24-page supplement to the April 1939 issue of *The Shakespeare Fellowship News-letter* in which Allen and Ward debated Canon G. H. Rendall and Mr. T. M. Aitken about their theory). Whittemore gives an updated overview on the Tudor Heir theory on pages xxxv-xxxvi of *The Monument*. Baconians also had considered the royal factor in their analysis of the Sonnets and contemplated how that factor figured into the authorship debate, often by concluding that when Shakespeare speaks of something as "royal," he literally means it.

⁴ Another variation of this theory is that Oxford himself is a son of Elizabeth who, born in 1548, was her first child at a time when rumors circulated of her possible impregnantion by the Lord Admiral, Thomas Seymour; in response, the 30-year old William Cecil (later Lord Burghley) came to her aid during this crisis and remained at her side for the next 50 years, sheltering and educating Oxford—eventually even marrying Oxford to his daughter. If Oxford, however, were both the son of Elizabeth and the father of Southampton by her, that would constitute incest—a

sexual practice far more common in the Elizabethan world than often supposed, but hateful to the ears of Victorian-minded moralists who are scandalized that Shakespeare could have been a practitioner of such a sexual abomination. Many studies, however, have been written on the extensive theme of incest in Shakespeare. If incest is the deep, dark secret at the core of the Shakespeare problem, that would explain, of course, much about the imposition of secrecy on the authorship then and account for the perpetuity of the secrecy and reluctance to pursue its implication that continues today; for more on this, refer to Professor Daniel Wright's address to the Shakespeare Oxford Society in October 2008, "All My Children: Royal Bastards and Royal Policy."

⁵ Throughout the Tudor dynasty, especially after Henry VIII's break with Rome, treason charges against political opponents became the standard means of applying political control, and the lesser charge of "misprision of treason" became a useful bargaining chip for the Crown, utilized on a case-by-case basis. See Bellamy's *The Tudor Law of Treason* for a history of how this practice evolved.

⁶ Southampton then embarked upon a storied political career that culminated in his becoming a political opponent of James in the early 1620s, allied with—surprisingly?—the 18th earl of Oxford, Henry de Vere. And at this same moment in history the First Folio (1623) was published.

⁷ Myers cites from Cobbett's *Complete Collection of State Trials* (London, 1809-28) as his source on Lee's trial.

⁸ This is where, in my view, Joseph Pequigney and his version of the homosexual theory of the sonnets (and, for that matter, all the gay sexual theorists of the Sonnets) wander astray, for although Pequigney also looks at the connections among these same key words, he departs in many conjectural directions after doing so. For example, on page 104 of *Such is My Love*, while discussing Sonnet 35, he observes that "trespass" (35.6), some "ill-deed" (34.14) and a "sensual fault" (35.9) constitute the "cause of the quarrel [between the Poet and the Youth]." He then notes, however, that E.A.M. Coleman, in *The Dramatic Use of Bawdy in Shakespeare*, has remarked that "fault" frequently occurs in early modern English with a "sexual flavour" and so concludes that the modifier "sensual" confirms that the "fault" is somehow sexual.

Here, therefore, is someone who looks at this same linkage of words ("trespass" and "fault") as clear referents to something that is going on between the Poet and the Youth but who provides only subjective speculation with no historical context outside the Sonnet to inform his interpretation. As we shall see, Southampton himself referred, in writing, to his participation in the Rebellion as his "fawte, i.e., fault," and Whittemore, in his glosses on Sonnet 35, supplies several examples of "sensual" being used within this period in distinctly non-sexual contexts—including one derived from William Cecil, Lord Burghley, who wrote in 1584 that "I favor no sensual & willful recusants" (qtd in *The Monument* 250).

[9] None of the major recent books on the sonnets—Booth (1977); Kerrigan (1986); Vendler (1997); Duncan-Jones (1998)—has anything to say about Shakespeare's meaning in using the word "crime." It is not even *mentioned* in their extensive glosses of words in the Sonnets. This absence of any discussion about "crime"—and its centrality in interpreting the meaning of the Sonnets—shows how the absence of a real historical context clouds the judgment of anyone tackling the Sonnet mystery. It also is of interest to note that both Booth and Duncan-Jones, in discussing Sonnet 120, observe that comparisons can be made back to Sonnet 34. Duncan-Jones specifically suggests that the use of the word "salve" in both sonnets may be related. But neither Booth nor Duncan-Jones ventures any farther than this, and they do not consider the possible interconnections between such vital words as "ransom" in Sonnet 34, "trespass" in Sonnet 35, and the use of both words ("ransom" and "trespass") in Sonnet 120. So the notion that the Poet is talking about the same event, using the same language in Sonnets 34-35 and 120, is absent from their commentary, let alone any consideration that both instances of "trespass" may be referring to a *real* "crime."

[10] Kositsky and Stritmatter wrote in response to articles by William Boyle and Hank Whittemore in *Shakespeare Matters* (Summer 2004)—not to Whittemore's *The Monument*, which had yet been published—and so were unaware of Whittemore's explanation for this. Yet, astonishingly, they dismissively write in their article: "Doubtless reply will be made that we have not waited to evaluate the entirety of the evidence contained in Mr. Whittemore's book.

This is true but also irrelevant. No larger case which depends on the kind of examples cited in these two articles can be regarded as a sound one" (13).

[11] It is interesting to note how this aspect of Tarquin can be seen more in Essex than Southampton. Chris Fitter, commenting on how he sees Essex reflected in *Richard II*, writes, "Shakespeare's motivation for freezing the career of the hot and headlong young nobleman in a lucid frost of maximal suspicion must remain, of course, conjectural" (Fitter par. 45), and in describing Essex as "hot and headlong," he also could be describing Tarquin in *Lucrece*. This view of Essex and its possible parallel with Tarquin touches on my growing suspicion that the "graver labor" of Lucrece may also (like *Richard II*) have been part of a broader 1590s succession politics agenda, perhaps intended as a cautionary tale that may well have been anticipating what came to pass in 1601 and warning Southampton to beware of his relationship with Essex.

[12] In *Webster's New World Dictionary*, "sensuous" is defined as follows: "1. Of, derived from, or perceived by the senses, 2. Enjoying sensation." "Sensual" is defined as: "1. Of the body and the senses *as distinguished from the intellect* [emphasis added]. 2. Connected or occupied with sexual pleasure." It is this first definition of "sensual" that is closest, I believe, to Shakespeare's intent in depicting Tarquin's thinking as he anticipates taking (raping) Lucrece. This is why so much of the poem begins with his "soliloquy," preoccupied with the consequences of what he is about to do, but with his intellect unable to control his senses.

[13] A 2001 article ("Tarquin Dispossessed") in *Shakespeare Quarterly* by Catherine Belsey contains many interesting observations on the political ramifications of Tarquin's act, Lucrece's response and the subsequent political fallout. I have drawn much from her observations, especially regarding the notion of what it means to be "dispossessed." She does not, however, discuss the semantic—and possibly legal—subtleties of "treason" vs. "trespass."

[14] There are several good reasons why "of treason" would not be used. First, it would make the actual historical context too obvious. Second, it may not scan right for the poet in composing this sonnet. Third, if Shakespeare's use of the words "treason" and "trespass" do represent a difference in his mind—and

perhaps also in law—over degrees of culpability (as in Lucrece), then that is one more reason not to use the word "treason" in the middle hundred sonnets, particularly if he genuinely believes that Southampton did not actually commit a treasonable offense (his judicial conviction notwithstanding). It also is interesting to note that the only appearance of the word "treason" in the Sonnets is in Sonnet 151, where it appears along with the only three instances of the word "conscience." Its usage here (" . . . I do betray / My nobler part to my gross body's treason"—lines 5-6) may correspond to what we have been considering about Tarquin in *Lucrece*, i.e. that his "treason" is his surrender to his "sensual" urges because of his "frozen conscience." There is not space in this essay to explore the larger meaning of this sole appearance of the word "treason," coupled with "conscience," nor why the Poet uses it to describe himself *vis à vis* the Dark Lady (Elizabeth) rather than the Youth (Southampton) who was convicted of that crime.

[15] Whittemore provides several examples from the Shakespeare plays in *The Monument* (see, for example, p. 248).

[16] The well-known legal concept of misprision is repeated over the centuries in such authorities as Edward Coke's *Institutes of the Laws of England* and William Blackstone's *Commentaries on the Laws of England*.

[17] The exact quote from Duncan-Jones (in her gloss of line 11) is: "'upon misprision growing' means coming into existence as the result of a false estimate" (284).

[18] Southampton's letters, as Whittemore notes in *The Monument* (301-302), are virtually Shakespearean in their pleas for mercy from the Queen, but they are also savvy in laying the groundwork for a commutation of his conviction for treason to one of conviction for "misprision of treason" and its accompanying life sentence rather than death sentence (301-202).

[19] Sir Walter Raleigh, in a letter to the Privy Council begging for his life after his conviction for treason in November 1603, wrote, "For a greater gift none can give, or receive, than life . . ." (qtd in Hume 199). Raleigh's death sentence was, indeed, later commuted to misprision of treason, which, incredibly, is what Attorney General Edward Coke said is all that he was accusing him of in the first place. Raleigh's treason conviction was, however, reinstated (as it could be, since he was never pardoned), and he was executed in 1618 (Hume 281).

[20] It is interesting to note that Professor Helen Vendler had been sent an early draft of Whittemore's work in spring 1999, and she wrote a letter to Shakespeare Oxford Society Trustee Elliott Stone in reply, declaring, "I am no historian, and have by now learned the limits of my own interests, which are rhetorical and not historical."

[21] For the record, we should note that Stritmatter believes that Southampton likely *was* a putative Tudor heir, as demonstrated most recently in his 2004 article on *Venus and Adonis* in the *Tennessee Law Review* (216). Lynne Kositsky, his co-author in critique of the Monument Theory, does not, however, accept the "Tudor Heir" theory. And as readers may have discerned by now, it is being postulated in this essay that the Monument Theory of the Sonnets (with the Essex Rebellion at its center) is a clinching argument *both* for Oxford being Shakespeare and for Southampton being the Fair Youth *and* a candidate for the succession.

[22] The Essex Rebellion context of *The Phoenix and the Turtle* has been explicated in Anthea Hume's "Love's Martyr, The Phoenix and Turtle, and the Aftermath of the Essex Rebellion." While the author is primarily concerned with Robert Chester's *Love's Martyr* as a political allegory about the failed Essex Rebellion and the succession issue (with the Phoenix representing the Queen, and the Turtle the "loyal and loving subjects of the Queen" [57]), she also discusses Shakespeare's role in the 1601 collection and his unique take on the succession issue (Shakespeare's Phoenix alone *does not arise from its ashes*, but is instead described as "leaving no posterity . . . t'was married chastity," ll. 59-60). Oxfordians William Plumer Fowler, Dorothy Ogburn and Professor Daniel Wright also have discoursed on this poem, making sense of its enigmas by positing that it is about Oxford (Turtle), Elizabeth (Phoenix) and Southampton (Rarity) and the end of a dynasty (Tudor) because the Phoenix *will not acknowledge* her posterity. Hume posits that the Turtle is the people of England, which explains how the chaste Virgin Queen could leave "no posteritie." Oxfordians Fowler, Ogburn and Wright, however, argue that "married chastity" and "no posterity" represent something more tangible, i.e., a real but

unacknowledged heir. Still, all four (Hume, Fowler, Ogburn and Wright) agree that the outcome was the same—the Tudor dynasty "unofficially" ended with the Essex Rebellion.

[23] By the "how and why of the authorship problem" I mean the situation that occurred after the author's death. It is a "given" for all anti-Stratfordians that the true author wrote anonymously during his lifetime. The greater mystery, heretofore, is why the attribution to the Stratford man took place, and why it has, until now, endured for four centuries. The Monument Theory of the sonnets, plus the Tudor Heir theory regarding the crisis of the succession, provide compelling "reasons of state" for this situation, i.e., the attribution of the works of "Shakespeare" to the Stratford man, Shaksper, in order to de-politicize the works and leave them sanitized of any supposed relationship to politics and people at the Court.

Works Cited

Akrigg, G.P.V. *Shakespeare and the Earl of Southampton*. Cambridge: Harvard, 1968.

Allen, Percy and B.M Ward. *An Enquiry into the Relations between Lord Oxford as "Shakespeare," Queen Elizabeth and the Fair Youth of Shakespeare's Sonnets*. London, 1937.

Bellamy, John. *The Tudor Law of Treason*. London: Routledge, 1979.

Belsey, Catherine "Tarquin Dispossessed; Expropriation and Consent in *The Rape of Lucrece*." *Shakespeare Quarterly* 52.3 (2001): 315-335.

Blackstone, William. *Commentaries on the Laws of England*. Oxford: Clarendon, 1765.

Booth, Stephen. *Shakespeare's Sonnets*. New Haven: Yale, 1977.

Boyle, William. "With the Sonnets Now Solved . . ." *Shakespeare Matters* 3.4 (2004): 1, 11-15.

—. "The 1987 Moot Court Trial." *Shakespeare Oxford Newsletter* 33.3 (1997): 1, 6-8.

Camden, William. *Anno Domini* 1601. <http://www.philological.bham.ac.uk/camden/1601e.html>

Cobbett, William and T.B. Howell, eds. *Cobbett's Complete Collection of State Trials*. 34 vols. London, 1809-28.

Coke, Edward. *Institutes of the Laws of England*. London, 1628.

Colman, E.A.M. *The Dramatic Use of Bawdy in Shakespeare*. London: Longman, 1974.

Devereux, Walter Bourchier. *Lives and Letters of the Earls of Essex in the Reigns of Elizabeth, James I and Charles I*. 2 vols. London: Murray, 1853. <http://books.google.com/books?dq=devereux+lives+and+letters&printsec=frontcover&source=web&sig=RVjfVx3v0cAmtL0RbHDqEfxT_U&id=loc3EN7A75wC&ots=p7tgfNA2sx&output=htm>.

Donrow, Herbert S. *The Sonnets in England and America: A Bibliography of Criticism*. Westport: Greenwood, 1982

Duncan, Owen. "The Political Career of Sir Henry Neville." Diss., Ohio State University, 1974.

Duncan-Jones, Katherine. *Shakespeare's Sonnets*. London: Nelson, 1997.

Fitter, Chris. "Historicising Shakespeare's *Richard II*: Current Events, Dating and the Sabotage of Essex." *Early Modern Literary Studies* 11.2 (2005). <http://purl.oclc.org/emls/11-2/fittric2.htm>.

Fowler, William Plumer. *Shakespeare Revealed in Oxford's Letters*. Portsmouth: Peter Randall, 1986.

—. *Shakespeare's "Phoenix and Turtle": An Interpretation by William Plumer Fowler, With a Supplementary Exegesis by Dorothy Ogburn*. Portsmouth: Peter Randall, 1986.

Furness, Mrs. Howard Horace. *A Concordance to Shakespeare Poems*. 1874. New York: AMS, 1972.

Gray, Henry David. "Shakespeare's Last Sonnets." *Modern Language Notes* 32.1 (1917): 17-21.

Harrison, G.B. *The Elizabethan Journals*. London: Routledge, 1938.

Hayashi, Tetsumaro. *Shakespeare's Sonnets: A Record of 20th Century Criticism*. Metuchen, NJ: Scarecrow, 1972.

Hotson, Leslie. *Mr. W. H.* London: Rupert Hart-Davis, 1962.

Hume, Anthea. "Love's Martyr, The Phoenix and Turtle, and the Aftermath of the Essex Rebellion," *Review of English Studies* 40.157 (1989): 48-71.

Hume, Martin. *Sir Walter Raleigh*. New York: Knopf, 1926.

James, Brenda and William D. Rubinstein. *The Truth Will Out*. Harlow: Longman, 2005.

Keeton, George W. *Trial for Treason*. London: MacDonald, 1959.

Kerrigan, John. *Shakespeare's Sonnets*. London: Penguin, 1986.

Kositsky, Lynne, and Roger Stritmatter. "Critique of the Monument Theory." *Shakespeare Matters* 4.1 (Fall 2004): 1, 10-14.

Lacey, Robert. *Robert, Earl of Essex*. London: History Book Club, 1970.

Massey, Gerald. *Shakespeare's Sonnets Never Before Interpreted*. London: Longmans, 1866.

Myers, James P. "'Murdering Heart . . . Murdering Hand': Captain Thomas Lee of Ireland, Elizabethan Assassin." *Sixteenth Century Journal* 22.1 (1991): 47-60.

Nichols, John. *The Progresses, Processions and Magnificent Festivities, of King James the First, His Royal Consort, Family and Court*. 4 vols. London, 1828.

Ogburn, Charlton Jr. *The Man Who Was Shakespeare*. McLean, VA.: EPM, 1995.

Parsons, Robert. *Conference about the Next Succession to the Crowne of England*. Amsterdam, 1594; London, 1595.

Pequigney, Joseph. *Such is My Love*. Chicago: University of Chicago, 1985.

Rastell, John. *The Exposicions of the Termes of the Lawes of England*. London: Richard Tottell, 1567.

Roberts, Clayton, and Owen Duncan. "The Parliamentary Undertaking of 1614." *English Historical Review*. 93.368 (1978): 481-498.

Rowse, A. L. *Shakespeare's Southampton*. New York: Harper & Row, 1965.

Schiffer, James. "Reading New Life into Shakespeare's Sonnets: A Survey of Criticism." *Shakespeare's Sonnets: Critical Essays*. Ed. James Schiffer. New York: Garland, 1999. 3-71.

Shakespeare, William. *Rape of Lucrece*. From *The Riverside Shakespeare*. New York: Houghton Mifflin, 1974.

Shakespeare, William. *Shake-speares Sonnets*. 1609. London: Thomas Thorpe, 1977.

Stopes, Charlotte C. *The Life of Henry, Third Earl of Southampton*. 1922. New York: AMS, 1969.

Stritmatter, Roger. "A Law Case in Verse: *Venus and Adonis* and the Authorship Question." *Tennessee Law Review* 72.1 (2004): 171-219.

Thatcher, David, "What a Lark: The Undoing of Sonnet 29." *Durham University Journal* 55.1 (1994): 59-66.

Vendler, Helen. *The Art of Shakespeare's Sonnets*. Cambridge: Harvard, 1997.

—. Letter to Elliott Stone. 8 June 1999.

Whittemore, Hank. *The Monument*. Marshfield, MA: Meadow Geese Press, 2005.

Wright, Daniel L. "All My Children: Royal Bastards and Royal Policy." The Shakespeare Oxford Society / Shakespeare Fellowship Annual Conference. White Plains, NY. 9 October 2008.

—. "Phoenix Rising: Recovering Authorial Intent in Interpreting Shakespeare's 'Phoenix and Turtle.'" The 13th Annual Shakespeare Authorship Studies Conference. Concordia University. Portland, OR. 18 April 2009.

Mythopoesis of Resurrection: Hesiod to Shakespeare
The Winter's Tale and Pericles, Prince of Tyre

Earl Showerman, M.D.

Two of Shakespeare's romances, *The Winter's Tale* and *Pericles, Prince of Tyre*, share remarkably similar elements of plot, nomenclature, characterization, dramaturgy, and symbolic geography. Both stories tell of kings who suffer extreme loss and long grief, of redeeming, virtuous daughters, and of resurrected sainted queens. Both end in cathartic reunions, and are dominated by the divine twins, Apollo and Diana. This paper proposes to link these two romances, first by direct comparison and then by tracing their mutual root in the mythopoetic treatment of human resurrection from the earliest Greek lyric poets through the literature of the Golden Age of Athens, Ovid, and the old English poets, Geoffrey Chaucer and John Gower.

We will follow the resurrection stories of three queens: Alcestis, Hermione and Thaisa; and of three physicians, Lord Cerimon, Hippocrates and Asclepius, whose careers will provide the key to understanding Shakespeare's inspired vision of the mystery of birth, death and rebirth. In *The Sovereign Flower*, G. Wilson Knight referred to the statue scene of *The Winter's Tale* as the "most strikingly conceived and profoundly penetrating moment in English literature" (240), and similar praise is rendered for the scene depicting Thaisa's resuscitation in Act III of *Pericles*. Our goal here will be to unveil the matrix of Greek myths, poetry and history that informs Shakespeare's profoundly romantic artistry.

I bring to these literary works the experiential perspective of 30 years served as an emergency physician where I was intimately involved in numerous critical resuscitations of the nearly dead and recently departed. For many years, I supervised and trained physicians, paramedics and nurses in advanced cardiac life support, eventually specializing in teaching the ethics of resuscitation. The ancient techniques and attitudes toward life-saving measures became my provenance, the teachings of Hippocrates and the mythography of his god, Asclepius. Shakespeare, I now believe, was well aware of Hippocratic ethics and practices, and modeled his most revered physician, Lord Cerimon, on the mythic Greek physicians, the *heros iatros*, who were reputed to have raised the dead. It is their art, knowledge and divine practice that provides the most spiritual and mysterious dramatic moments in the entire Shakespeare canon.

At the Ann Arbor Shakespeare Authorship Conference, I presented evidence that *The Winter's Tale* is populated with characters representing ancient Greek heroes and demigods, and is ruled by the pervasive, prophetic influence of Apollo. Many scholars, who published over 100 years ago, have also convincingly identified *Alcestis* (438 BCE) as the source for the resurrection of Queen Hermione in the statue scene. These findings have been recently reported in *The Oxfordian X* in my article "'Look down and see what Death is doing'—Gods and Greeks in *The Winter's Tale*." Euripides' tragicomedy *Alcestis* in fact does have a near-identical final scene in which a presumed-dead and much-revered queen returns from the underworld and is reunited with the king.

The presented evidence of allusions to Greek history, myth and drama in *The Winter's Tale* will be briefly reviewed here before a similar analysis is undertaken with *Pericles*. The similarities between *Pericles* and *The Winter's Tale* are immediately evident, despite the archaic, almost gnomic style of the first two acts of *Pericles*, which most scholars suggest is an indication of co-authorship. Both plays have revered queens and virtuous daughters who are lost to their kings, but later restored. Both employ narrators, and both have 15-16 year gaps between disaster, death and reunion. Both queens are post-partum when they apparently die and both daughters are named for their birth circumstances. In both, music and prayer are incorporated into the scenes of resurrection, and both plays employ providential tempests, dream prophesy, statues, and sacred ceremony. Remarkably, both are populated by characters named after famous Greeks from antiquity: mythic figures, kings, warriors, politicians, and poets. Both follow their primary sources very closely, but with significant and symbolic exceptions in Shakespeare's plots, characterization, nomenclature, and geography. Finally, both are ruled by related pagan gods, the immortal twins, Apollo and Diana. *The Winter's Tale* and *Pericles* are linked in highly significant ways that warrant this direct comparison, one that leads us ultimately through 2,000 years of poetic license on royal immortality.

Alcestis is the only extant 5th century tragicomedy and the only Greek drama to portray a human resurrection. Although it challenges the traditional view of Shakespeare's Greek literacy, a mythopoetic line of human resurrection can be traced back even further to the earliest Greek poetry of Hesiod and 200 years later of Pindar. Ovid's *Metamorphoses* and Chaucer's *Legend of Good Women* are two other sources that may have influenced Shakespeare's powerful and inspired vision of resuscitating the dead. To establish these links between the Greek poetic traditions and Shakespeare, we will first consider the Greek sources of plot, dramaturgy, and characters for both *The Winter's Tale* and *Pericles*, and then trace out the historic, mythopoetic representations of Asclepius and Alcestis, the Greek doctor and royal patient in our primary case study.

The importance of these relationships between Shakespeare and the Greek canon strikes at the heart of the authorship controversy, since it has been universally accepted

over the past 100 years that the Stratford Grammar School would not have given William Shakespere the ability to read untranslated Greek poetry. In his 1903 edition of *Classical Mythology in Shakespeare* Yale University Professor Robert K. Root voiced the consensus that has reigned ever since: "It is at any rate certain that he nowhere alludes to any of the characters or episodes of Greek drama, that they exerted no influence whatsoever on his conception of mythology" (6). A. D. Nutall in "Shakespeare and the Greeks," from *Shakespeare and the Classics* (2004), edited by Charles Martindale and A.B. Taylor, summarizes the current expert opinion on Shakespeare's "lesse Greek."

> That Shakespeare was cut off from Greek poetry and drama is probably a bleak truth that we should accept. A case can be made—and has been made—for Shakespeare's having some knowledge of certain Greek plays, such as Aeschylus' *Agamemnon*, Euripides' *Orestes*, *Alcestis*, and *Hecuba*, by way of available Latin versions, but this, surely, is an area in which the faint occasional echoes mean less than the circumambient silence. When we consider how hungrily Shakespeare feeds upon Ovid, learning from him, or extending him at every turn, it becomes more evident that he cannot in any serious sense have found his way to Euripides. (210)

Although Emrys Jones does describe a connection between Euripides' *Hecuba* and *Titus Andronicus* in *The Origins of Shakespeare* (1977), he suggests that Shakespeare would have known the Greek dramas through available editions of Latin translations. However, the early Latin translations of Euripides' dramas were mostly limited to *Hecuba* and *Iphigenia of Aulis*. *Alcestis*, the play that presents a royal resurrection, did have an early Latin translation by the renowned Scottish scholar, George Buchanan, but it was published in

France in 1567, and therefore would seem an unlikely source for the youth from Stratford. Jonathan Bate, in *Shakespeare and Ovid* (1993), reiterates the anything-but-Greek case by positing a link through Ovid:

> Despite the resemblances between *The Winter's Tale* and *Alcestis*, *Titus Andronicus* and *Hecuba*, it cannot be proved that Shakespeare knew any of the plays of Euripides. But there is no doubt he derived a Euripidean spirit from Ovid. Euripides taught Ovid what Ovid taught Shakespeare: an art of tragicomedy, a way of writing about the mind under stress of extreme passion, a sensitivity to female suffering. (239)

However, just a year later in his 1994 essay, "Dying to Live in *Much Ado about Nothing*", Bate argues that the final scenes of both *Much Ado* and *Winter's Tale* were likely based on Euripides' *Alcestis*. Bate may be the first Shakespeare scholar in nearly 100 years to make this claim and his argument mostly follows the same reasoning of previous scholars. He asserts that temporary consignment to the grave is an effective comedic device, that good comedy must be close to tragedy, and that an audience shares a vicarious rebirth through the return of Hero and Hermione:

> ....One way of putting it would be to say that *The Winter's Tale*, with its hinged tragicomic structure, is the logical conclusion of Shakespeare's work. That play is certainly the fully matured reworking of *Much Ado*. The temporary consignment to the grave is not only an analogue for the audience's experience in the theatre, and for the tragic element in comedy, it is also central to most myths and religions.... Shakespeare made much of certain classical myths of temporary death and rebirth—the dying god, Adonis; Proserpina, goddess of spring, who dies to live and who is the archetype of Marina and Perdita; Orpheus bringing Eurydice back from the underworld.

The ultimate "source" for the Hero plot of *Much Ado* is a Greek myth, that of *Alcestis*. Shakespeare could have known a Latin translation of Euripides' play on the subject; he certainly received the story at secondhand through the prose romances that were the direct sources of *Much Ado about Nothing*. (79)

G. Wilson Knight senses a more direct connection between Shakespeare's romances and the 5th century Greek dramas. In Chapter II, "The Writing of Pericles," in *The Crown of Life* (1969), he observes:

> ...with the Renaissance great drama, silent since Aeschylus, Sophocles and Euripides and their Roman followers, returns. The step from Aeschylus to Shakespeare is very easy: in spite of Shakespeare's obvious Christian sympathies, the two dramatists seem more contemporaneous than either with Dante. They breathe the same air of questioning adventure, sharing the same brooding sense of blood and death as vast antagonists to the soul of man. (35)

The Winter's Tale —Alcestis, Apollo and the Cast of Greeks

The Winter's Tale derives its central plot from Robert Greene's 1588 romance, *Pandosto. The Triumph of Time*. According to the *Arden* editor, there are more verbal echoes from *Pandosto* in the play than any other novel used by Shakespeare as a source. However, the differences between Greene's prose and Shakespeare's poetic romance are as striking as the similarities. Shakespeare deftly transforms the conclusion of Greene's morally troubling novel that ends with the suicide of the incest-driven, guilt-ridden king, into an Apollonian paean of forgiveness, redemption, resurrection and reunion. The death of Bellaria becomes the resurrection of Hermione; Pandosto's enduring lust, jealousy, and self-destruction becomes Leontes' devotion and redemption.

Shakespeare's *dramatis personae* include important characters absent in Greene, including Paulina, Antigonus, and Autolycus, and the major characters are cleverly renamed, mostly after legendary Greeks and Romans. Plutarch, Euripides, Herodotus and Homer provide the names: Three successive Kings of Sparta, King of Macedonia, King of Sicily, Second founder of Rome, conqueror of Britain, Greek and Trojan princesses, and the son of Hermes. The preeminence of Apollo's Oracle, and the remarkable dramaturgic similarities of the statue scene and *Alcestis*, suggest that a Renaissance imitation of Greek historic, mythic and dramatic literature informs this inspired romance.

While many Shakespeare editors have suggested a connection between the miraculous final scene of *The Winter's Tale* and the story of Pygmallion in Ovid's *Metamorphoses*, and most also acknowledge a symbolic connection to the Demeter-Persephone myth, few even mention Euripides' *Alcestis*, where a veiled and mysteriously silent queen is returned from the land of the dead to a grieving and deeply touched King, one who vowed never to remarry and who promised to worship a substitute statue of his dearly departed wife.

The connection of these two final scenes from Euripides and Shakespeare was first dramatically represented in a 1780 Johan Zoffany portrait of the young, talented aristocratic Elizabeth Farren as Hermione. Ms. Farren, future star of Drury Lane and Countess of Derby, is shown holding back her veil and leaning on a pedestal which depicts two scenes from Euripides' *Alcestis*. In the lower, darker circular bas-relief, Hercules is shown lunging at Death to grapple for possession of Alcestis; in the upper, lighter panel, the unveiled queen is holding King Admetus' hand.

Since then, a number of scholars in-cluding W.W. Lloyd (1856), Israel Gollancz (1894), A.E. Haigh (*The Tragic Drama of the Greeks* -1896), H.R.D. Anders (*Shakespeare's Books* -1904), and William Theobold (*The Classical Element in the Shakespeare Plays* -1909) have all recognized Euripides' tragi-comedy as the primary source for this striking scene, perhaps Shakespeare's most sublime dramatic achievement. The archetypal configuration of resurrection provides the mystery and spiritual power in *The Winter's Tale*, and its primary source is rooted in the ancient poetry of Hesiod, Pindar and Euripides. Most scholars over the past 100 years, however, have entirely ignored this possibility, focusing instead on Demeter-Persephone and Pygmallion.

Charles Frey in his *Vast Romance* study of Shakespeare's *Winter's Tale* explores the mythic dimension of the play through its association with Sicily, where the goddess Ceres, mother of Proserpina, was considered to be the queen in some accounts. He also notes, citing the lexicon of Hesychius of Alexandria, that Hermione "is a name that occurs as a title of Demeter and Persephone, the Greek names, of course, for Ceres and Proserpina" (62). He argues that Shakespeare's insistence on the likeness of Hermione and Perdita tends to reinforce the mythic associations of Helen of Troy and her own daughter, Hermione. These multiple associations "rise up behind mother and daughter in the play, lending them no specific analogues so much as a special ambience, an implication of greater forces that are surfacing by means of these characters" (62). Adding the obvious associations between Flora and Perdita, he summarizes his view of the importance of these mythic influences:

Shakespeare allows the myths of Hermione and Ceres, and of Proserpina and Flora to blend in the observer's mind into a persistent sense of normally remote natural and supernatural powers that are represented by and working creatively through human actions. His use of mythic materials parallels and perhaps feeds

upon that of Golding, who also po-
eticizes the Proserpina myth toward
dream. (63)

Many other scholars have noted the
extraordinary parallels between Perdita
and Persephone and between Hermione
and Demeter. In *Shakespeare and the Greek
Romance: A Study of Origins* author Carol
Gesner also considers *The Winter's Tale* as a
"conscious adaptation of Greek romance to
the stage" (116):

> On first reading, the exposure of
> Perdita and the pastoral fourth
> act suggest Longus as the major
> Hellenistic influence. Reflection,
> however, leads inevitably to recog-
> nition of Heliodorus as the central
> romance inspiration, perceptibly
> shadowed by the ever-elusive Chari-
> ton. (116)

Gesner writes that Act IV is filled with
the conventions of pastoral literature, and that
there are intriguing plot parallels to Longus'
Daphnis and Chloe, translated by Angel Day
in 1587. Noting, however, that the association of the shipwreck with Apollo's oracle and
the exposure and restoration of Perdita is
"Heliodoran in concept" (119), she argues
that the third century Greek's Aethiopica, a
novel indebted to the works of Homer and
Euripides which proved immensely influential
to writers throughout Europe, was the more
likely primary source for Shakespeare. Thomas
Underdowne's 1587 translation of Heliodorus
was dedicated to Edward de Vere.

> Coupled with the splendor and
> supple beauty of the poetry, it is the
> great deviation from *Pandosto* back
> to Greek romance in the restoration
> of the supposedly dead queen to
> her husband that lifts *The Winter's
> Tale* into what may be both the
> intellectual and artistic culmina-
> tion of the ancient narrative and
> thematic materials.... By restoring
> the queen Shakespeare made it pos-

sible to read the play concurrently
as drama of the human experience
of repentance and forgiveness; as allegory of the Christian redemption
theology; and as a restatement of the
Ceres-Persephone myth, the ancient
explanation of the seasonal cycles of
death and fertility; of growth, decay,
and regrowth; and by extension,
as symbolic of human life cycles.
(124)

Shakespeare scholars Jonathan Bate and
Charles and Michelle Martindale see more
of an Ovidian influence, primarily through
the story of Pygmallion in *Metamorphoses
X*. Although the story of a statue brought
to life certainly parallels Shakespeare's illusion, Ovid's poetry is far more erotic than
the reverential dramatic tone in Shakespeare
and Euripides. Hallet Smith *The Riverside*
edition is more inclusive in his comparison
of these two accepted mythologems for both
Pygmallion in the statue scene, as well as
Proserpina in connection with Perdita. He
adds that, "although the posing of a woman
as a statue may seem silly enough to a reader,
Shakespeare's audience was accustomed to
it in the court masques, and the scene has
proven strikingly effective on the public stage"
(1566). A.L. Rouse asserts that Lyly and Mar-
ston also employed the device of the living
statue. J.H.P. Pafford, editor of *The Arden
Shakespeare* (1963), however, also includes a
reference to *Alcestis* as a possible classic source
in his introduction:

> Many have noted Shakespeare's in-
> debtedness to Ovid's *Metamorphoses*,
> which he knew well, probably in
> Latin as well as in Golding's transla-
> tion. One relationship is in the story
> of the rape of Proserpine.... Another
> is in Autolycus, and yet another is
> in the story of the ivory statue of a
> woman made by Pygmallion and
> at Pygmallion's prayer given life
> by Venus, from which Shakespeare
> probably took the idea of Hermione

as a statue. However, in the revealing of the statue there are several striking parallels with the *Alcestis*. (xxxxiv)

W.W. Lloyd's comments from 1856 included in Horace Howard Furness' *New Variorum* edition of 1898 are perhaps the most compelling of all critics who have considered *Alcestis* a model for the statue scene of *The Winter's Tale*.[1] Lloyd particularly notes the parallels in increased dramatic tension, the agitation of the kings and the elevated dignity of the silent queens. A.E. Haigh's analysis of *Alcestis* published in *The Tragic Drama of the Greeks* (1896) includes a similar comparison to *The Winter's Tale*. Haigh makes the point that this play is the only extant example of Greek tragicomedy, that it was produced as a substitute for the customary satiric drama that followed a traditional trilogy, and that it won second prize.

> Every critic has admired the pathos and dramatic effect of the final scene, in which Alcestis is brought back disguised as a stranger, and received at first with reluctance, until she is gradually recognized. Two points in the scene deserve notice. The first is the curious resemblance to the conclusion of *The Winter's Tale*, where Leontes is taken to see, as he imagines, the statue of his dead wife, and finds instead the living Hermione. Second is the silence of Alcestis, after her return from the grave. The silence is due, not to the theatrical exigencies, and the absence of a third actor, as some critics have supposed, but to the deliberate choice of the poet. For one who has just been restored from the darkness of the tomb, no form of words could be as appropriate as the mute and half-dazed torpor in which she stands. (285)

As H.R.D. Anders also wrote over 100 years ago in *Shakespeare's Books*, "The striking resemblance in the closing scene of *The Winter's Tale* where Hermione reappears as a statue, to the last of Euripides's *Alcestis* has often been noticed. I have no doubt but that the story of Admetus and Alcestis was known to Shakespeare" (286).

There are a number of other thematic and dramaturgic similarities between *The Winter's Tale* and *Alcestis*, which are worth noting:

- First, there is **preeminent and prophetic Apollo** in both plays. Apollo gives the first 27 lines of *Alcestis*, and discourses with Death for the next 50 while there are over 25 allusions to Apollo or his Oracle in *The Winter's Tale*.
- Both kings, Admetus and Leontes, **express refusal of remarriage** and demonstrate "**soul-piercing**" contrition before their disguised queens in the final scenes.
- **Language of idealization** is used to describe Alcestis and Hermione, and both queens are associated with tombs that are described as shrines.
- In Alcestis Admetus promises to commission a **substitute statue of Alcestis**, one he vows to adore.
- Both dramas feature highly **dramatic hand gestures**, and employ **music and prayer** in the resurrection scenes.
- Both dramas are populated by renown **Greek mythic and historic characters**

Apollo's prologue in *Alcestis* links the drama to the Olympian gods and the fate of Asclepius, who was struck down with a thunderbolt for the sin of raising the dead.

> The cause was Zeus. He struck Asclepius, my son, full in the breast with a bolt of thunder, and laid him dead. Then in wild rage I slew the

Cyclopes who forge the fire of Zeus. To atone for this my Father forced me to labour as a hireling for a mortal man; and I came to this country, and tended oxen for my host. To this hour I have protected him and his. I, who am just, chanced on the son of Pheres, a just man, whom I have saved from Death by tricking the Fates. The Goddesses pledged me their faith. Admetus should escape immediate death if, in exchange, another corpse were given to the Under-Gods. One by one he tested all his friends, and even his father and the old mother who had brought him forth—and found none that would die for him and never more behold the light of day, save only his wife. Now, her spirit waiting to break loose, she droops upon his arm within the house; this is the day when she must die and render up her life.

Apollo goes on to challenge Death and makes a prophecy that Hercules will come and wrestle Alcestis from Death. Although Zeus and other Olympians are alluded to in the play, none receives the central focus that rests on Apollo. At the midpoint of the drama, the chorus of young women sings a pastoral paean to Apollo:

Strophe I
O house of a bountiful lord,
Ever open to many guests,
The God of Pytho,
Apollo of the beautiful lyre,
Deigned to dwell in you
And live a shepherd in your lands!
On the slope of the hillsides
He played melodies of mating
On the Pipes of Pan to his herds.

Antistrophe I
And the dappled lynxes fed with
    them
In joy at your singing;

From the wooded vale of Orthrys
Came a yellow troop of lions;
To the sound of your lyre, O
    Phoebus,
Danced the dappled fawn
Moving on light feet
Beyond the high-crested pines,
    Charmed by your sweet singing.
        (*Alcestis* 568-576)

David Bergeron, in "The Apollo Mission in *The Winter's Tale*" (1995), reveals how Shakespeare also invested his play with manifold aspects of Apollo, and that even though the god does not appear on stage, as Artemis does in *Pericles*, his agency permeates the drama through the Oracle and beneficent actions of Camillo and Paulina toward Polixenes and Hermione. I would add the Shepherd for his protection of Perdita.

Of the twenty-nine references to Apollo in his canon, thirteen come in *Winter's Tale*. Three early comedies, *Love's Labour's Lost*, *A Midsummer Night's Dream*, and *Taming of the Shrew*, contain a few references; but then we skip all the way to *Winter's Tale* before Shakespeare alludes to Apollo again in comedy. Only in his late romance does Shakespeare refer to Apollo's power as an oracle. (Bergeron 362)

Bergeron identifies the major classical literary sources on the Oracle as the Homeric Hymn of Apollo, Aeschylus (*Eumenides*), Euripides (*Iphigenia of Taurus & Ion*), and especially Ovid (*Metamorphoses*). Pindar, Plato, Herodotus, Aristotle, Livy, and Lucan also wrote of the Delphic Oracle and Plutarch lived at Delphi and wrote extensively on its rituals in his *Moralia*. Bergeron further notes that a representation of the Oracle made its debut appearance on the Elizabethan stage in John Lyly's *Midas* (1589).

Shakespeare's use of "Delphos" for Delphi may represent a conflation of Delphi and the isle of Delos where Apollo was born;

Golding's translation of Ovid and Greene similarly use "Delphos" as the location of the Oracle. The Oracle of Delphi was situated in central Greece on Mount Parnassus. In antiquity it was reported to be infallible, although many of its famous prophesies were enigmatic. The Oracle was credited with predicting the defeat of the Persians by the Athenians and was the only Oracle to pass the Test of Croesus. Delphi accumulated fabulous wealth in art and other treasures during the 6th and 5th centuries, and instituted the Pythian Games, which rivaled the games at Olympia. The priestesses, or Pithia, were believed to go into an ecstatic union with Apollo in the Temple *omphalos*, the "center of the universe."

Apollonian agency is directly represented in *The Winter's Tale* through the descriptions of the Oracle by Cleomenes and Dion, and when the Oracle is presented formally at the Queen's trial, the seals are ceremoniously broken and the judgment of Hermione's innocence and Leontes' sin proclaimed. Apollo acts indirectly through the protections and prophecies of Camillo, Paulina and the Shepherd. He is also identified with Florizel, for his shepherd's disguise and his direct allusion to "the fire-rob'd god, Golden Apollo, a poor humble swain as I seem now" (4.4.29-31).

According to the ancient tradition, Apollo has knowledge of the past, present, and future, and since time heals, we see in Apollo the healer at work through Leontes' transformative contrition and deep grief. Bergeron suggests that:

The play's preoccupation with time, I am suggesting, grows from a keen interest in Apollo who brings his aid in the unfolding of time. Or to state it another way: Apollo gives the gift of time in this play as part of his help—a time that turns out to be efficacious in the ways that we and Leontes could not have anticipated. (369)

He further notes how the healing power of art, poetry and music are also Apollonian at-

tributions, which have very dramatic effects in Shakespeare's romance.

We recall that traditions link Apollo to the Nine Muses, to music and art. Paulina creates a complete Apollonian moment at her house where music, art, and theatre interconnect at a propitious time. Like Romano and like Apollo, Paulina sculpts this experience to produce mystery, wonder, faith, and eventually catharsis. (377)

The dramaturgic similarities between the final scenes of *Alcestis* and *The Winter's Tale* are detailed in my recently published paper on "Gods and Greeks" in *The Oxfordian X*. Most relevant to our present concerns are the almost identical reactions of the two kings when they first see the mysterious vision of their returned queens: While Admetus says, "O woman, whosoever you may be, you have the form of Alcestis, and your body is like hers.... When I look upon her ...my heart is torn asunder—tears flow from my eyes.... I taste the bitterness of my sorrow" (1054-1065). Leontes says, "Her natural posture! / Chide me, dear stone, that I may say indeed / Thou art Hermione;" and "Now piercing my soul. O, thus she stood" (5.3.23-34).

Language used to describe both Hermione and Alcestis reflects Neoplatonic idealization. Hermione is described as "most sacred lady", "sovereignly ...honorable", "gracious", "sweetest companion", "perfect woman", "peerless", "unparall'd", and "sainted spirit". Alcestis is also described as a "sainted or blessed spirit" (*makaira daimon*), "the best and the dearest of women," "noble and virtuous," "sacred lady." A.E. Haigh comments:

… there is perhaps no character in ancient poetry which has aroused deeper admiration than that of Alcestis, the devoted wife and tender-hearted mistress, whose presence in the house is like a gleam of sunshine, and whose affectionate regard for even the humblest member of the household is shown, during her dying moments, by her tender words of farewell. (222)

Finally, both tragicomedies employ elaborate hand gestures, what could be called the "dialogue of hands." Both Charles Frey in *Shakespeare's Vast Romance: A Study of The Winter's Tale* (1980) and B.J. Sokol in *Art and Illusion in The Winter's Tale* (1994) make specific note of the play's many dramatically symbolic hand gestures and allusions. "paddling palms, and pinching fingers" (1.2.115) and "virginalling" (1.2.125) serve to inflame Leontes' jealousy. Frey observes:

In that single instant of handclasps transferred through Hermione, Camillo's image of the kings who "shook hands, as over a vast" explodes into suspicion. The gesture that to Hermione and Polixenes means love and confidence to Leontes means a lascivious breach of trust. (122)

The comic quality of hand gestures is quite evident in the series of exchanges between Clown and Autolycus in Act IV and V, but in the statue scene hand gestures reach the apex of their healing power through their being seen, touched and kissed. Romano's hands are said to have created a living art, "life as lively mock'd" (5.3.19). Perdita asks to kiss the hand of her mother's statue, but Paulina restrains her until the moment of reanimation. Instructing Hermione to descend from her pedestal, says tells Leontes:

>   Do not shun her
> Until you see her die again; for then
> You kill her double. Nay, present your hand: (5.3.105-7)

B.J. Sokol identifies Shakespeare's theatric dramaturgy with the hand gestures of early Renaissance statues, which portrayed "the light of inner being through outward forms by means of a detailed 'theory of Signs'" (178).

Hermione is both statue and lover in a culture with a code of gestures for both, so the disposition of her hands when she plays the statue would seem to be crucial. A guide to what might be achieved could be found in the teachings of the *hypocrisis*, the fifth stage of classical rhetoric, or in allied traditions of acting gestures. (178)

In Euripides' *Alcestis*, dramatic hand actions and metaphors are also emphatic. Death accuses Apollo of having a "lawless grasp" (28); the Chorus of young women beat their hands as a sign that Alcestis has died; the dying queen "held out her hand to each" (196); Hercules won her back to "my hands" (1031) and trusts only Admetus' "right hand" (1115) with the resurrected queen. Hands are Alcestis' last gift to Admetus before her death:

> Alcestis: O my children, you have heard your father say never will he set another wife over you and never thus insult me.
> Admetus: Again I say it and will perform it too!
> Alcestis (*placing the children's hands in his*): Then take these children from my hand.
> Admetus: I take them, dear gifts from a dear hand. (371-375)

The visual language, the dialogue of hands, in both of these plays, and the numerous allusions to hands, is evidence of a direct relationship between Euripides' and Shakespeare's tragicomedies, one that has not received previous scholarly attention. Perhaps this should not be so surprising since hand gestures involve the dramatic imagination in ways that go beyond analyses of text and speech, and involve the artists like Elizabeth Farren who use their bodies as well as their voices to tell the story.

J.H.P. Pafford of *The Arden Shakespeare* (1963) asserts correctly that Shakespeare chose the characters' names for his play from

Plutarch. Pafford fails, however, first to identify most of the historic and mythic characters themselves, and more importantly to then recognize them as an integrated group of personalities, connected either historically or poetically. Howard Hunter Furness (*The New Variorum* Edition of 1898) was perhaps the first scholar to note Shakespeare's reliance on Plutarch, almost never on Greene's *Pandosto*, in selecting his characters' names. He too admits ignorance regarding their meaning:

> In his nomenclature, Shakespeare is never merely servile in following his originals; but exercises a remarkable independence, sometimes simply adopting, sometimes slightly varying, sometimes wholly rejecting, the names he found in them. It is difficult to imagine that this conduct was merely arbitrary and careless. Euphony must of course have had its influence; often there must have occurred other considerations of no trifling interest, if only we could discover and understand them…. Shakespeare's names are curiously—often barbarously—much by Providence,—but assuredly not without Shakespeare's cunning purpose—mixed out of the various traditions he confusedly adopted, and languages, which he imperfectly knew. (1)

That Plutarch and earlier Greek poetry name sources for *The Winter's Tale* is rarely discussed in traditional criticism. Interestingly, Shakespeare's nomenclature refers directly to historic personalities in 5th century Greece, and includes three sequential rulers of Sparta from the period of the heroic battles with the Persians through the first years of the Peloponnesian War. The integrated nature of Shakespeare's naming scheme can be revelatory. For instance, Paulina's expressed faith in the worthiness of Alexander the Great's successor in Act 5 is a subtle allusion to Antigonus I, King of Macedonia and the

very man after whom her deceased husband was named. Similarly, Antigonus' fateful plea that birds should nurse the abandoned baby Perdita, and that the animals show pity, is a clear allusion to the animistic rescues of the infants Romulus and Remus, founders of Rome, and of Paris of Troy. Here, arranged alphabetically, are the likely relevant historic and mythic classical sources of the major character names in *The Winter's Tale*:

Antigonus: Antigonus I (382-301 BCE) was a renowned general under Alexander the Great and ascended the throne of Macedonia briefly after Alexander's death, only to be deposed by Lysimachus at the battle of Ipsus.

Archidamus: Archidamus II, King of Sparta (reigned 469-427 BCE) ruled during the first phase of the Peloponnesian War, aka Archidamian War. A personal friend of Pericles of Athens, he attempted to keep the peace but was overruled by the Spartans.

Autolycus: Autolycus was the son of Hermes, God of Thieves, and the beautiful maiden, Chione. He was among the Argonauts, taught wrestling to Hercules, and became a renowned thief who could make himself invisible. Grandfather of Odysseus.

Camillo: Camillus (446-365 BCE) or Marcus Furius Camillus was reported by Plutarch in his *Parallel Lives* (75 A.C.E.) as being "in the highest commands, and obtained the greatest successes, was five times chosen dictator, triumphed four times, and was styled the second founder of Rome" (153).

Cleomenes: Cleomenes, King of Sparta (reigned 521-491 BCE) was the subject of both Herodotus and Plutarch. Although accused of being slightly mad, Cleomenes was the undisputed leader of the Peloponnesian League, and ruled Sparta for 30 years.

Dion: Dion, King of Sicily is described in Plutarch as the 4th century ruler of Syracuse, and a friend and ardent follower of Plato. His bringing Plato to the court of Dionysius II was disastrous, resulting in the philosopher's being sold into slavery.

Hermione: Hermione is in Homer, Euripides, Plutarch, and Ovid. The daughter of Menelaus and Helen of Troy, she is first promised to Agamemnon's son, Orestes, but awarded in marriage to Neoptolemus (Pyrrhus) at the conclusion of the Trojan War. She appears as a female character in only one other Elizabethan drama, *Horestes* (1567). Hermione is portrayed in several dramas of Euripides, with radically different treatments of her character. In *Orestes* (408 B.C.E.) she is depicted as an honorable and innocent Spartan princess who becomes a hostage, threatened with death by a very disturbed, homicidal Orestes. During the Peloponnesian war, Hermione was portrayed as a murderously jealous, hysterical monarch in *Andromache* (420's BCE). Ovid's *Heroides* includes Hermione's 120-line appeal to Orestes to save her from Pyrrhus.

> Pyrrhus, Achilles' son, in self-will the image of his sire, holds me in durance against every law of earth and heaven. All that lay in my power I have done—I have refused consent to be held; farther than that my woman's hands could not avail. . . . I had been made a slave, carried away by the barbarian rout with the daughters of Greece. Less misused by the victorious Achaeans was Andromache herself, . . . (99)

Leontes: Leonidas I, King of Sparta succeeded his half-brother, Cleomenes in 489 BCE and was renowned as the leader of the Spartans at the battle of Thermopylae against Xerxes of Persia in 480, the legendary Gates of Fire. Some sources suggest he took only a small force to the battle because he knew he was likely going to his doom, since the Oracle of Delphi had foretold that victory would require the death of one of the Spartan kings. Athaneus includes a long speech by Leonidas

mocking the nature of women.

Paulina: Gaius Suetonius Paulinus became governor of Britain in 58 A.D.E., during the reign of Emperor Claudius. Earlier in his career, he was the first Roman general to cross the Atlas Mountains. Although vastly outnumbered by the Druid army during a revolt in 61, his legions destroyed the Britons, and wreaked a most severe revenge.

Perdita: Perdita derives from the Oracle in *Pandosto*, "that which is lost," and the reason for the name is specifically given (3.3.33). However, Paris of Troy was born to almost the identical circumstances of Perdita in which an oracle passes judgment and an infant is abandoned to die of exposure, only to be rescued and raised by a shepherd.

Polixenes: Polyxena of Troy was the youngest daughter of King Priam and Queen Hecuba, and was noted for her beauty and close relationship with Troilus, son of Hecuba and Apollo. After the sack of Troy, in one of the greatest sins committed by the conquering Greeks, she was sacrificed on the demand of the ghost of Achilles.

Bear: She-Bear who in legend nurtures the abandoned infant Paris for 5 days and saves his life. Antigonus' lines at the end of act 2, when Perdita's fate is placed in his charge suggest animistic rescue by the birds, wolves and bears.

> Come on, poor babe:
> Some powerful spirit instruct the kites and ravens
> To be thy nurses! Wolves and bears, they say,
> Casting their savageness aside, have done
> Like offices of pity. (2.3.184-7)

Before concluding and passing on to *Pericles*, I would like to comment on the allusion to "that rare Italian master, Julio Romano" (5.2.96). Giulio Romano (1492-

1546) was Raphael's most talented student, headed the Roman school of painting and was a personal friend of Baldasarre Castiglione, who brought the artist to Mantua. Romano was famous for his Pallazo de Te, his memorial sculptures, his paintings of Apollo, and for the monumental murals depicting scenes from the Trojan War, the Judgment of Paris, and the rape of Helen. He also created hundreds of erotic engravings, known as "the postures," a word Leontes uses to describe Hermione's statuesque form. Romano is the only artist Shakespeare directly alludes to in the entire canon, and his stylish realism fits perfectly with the poet's representation as art that "would beguile Nature" (Magri 55).

Finally, a discussion of resurrection in Renaissance drama would not be complete without acknowledging the possibility of a Hermetic influence. In *Tragedy and After: Euripides, Shakespeare, Goethe*, Ekbert Faas recognizes that Hermione's resurrection lacks any of the hints for its being a Christian parable, but rather is depicted "as a kind of Hermetic magic," "Lawful as eating." Quoting Frances Yates *Shakespeare's Last Plays: A New Approach* (1975), Faas suggests Shakespeare was using imagery and dramaturgy of magic derived from the Asclepius dialogue of the Egyptian, "Hermes Trismegistus":

> This may or may not be a direct allusion "to the famous god-making passage in the Asclepius." But the notion, reported in the Hermetic text, of how the old Egyptian priests, frequently to the accompaniment of music, used to infuse their statues of the gods with life, was widely enough known to be recognized by at least some members of Shakespeare's audience.
>
> (*Shakespeare's Poetics* 144)

Francis Yates argues that these dialogues had a great influence in the Renaissance and were associated with Hermeticism, Neoplatonism, and the magical-religious teachings of Giordano Bruno. Suggesting that the "life-infusing" magic of the statue scene may be seen as a metaphor for the artistic process, Yates concludes that Shakespeare was not only familiar with the *Asclepius*, but also found it profoundly important.

> The bringing of life to Hermione is in fact the core of the message of the play, the return of life of a lost and banished goodness and virtue. . . . The episode of Paulina's daring magic, with its allusion to the magical statues of the *Asclepius*, may thus be a key to the meaning of the play as an expression of one of the deepest currents of Renaissance magical philosophy of nature.
>
> (*Majesty & Magic* 91)

Although this is an intriguing possible source for an allusion to the Greek god of healing, and his role in resurrection and sacred reanimation rites, the better probability, based on all the dramaturgic and "Apollonian" similarities between the plays, is that the Greek Asclepius, as reputed savior of the dead in *Alcestis*, is the more credible inspiration for Shakespeare. However, in our analysis of *Pericles* we will again encounter the Egyptian.

In summary, *The Winter's Tale* is beholding to Euripides' *Alcestis* for the magical scene that elevates the drama far beyond the reach of Greene's Pandosto. Shakespeare also shows great respect for Apollo's Oracle and seems remarkably familiar with the Greek canon, using character names drawn from both myth and the ranks of the heroic kings of the 5th century.

Pericles, Prince of Tyre — Cast of Greeks, Artemis and Cerimon

Although *Pericles* was not included in the First Folio, it has generally been accepted into the canon since first being printed in quarto in 1609. Whether the textual problems reflect a memorial reconstruction, or Shakespeare was co-authored, the quaint language of the first two acts differs significantly from the power and beauty of the poetry that follows. G. Wilson Knight wrote "Pericles is the result of no sudden vision: It is Shakespeare's total poetry on the brink of self knowledge" (73). Whatever its dramatic and poetic flaws may be, *Pericles* was extremely popular in the early 17th century.

Pericles, like *The Winter's Tale*, is also populated by characters Shakespeare named from Greek sources including Plutarch and the 5th century BCE poets and historians. For plot he precisely follows his primary source, story of Apollonius of Tyre in *Confessio Amantis* by John Gower (1330-1408) who was a personal friend of Geoffrey Chaucer. The story of Apollonius probably dates back to an unknown Greek romance of the 3rd century because of similarities with Xenophon's *Ephesian Tale*. The other sources we will consider here include the *Corpus Hermeticum*, Greek lyric poetry, and Ovid's *Metamorphoses*. There are also hidden religious allusions in *Pericles* that may have not been noted by previous scholars, and a definite suggestion of Hermeticism. Like Gower's plot, Shakespeare also follows Gower's symbolic geography, except for one highly significant change, that of choosing Mytilene as the location of Marina's brothel experience and of her healing reunion with Pericles in Acts IV and V.

The presiding deity of this play is Diana, sister to Apollo. Neptune does provides repeated providential tempests and is honored at the festival in Mytilene, but it is Diana who provides protection for Thaisa and Marina, and who appears prophetically in *Pericles* dream, directing him to her Temple at Ephesus where he will be happily reunited with his queen at the conclusion of the play. Unlike *The Winter's Tale* where Hermione's restoration is portrayed as art becoming life, in *Pericles* the raising of Thaisa is enacted as a mysterious medical art performed by Lord Cerimon. Cerimon is a "natural magician and sage" who "serves as a moral touchstone in the play" according to Pelican Shakespeare editor Stephen Orgel (xli). Cerimon's skill and beneficence reflects a profound understanding

of Hippocratic ethics and of the physician's legendary powers. Cerimon's ritual of resurrection invokes the assistance of both Apollo and Asclepius, whose life and death will be explored in our concluding argument.

Shakespeare's *dramatis personae* in Pericles reflects a similar renaming method that he employed in *The Winter's Tale*. Nonetheless, several characters are named identically, including the evil, incestuous King Antiochus, the envious, murderous Dionyza of Tarsus, and mage, Lord Cerimon. Shakespeare expands the role of Gower's noble Tyrian, Hellanicus, and renames him Helicanus, perhaps in tribute to Hesiod (c.700 BCE) who received his poetic inspiration from the Muses on Mount Helicon. Tharsia, the daughter in Gower's tale, becomes Thaisa, the resurrected mother and high priestess of Diana's Temple at Ephesus.

Apollonius becomes **Pericles**: Apollonius in Gower is clearly associated poetically with his namesake because he is described as master of the harp and song like "Apollo, god of the heathens." Stephen Orgel notes the importance of these names: "To replace the name Apollonius with Pericles, the Athenian statesman and military hero, was to move the story from the world of fantasy into the world of statecraft and action" (xl). Some scholars have suggested that Pericles is actually named after Phillip Sydney's character Pyrocles from the *Arcadia* because of the marginal euphony and because of certain elements of Sidney's portrayal.

I believe there is much more evidence to support **Pericles of Athens** as the model for the suffering king. Pericles (c.495-429 BCE) was the most renowned "first citizen" of Athens during the Golden Age and was its primary leader for 30 years. He was referred to as being "Olympian" for his historic stature, and greatly admired for his democratic leadership, rhetorical brilliance, and support of the arts throughout his life. He was archon for the production of Aeschylus' *The Persians* in 472 BCE, and when he later came to power he insisted the Athenians rebuild the temples on the Acropolis that had been destroyed by the Persians in 479. The construction of the Parthenon, with its fabulous architecture, famous (Elgin) sculptures, including the golden statue of Athena, was commissioned to his friend Phidias.

Pericles introduced populist social policies and led the Athenians as they grew to dominate the Delian League. His personal connections included the Sophist philosopher Anaxagoras and Greece's most famous hetaera, Aspasia, by whom he had an illegitimate son. He led the Athenians in a number of battles, including the Battle of Delphi, but at the end of his life was accused of corruption and bears some responsibility for starting the Peloponnesian War in 431. Thucydides and especially Plutarch treat Pericles with great respect in their histories. He was, however, blamed for Athens' plague by Sophocles in his *Oedipus The King* (429) and was also criticized by Plato in *Gorgias*. Pericles died in 429, still grieving for the deaths of his two legitimate sons who also suffered the plague.

There are distinct similarities in the literary and historic portrayals of Pericles of Tyre and of Athens. Both were highly intelligent, generous, loved by their people, and associated with the arts. Both also suffer the loss of a child and are threatened by unhappy nobility. Finally, both were opposed by Cleon.

Stranguilio becomes **Cleon of Tarsus:** Cleon in *Pericles* is clearly based on **Cleon of Athens** (d. 422BCE), a rich Athenian merchant, and leader of the opposition party during Pericles' last years. Cleon rose to power after Pericles' death and gained particular notoriety for his proposed policy of exterminating all the citizens of Mytilene after an Athenian military victory. His death resulted in a temporary suspension of the Peloponnesian War with the Peace of Nicias. He was reviled by both the comic playwright Aristophanes and by the historian Thucydides. In *Pericles* Cleon is portrayed as weak and easily manipulated by his conniving wife, Dionyza, who attempts to have Marina assassinated because of her envy of Marina's

beauty, art and virtue.

Arcestrates becomes **Simonides, King of Pentapolis:** Simonides is the good king in *Pericles* who is loved by his people, and who acknowledges and hosts Pericles even though the prince has lost everything in a tempest save his father's rusty armor. Simonides also subtly encourages Pericles' match with his love-struck daughter, Thaisa. **Simonides of Ceos** (c.556-459 BCE) is the likely personality Shakespeare used to name his kind king. The historic Simonides was a canonical lyric poet along with Sappho and Pindar whose work in included in the *Greek Anthology*. He lived in both Athens and Thessaly and wrote elegies and paeans to Apollo, as well as patriotic poems celebrating the Greek battles with the Persians at Marathon and Thermopylae. Simonides once even gained the victory over Aeschylus in the Athenian trilogies competition.

Athanagoras becomes **Lysimachus:** Regarding this name change Pelican editor Stephen Orgel comments:

> Athenagoras becomes Lysimachus (and) the change, if history is relevant, is not trivial: Athenagoras was an early Christian philosopher, who wrote a treatise on the Resurrection, and should be very much in tune with the play. Lysimachus, however, was one of Alexander's generals, who became ruler of Macedonia and was notorious for his tyranny and cruelty. Perhaps this is another case in which Pericles fails to see beyond the surface—and perhaps Jacobean audiences with classical educations did not foresee a happy future for Marina. (xxxviii)

Actually, Lysimachus is ironically even more relevant to *Pericles* than Athenagoras, precisely because, like the historic Pericles in Athens, he rebuilt Ephesus in 292 BCE, which was to become known as the "first and greatest metropolis of Asia," and home to the world-famous Temple of Diana where our play concludes. Lysimachus was King of Thrace and of Asia Minor, joined the coalition that defeated Antigonus I at the Battle of Ipsus, and later fought Antigonus' son, Demetrius.

Cerimon's unnamed servant becomes **Philemon:** Philemon is most probably named after Philemon of Athens (c.362-262 BCE), a poet and prolific playwright of the New Comedy that was a rival to Menander. Only two of Philemon's plays, *Mercator* and *Trinummus*, have been preserved in Latin translations by Plautus. Philemon won repeated victories in the competitions and lived to be over 100 years old. Philemon also appears as the worthy husband of Baucis in Ovid's *Metamorphoses VIII*.

Tharsia becomes **Marina:** The characterization of Marina is largely based upon Gower's Tharsia. This includes the period of maintaining her virtue while enslaved at the brothel in Mytilene. There are many remarkable parallels between Marina and Perdita besides the topical and prophet reasons given for their names. Both are princesses, separated from their families during providential tempests. Both are condemned to death by enraged, jealous tyrants, and both escape death by sea voyages. At the same age both are rescued by disguised but noble suitors, and both help heal their soul-sick fathers, followed by their immediate reunions with the mysteriously resurrected and sanctified queens. Marina, raised at court, is described as Mistress of the Arts, superior in discourse, in virtue, majesty and modesty, "sings like one immortal" and "dances goddesslike" (5.1.3), creating needle work that "composes natures own shape" (5.1.6). She prays only to Diana and is protected by the Goddess. Perdita, raised by the Shepherd, is Mistress of Nature and the Feast, identified with flowers and a natural grace and wit, queen of "curds and cream" (4.4.161), who "dances featly" (4.4.178). She is compared to Persephone and Flora.

Tharsia and Marina's character may actually be drawn from the lives of famous Greek women of antiquity. One is the poet **Sappho** (c.630-570 BCE) who lived on the isle of Lesbos, and was a one-time resident of Mytilene, the capitol. She wrote sophisticated, passionate poetry, often addressed to women, and was greatly admired by Plato, Aristophanes, Ovid and Horace. At one point in her life, she was exiled to Sicily where she was welcomed in Syracuse with a statue dedicated in her honor, a motif also related to Marina. Sappho produced many volumes of lyric poetry, but only a few poems and fragments remain. Still, she is ranked with Pindar as the greatest for lyric and choral poetry. Many scholars believe there is evidence that Sappho instructed young women in music and letters, thus in so many ways giving a topical reason for situating Marina in Sappho's capitol, Mytilene.

The other famous Greek model for Tharsia-Marina may be the lifelong love of Pericles of Athens, **Aspasia** (c.470-400 BCE). The most renowned hetaera of the Golden Age, Aspasia was praised for her beauty, wisdom, and rhetoric, and received the attentions of Plato, Aristophanes, Xenophon, Thucydides, Plutarch, Cicero and Lucian. She is alleged to have operated a brothel and was once accused by her critics of corrupting the women of Athens. Tried for impiety, she was ultimately exonerated through the intervention of Pericles. Some scholars maintain that Aspasia is the model for Socrates teacher, Diotima, in Plato's *Symposium*. While some scholars believe she wrote Pericles greatest orations, others are less complementary, even blaming her for starting the Peloponnesian War.

John Gower no doubt meant indirect praise of a courageous philosopher and religious figure by naming his Prince of Machilenta Athanagoras. As Stephen Orgel has argued, **Athenagoras** of Athens (133-190 CE) is a very appropriate figure for a theological allusion in the story of Apollonius. An influential Platonist philosopher who converted to Christianity and was an advocate for monotheism, Athenagoras' writings included *Apology, a Treatise on the Resurrection*, and famous appeals to Emperor Marcus

Aurelius for mercy for Christians who had been charged with atheism. Shakespeare also includes allusions to theologians in *Pericles*, but in a much more subtle and satiric way, one that may have gone unrecognized by previous scholarship.

The first of these religious figures is **Juan de Valdés** (c.1509-41), a Spanish religious writer whose *Diologo de Mercurio y Caron* criticized the corruptions of the Spanish Catholic Church and resulted in his exile to Naples where he enjoyed the protection of the Pope, partly because he had upheld the validity of Henry VIII's marriage to Catherine of Aragon. In *Pericles*, he is referred to by the murderous Leonine as "the great pirate Valdes" (4.1.96) whose minions have abducted, and therefore mercifully saved, Marina. In Naples, Valdés was surrounded by a coterie of scholars, poets and Italian Protestants, including Vermigli, aka Peter Martyr. Vermigli left Naples after Valdés death, eventually traveled to England and became an immensely influential Reformation theologian.

Valdés was openly criticized in 1567 as being unsound on the holy trinity by several other theologians, including **Francis David**, aka **Ferenc David** (1510-79), the Calvinist Bishop of the Hungarian Church in **Transylvania**. In *Pericles*, Pander laments how bad the prostitution business has been, and recalls how the "poor Transylvanian is dead that lay with the little baggage" (4.2.20). Coming just 25 lines after the allusion to the "great pirate Valdes," it seems quite likely that the author is slyly referring to Francis David who studied at Wittenberg, and was an anti-Trinitarian with doubts about the scriptural basis for the holy ghost. He is credited with the expression "We need not think alike to love alike" and is thought of as one of the founders of Unitarianism. He was later convicted of "innovation" and died in a Catholic prison.

While Shakespeare employs a villain and bauds to comment on Protestant reformers, he has Lord Cerimon, the healer who can raises Thaisa, make a direct allusion to the "**Egyptian** that had nine hours lain dead"

(3.2.85), most likely **Hermes Trismegistus**. Like in *The Winter's Tale*, there is a clear possibility that the author was familiar with the Corpus Hermeticum including the *Asclepius*, the collection of Greek mystery texts from Alexandria, written most probably during the 2nd and 3rd centuries. The *Hermetica* was translated into Latin by the Italian scholar Ficino in 1471, and was considered to reflect the apex of pagan philosophy during the Renaissance. It addressed issues of Gnosticism, astrology, alchemy and magic, including the reanimation of sacred statues to musical accompaniment.

Our understanding of *Pericles* is enhanced when we consider how Diana's influence dominates this drama the way her twin, Apollo, is central to *The Winter's Tale*. There are numerous allusions to Diana throughout the play; she appears to Pericles in a prophet dream, and the final scene takes place at her world famous temple at Ephesus where Thaisa has become the high priestess. Both Thaisa and Marina place their lives under Diana's protection, and Pericles himself swears by her to remain "unscissored" (3.4.28) until Marina is married.

Diana-Artemis is the goddess of the hunt, as well as of chastity, fertility and childbirth. She even helped her mother deliver her younger twin, Apollo. She revered throughout Greece, and was depicted as a multi-breasted deity in the antique statue of the "Lady of Ephesus." All Athenian young girls served for a year in her temple at the nearby sanctuary in Brauron, and were referred to as *arktoi*, "she-bears." during their service. The ancient symbols identified with Diana include the silver bow, lyre, moon, nature, and the Amazons. During the Renaissance, Queen Elizabeth was very closely identified with Diana, England's "mortal moon." Just as Apollo is appropriate as the presiding influence in a drama of destructive sexual jealousy and the healing power of time and good counsel, so Diana is perfectly matched to *Pericles*, a story that hinges on the beneficence of the goddess in preserving Thaisa through childbirth and protecting Marina's virtue.

Pericles has imbedded symbolic geography that owes its origins to Gower's Apollonius. The medieval story, like Shakespeare's, begins at the court of Antiochus in **Antioch**, which was the largest city in the world after Rome and Alexandria during the Hellenistic period. The Temple of Pythian Apollo was a landmark in this Seleucid empire capitol, a multi-cultural Mecca. Praised by Cicero for its achievements in arts and letters, its citizens nonetheless also had a reputation for dissolute behavior. Sts. Peter and Paul both preached at Antioch. Ancient **Tyre** was a city on the Lebanon coast during the reigns of David and Solomon. Tyre was sequentially conquered by Alexander the Great and Antigonus I, and later during the First Crusade. **Tarsus** was a Greek city on coast of Turkey, which also had a literary reputation that rivaled Athens an Alexandria. Tarsus is where Anthony met Cleopatra, and the home of Paul of Tarsus.

Pentapolis was a group of cities on the coast of Libya with the port of **Apollonia** and capitol of Cyrene. **Simon of Cyrene** was the man who was forced to carry the cross of Jesus through Jerusalem. In Gnostic traditions, Simon is reputed to have died on the cross in lieu of Jesus. The name of this ancient port and the closeness of Simon's name to Shakespeare's King Simonides of Pentapolis suggest that both Gower and Shakespeare educated their audiences by using famous names and symbolic geography. **Ephesus** was no exception, an Athenian city on the Aegean coast of Turkey; it was renowned for the Temple of Artemis, and its theatre, and library. After it was rebuilt by Lysimachus, it became the greatest city in Roman Asia, and gained fame among Christians for St. Paul's gospel. The Temple of Artemis was one of the ancient Wonders of the World.

Shakespeare departs from his source only in one location and that is the substitution of **Mytilene** as the domain of Lysimachus and the brothel where Marina has enchanted the nobility with her arts of discourse, song, and embroidery, and completely frustrated the scheming of Pander, Bawd, and Boult. Mytilene was the capitol of the Isle of Lesbos, home of the lyric poets Sappho and Alcaeus. During the Peloponnesian War, Cleon of Athens attempted to exterminate the male citizens of Mytilene, but was overruled by the Athenian generals. Thus, it would appear the mythopoetic lines in *Pericles* are composed of historic, geographic, and religious symbols, that the story is supported by manifold, embedded, archetypal roots.

Finally, we come to **Lord Cerimon**, of whom Pericles says at the end of the play, "The gods can have no mortal officer more like a god than you" (5.3.62). Cerimon is the embodiment of Renaissance mage, combining mystical medical knowledge with the soul of charity. According to Eva Turner Clark, his name derives from the Latin *coerimonia*, meaning the sacred, the divine. In the *Medical Mind of Shakespeare* (1986), Aubrey Kail writes: "Cerimon is not only a physician, but also a nobleman, a lord of Ephesus, and a mystic who is endowed with extraordinary healing powers. It is not surprising therefore that Shakespeare's greatest tribute to the medical profession is stated by Cerimon" (28). Similarly, F. David Hoeniger praises Cerimon's art in *Medicine and Shakespeare in the English Renaissance* (1992):

> The authorities he consults presumably include Galen, Hippocrates, and more modern works.... He has learned not merely from books, but also from practice; he has tested his herbal and medicines, There is no other speech like his devoted to the medical art in the whole range of Elizabethan, Jacobean or Caroline drama.... Cerimon exemplifies the Hippocratic ideal in medicine. (66-7)

Francis Yates sees Cerimon as an almost Christ-like figure, possessing divine healing powers and motivated by his pure benevolence and charity.

We seem to sense here the new

ideal of the physician spreading in Europe through the influences of Paracelsus, in whom new medical skills are combined with a reputation for new magic. Cerimon uses 'musical therapy' in his healing, and his power of bringing to life again seems a miracle to the beholders. (88-9)

In the description of his art, Cerimon waxes philosophic:

> I hold it ever
> Virtue and cunning were endowments greater
> Than nobleness and riches. Careless heirs
> May the two latter darken and expend:
> But immortality attends the former,
> Making the man a god. 'Tis known, I ever
> Have studied physic, through which secret art,
> By turning o'er authorities, I have,
> Together with my practice, made familiar
> To me and to my aid the blessed infusions
> That dwell in vegetatives, in metals, stones;
> And can speak of the disturbances
> That nature works, and of her cures; which doth give me
> A more content in course of true delight
> Than to be thirsty after tottering honor,
> Or tie my pleasure up in silken bags,
> To please the fool and death.
> (3.2.25-41)

In his ritualized resurrection of Thaisa, Lord Cerimon first calls upon Apollo for understanding, "perfect me in the characters" (3.2.68) and then upon Asclepius for guidance (3.2.110), both pointing to the Hippocratic Oath, which begins, "I swear by Apollo, Asclepius, Hygeia and Panacea, and I take to witness all the gods...." He offers a prognosis that suggests Hermetic wisdom: "Death may usurp on nature many hours, / And yet, the fire of life kindle again, / The o'erpressed spirits. I heard of an Egyptian / That has nine hours lain dead, / Who was by good appliance recovered" (3.2.83-7). His techniques for resuscitating the shocked, hypothermic queen include fire, warm clothing, and music: "The rough and woeful music that we have, / Cause it to sound, beseech you. / The viol once more. How thou stirr'st, thou block! / The music there! I pray you give her air. / Gentlemen, this queen will live." (3.2.98-93). "Viol" could also refer to a vial of warm oil used by Cerimon's servant in Gower's tale of Apollonius. Of this scene G. Wilson Knight comments:

> We have moved very far beyond gnomic rhymes and moral precepts; beyond psychological lessons and social comments; have advanced beyond ethic altogether to a dramatic disclosure metaphysical rather than moral, indeed visionary rather than metaphysical, as we watch life blossom and glow from the very jaws of death, warmed into renewed existence by Cerimon's fire and music. (57)

Shakespeare's physician is the exemplar of Hippocratic ethics and reflects knowledge of the Oath and the ritual practices of ancient Greece. Hippocrates (c.460-370 BCE), the father of western medicine, was trained at the Asclepieion in Kos and traveled throughout Greece to study and teach. His legend includes credit for curing the plague in Athens, and for raising the dead on at least one occasion. The *Hippocratic Corpus* describes a method based on observation, clinical assessment, disease classification and supportive treatment. The ethical teachings emphasized humility, discipline, patient confidentiality and the importance of honoring lineage of the *heros iatros*, the hero physicians. Hippocrates is a character in Plato's *Protagoras*, and claimed direct descent from Asclepius and Hercules.

Thus, there appears to be a direct connection from *Pericles'* Lord Cerimon to the legendary, miraculous healer tradition of ancient Greece. Ephesus was famous for its medical traditions and as the home of Soranus, Hippocrates 2nd century biographer.

In summary, *Pericles* matches *The Winter's Tale* in its romantic plot, symbolic geography, characterization, antique nomenclature, presiding deity, and ceremonious resurrections. In *Shakespeare the Magus*, (2001), Arthur Versluis asserts that "The magus Cerimon is rather like the Hermetic psychopomp, who leads the initiate to rebirth, resurrecting him into new life; and in this respect he is indeed both a vehicle for the god's power, and a god himself" (50). Now, the literary source of this god-like archetype is before us, arising from an ancient song nearly 3,000 years old, the story of Asclepius.

Mythopoesis of Resurrection — Asclepius

The mythopoetic representation of pagan resurrection in the Greek, Roman and medieval canon, begins with the poetry of Hesiod, who wrote around 700 BCE. Among Hesiod's works are *The Theogony*, concerning the origins of the world and the gods, *Works and Days*, and *The Catalogue of Women*, a mythological recounting of the mortals who had mated with or been sired by the gods. While Asclepius and his two sons, Machaon and Podalirios, who were also gifted in the healing arts, are mentioned in Homer's *Iliad*, Hesiod is the first poet to recount the god's origins. In *Medicine: An Illustrated History*, Hesiod's rendition of the myth is well-summarized:

The story is that Coronis, a mortal woman, either voluntarily or unwillingly, succumbed to the sun-god, Apollo, but while pregnant with the god's child she married Ischys,

to whom in some versions she had been betrothed. Apollo killed Ischys, while his sister Artemis slew Coronis, but before her body was burned on the funeral pyre Apollo snatched the babe Asclepios, bringing him to the mountain retreat of Chiron, the centaur, who raised the child and taught him all there was to know about the healing arts, especially in regard to plants and medicines. When the boy grew to manhood, he became so skillful that he even brought a dead man back to life. Zeus, the chief Olympian god, fearing that that the afterworld would be depopulated if Asclepios continued to resurrect people, struck down the healer with a thunderbolt. Asclepios was then brought to heaven as a deity. (Lyons and Petrucelli 165-170)

Lyons and Petrucelli include additional commentaries on the myth as reported several hundred years later by Pindar, one of the greatest Greek lyric poets of the 5th century. In Pindar, the Olympian gods were sanitized of their arbitrary destructive fury by depicting Coronis as an adulteress who deceives both the god and Ischys, and by magnifying Asclepius' sin by having him demand a "salary of gold" for the resuscitation. William Race's translation of Pindar's third Pythian Ode gives details of Asclepius' many cures:

When people came to him with
     cancerous sores
Or with limbs wounded by grey
     bronze,
Or by a far-flung stone,
Or with bodies wracked by sum-
     mer fever
Or winter chill, he relieved them of
     their various ills
And restored them; some he tended
     with calming incantations,
To others he gave soothing potions
     or applied medicines

All over their bodies; still others he
    healed with surgery. (55)

In various versions of Asclepius' story, he is reputed to have raised many Greek heros from the dead, including Hyppolytus, Orion, Tyndareus, Glaucus and Lycurgus, brother of King Admetus. He accompanied Jason and the Argonauts on their quest for the golden fleece, and was the subject of many later writers including Euripides, Aristophanes (*Plutus*) and Ovid. In the second century, Pausanias (*Description of Greece*) and Apollodorus (*Bibliotheca*) also described in detail the temples, rituals, and miracles.

All the members of Asclepius' family possessed healing capacities: "His wife, Epione soothed pain, and his daughter Hygeia was the deity of health who came to represent prevention of disease. Panacea, another daughter presented treatment" (Lyons and Petrucelli, 170). The Temples of Asclepius were healing centers that, by the 4th century BCE, had spread throughout Greece and Asia Minor. The most famous of these temples was at Epidaurus where the suppliants were purified, and then allowed to sleep in the *enkoimitria*, an inner hall where the priests guided them in a ritual of dream healing. Pausanias reports that hymns and music were also performed at the temples. The cult of Asclepius established temples in Athens in 420 BCE, at the Acropolis next to the Temple of Dionysius, and in Rome, where the sanctuary was built on Tiber Island in 237 BCE.

Euripides poetically captured the tragic fate of Asclepius in *Alcestis*. Recall Apollo's prologue speech where the god says, "The cause was Zeus. He struck Asclepius, my son, full in the breast with a bolt of thunder, and laid him dead." Asclepius is alluded to again in *Alcestis* at the end of the first song of the Chorus:

He alone—
If the light yet shown for his eye—
Asclepius, Phoebus's son,
Could have led her back
From the land of shadows,

From the gates of Hades,
For he raised the dead
Ere the Zeus-driven shaft
Slew him with thunder fire…
        (123-130)

After the burial of Queen Alcestis, the Chorus laments the limitations of human knowledge and capacity for healing in the face of our ultimate mortality:

I have lived with the Muses
And on lofty heights:
Many doctrines have I learned;
But Fate is above us all.
Nothing avails against Fate—
Neither the Thracian tablets
Marked with Orphic symbols,
Nor the herbs given by Phoebus
To the children of Asclepius
To heal men of their sickness.
        (966-975)

Ovid's *Metamorphoses* includes long passages in several books on Asclepius's birth, and his healing skills and fate. Remarkably, Ovid even gives a detailed account of the historic moving of the god from the sanctuary at Epidaurus to Rome. This event is noted by classics professor C. Kerényi in his study, *Asklepios: Archetypal Image of the Physician's Existence* (1959). The Romans were suffering from a period of war and pestilence, and were told by their oracle of Apollo, the Sibylline Books, to invite Asclepios to Rome, suggesting that Asclepios was already widely recognized as a god of healing in Italy. "The transfer of a powerful new god from a foreign land to Rome demanded an elaborate ceremony to be executed with care and attentiveness—that is *religio*" (Kerény 9). Ten men, led by Quintus Ogulnius, were sent to Epidaurus to bring the god to Rome, and the essential features of this event were included in Arthur Golding's 1567 translation of Book XV of *Metamorphoses*:

Yee Muses whoo to Poets are present
    springs of grace,
Now shewe (for you knowe, neyther
    are you dulled by tyme or space)

How Aesculapius that is in the Tyber
    deepe
Among the sacred saynets of Rome
    had fortune for to creepe.
A cruell plage did heretofore infect
    the Latian aire,
And people's bodyes pyning pale the
    murreine did appayre.
When tyred of the burial of theyr
    friends, they did peerceyve
Themselves no helpe at mannes hand
    nor by Physicke to receive.
Then seeking help from heaven,
    they sent to Delphos (which
    dooth stand
Amid the world) for counsell to bee
    had at Phebus hand.
Beseeching him with helthfull ayd
    to succour theyr distresse,
And of the myghtye Citie Rome the
    mischief to redresse.
The quivers which Apollo bryght
    himself was woont to beare,
The Baytrees, and the place itself
    together shaken were.
And by and by the table from the
    furthest part of all
The Chauncell spake theis words,
    which did theyr harts with
    feare appal:
The thing yee Romanes seeke for
    here, yee should have sought
    more ny
Your countrye. Yea and nearer home
    go seeke it now. Not I,
Apollo, but Apollos sonne is hee that
    must redresse
Your sorrowes. Take your journey
    and with good handsell of
    success,
And fetch my sonne among you.
    When Apollos hest was told
Among the prudent Senators, they
    sercht what towne did hold
His sonne, and unto Epidawre a
    Gallye for him was sent.
                  (698-720)

Ovid's description includes a recounting of the deliberations in Epidaurus and the prophetic dream of the Roman ambassador of Asclepius who says to him, "Feare not, I will come and leave my shryne / This serpent which dooth wreath and knottes about this staffe of mine / Mark well, and make good heede therof: that when thou shalt it see, / Thou mayst it knowe. For into it transformed will I bee" (736-739). The next 100 lines of the poem describe the glorious journey of the chthonic God—Serpent to the royal welcome in his new home, the Temple on Tiber Island.

Book II of *Metamorphoses* also includes a detailed description of Asclepius' birth, and of the jealous wrath of Apollo when his faithful bird, Raven, told him that Coronis has lain with another. Ovid's description of Apollo's jealous fury is rich; frowning, the god cast his garland from his head, his color changed, and a "rage of yre ...boiled in his belking breast", and "set his heart on fire," such that he shot the "deadly Dart" into his lover's chest. Dying, Coronis reminds the god that by her being pregnant, "a couple" shall die.

Thus muche she saide: and with the
    bloud hir life did fade away,
Than all to late, alas too late gan
    Phebus to repent
That of his lover he had tane so
    cruell punishment.
He blames himself for giving eare so
    unadvisedly.
He blames himselfe in that he tooke
    it so outrageously.
He hates and bannes his faithful
    birde because he did enforme
Him of his lovers naughtinesse that
    made him so to storme.
He hates his bow, he hates his shaft
    that rashly from it went:
And eke he hates his hasty hands by
    whom the bow was bent.
He takes hir up betweene his armes
    endeavoring all too late
By plaister made of precious herbes
    to stay hir helplesse fate.

But when he saw there was no
   shift: but that she needes must
   burne,
And that the solemne sacred fire was
   prest to serve the turne,
Then from the bottome of his heart
   full sorie sighes he fet
(For heavenly powers with waterie
   teares their cheeks may never
   wet)
                    (II 768-783)

Ovid's verse describes how Apollo "could not abide to see his seede to ashes turne. / But tooke the baby frome hir wombe and from the firie flame, / And unto double Chyrons den conveyed straight the same" (791-3). Ovid's description of Apollo's fatal rage, grief, repentance, and rescue of his child may have relevance here as an archetypal pattern of jealousy and revenge, followed by grief and reconciliation, one that certainly governs Leontes' sinful actions and repentance in *The Winter's Tale*.

In *Greek Hero Cults and the Ideas of Immortality* (1921), Lewis Richard Farnell includes a description of an Epidaurian rendition of Asclepius' birth that includes another version of the familiar theme of attempted infanticide and rescue by both animals and a shepherd. Pausanias writes of an archaic tradition about the unnamed daughter of King Phleguas who was pregnant by Apollo,

and who bore the holy babe in the
neighborhood of Epidauros, and
ruthlessly exposed it on a mountain.
It was, however, nourished by a
she-goat and guarded by a dog; the
shepherd Aresthanas, who found it,
observed lightening playing around
it and retired in terror. The babe immediately grew up and acquired the
fame of the miraculous healer who
could raise the dead. (252)

The story of Apollo's wrathful condemnation of Coronis and the miraculous rescue
of Asclepius from his mother's funeral pyre,

recalls both Leontes' attempted execution of Hermione for infidelity, despite the judgment of the god's Oracle, and his ordering Perdita "to the fire" three times before she is taken away by Antigonus in *The Winter's Tale*. Similarly, Heracles, the *deus ex machina* in *Alcestis*, performs his twelve labors in expiation for the sin of having killed his wife and children in a fit of divine madness inflicted upon him by Hera, the jealous Queen of Olympus. In all these Greek tales of resurrection mythology there seems to be an archetypal construct of sexual jealousy, attempted revenge murder, banishment, rescue of the innocent, restoration and reunion.

Mythopoesis of Resurrection — Alcestis

While Alcestis' resurrection story is addressed by several other ancient sources besides Euripides, it is Geoffrey Chaucer's prologue to *The Legend of Good Women* that provides the most exalted account of her return from the dead, now as the patron of the poet and the beneficent wife of the God of Love.

Plato's *Symposium*, also known as *Agathon's Feast*, is a Socratic dialogue on the nature of eros written roughly contemporaneous with Euripides' tragicomedy. Phaedrus offers the first argument, and gives Alcestis as an example of the power of love to enable great valor in battle, including the capacity for self-sacrifice for the sake of the beloved. "He says, 'this is true of women as well as men. In speaking to Greeks I need no example to support this assertion beyond that provided by Pelias' daughter Alcestis'" (Poole 142). Similarly, in praise of a few good women in Greek mythology, the Greek historian Athenaeus makes report of Alcestis' virtues in his third century *Deipnosophistae*, where he asserts that in Chrysilla, Eubulus says:

O most worshipful Zeus! Shall I
then ever blame women? I swear,
may I die if I do, she is the best of
all our possessions. Even if Medea
was an evil woman, yet Penelope, at

least, was of great worth. Someone will say that Clytemnestra was an evil woman; I match against her the good Alcestis. (23)

The most important medieval source on Alcestis is Chaucer's *The Legends of Good Women*, which was dedicated to King Richard II's first wife, Anne of Bohemia. It was composed around 1385, late in his career, evidently in response to the offence taken by ladies at court for his unsympathetic portrayal of women in his earlier works, *Troilus and Criseyde* and *The Romance of the Rose*. *Legends* is incomplete, composed of fragments, but does include an extended Prologue of over 500 lines that features the poet's dream vision of Alcestis as the wife of the God of Love instructing him to mend his ways and tell the stories of the greatest women of antiquity who were martyred to love. In the much shorter poems that follow, the poet lauds the lives of Cleopatra, Thisbe, Dido, Hypsipyle, Medea, Lucrece, Ariadne, Phiomela, Phyllis and Hypermnestra. These *Legends*, mostly derived from Ovid, are less imaginative than the Prologue itself, which details the intervention of Alcestis to mitigate Cupid's anger. According to translator and editor Brian Stone, "The unifying device offered is the single theme of feminine steadfastness and masculine treachery as defined in Alcestis's final instructions to the poet" (Chaucer 154):

> During your lifetime you shall year
> by year
> Spend most part of your time in
> writing stories
> Extolling all the legendary glories
> Of virtuous women—virgins, honest wives—
> Who kept their faith in loving all
> their lives;
> And tell of traitors who were false
> to them
> And made of all their lives a stratagem
> To see how many women they could
> shame:

> For in your world that's counted as
> a game.
> Though love is not the thing on
> which you're bent,
> Speak well of it: that is your
> punishment. (471-480)

The God of Love then addresses the poet directly, asking him if he has recognized his benefactor as virtuous Queen Alcestis, "who took her husband's place and chose to die" (501),

> And so instead of him to go to
> hell;
> Whom Hercules brought out from
> there to dwell
> On earth again, by God, and live in
> bliss? (502-504)

The poet replies affirmatively, thanking the renowned Queen for her largess:

> Small wonder that high Jove
> Should set her as a star in heaven
> above
> For all her virtues as writes Agathon.
> (512-514)

Editor Stone's footnote on Agathon here identifies him as a poet and friend of both Plato and Euripides and suggests that he was most likely mentioned by Chaucer because of allusions to *Alcestis* in the *Symposium* (249). The Prologue concludes with the God of Love instructing the poet, upon his life, to write the legend of "this perfect wife."

Conclusion
The mythographies of Alcestis and Asclepius lead from Hesiod and Euripides to Chaucer and Shakespeare, and provide the archetypal framework for *The Winter's Tale* and *Pericles* as resurrection romances. These dramas are told with a Greek alphabet of myth, drama, romance, history, and geography, the recognition of which flies in the face of Ben Jonson's assertion about Shakespeare's "Lesse Greek" and challenges traditional assumptions about the importance of the

Greek canon as primary inspiration for our greatest Renaissance dramas. Shakespeare's *Winter's Tale* is a paean to Apollo, the poet's Muse, and *Pericles* is blessed by the presence of Diana in both dream and Temple. The Greeks of antiquity, the poets, playwrights, and politicians who supported them, those who invented the tradition of theatre and the drama, and retold the sacred myths, realizing their genius in public triumphs, inspired Shakespeare's rich, romantic vision and even populate his plays through clever device of a "Plutarchan" nomenclature.

The failure to acknowledge this over the past century of scholarship on these plays no doubt arises from the eminence of scholars who are discomfited over Shakespeare's familiarity with primary Greek sources. Most prefer to attribute Shakespeare's "Greek" to Golding's Ovid, North's Plutarch, and perhaps to rare Latin translations of Euripides' dramas.

Oxfordians, on the other hand, have reason to believe that the source of Shakespeare's "Greek" is very much closer to home, as Oxford's tutor, Sir Thomas Smith, that "noble Theseus of learning," was England's foremost Greek orator, and helped produce Greek dramas at Cambridge early in his career. Smith and William Cecil both possessed magnificent libraries with all the relevant titles we have been discussing listed in their catalogues. The greatest Greek and Latin translators of England were clustered around Oxford, Cecil and Gray's Inn: Arthur Golding (Ovid's *Metamorphoses*), Arthur Hall (Homer's *Iliad*), Alexander Neville (Seneca's *Oedipus*), George Gascoigne (*The Supposes, Jocasta*), Jasper Heywood (Seneca's *Troas, Thyestes, Hercules Furens*), John Studley (Seneca's *Agamemnon, Medea, Hyppolytus*), George Turberville (Ovid and Virgil) and Thomas Wilson (Aristotle and Cicero).

Ultimately the neglect of Shakespeare's Greek sources by contemporary editors points to the uncomfortable conclusion that the authorship question has limited scholarship by sins of omission and blanket presumptions based on the education available at the Stratford grammar school. By opening the door to the primary Greek sources and questioning the authorship of the canon, manifold possibilities for new and novel interpretations of Shakespeare's art are possible. It is time we resurrect our awareness of just how old and deeply ingrained are the mythopoetic lines of our living dramatic arts.

Note

[1] W.W. Lloyd: "*The Alcestis* of Euripides, both in treatment and incident, has many points of analogy with *The Winter's Tale*... Admetus, fated to die, is by favour of Apollo permitted to prolong his life by furnishing Death with a voluntary substitute. He urges the duty upon his aged parents, who repudiate the proposal with very marked reflections on its unreasonableness...; and when his wife, Alcestis, becomes the volunteer, he grieves at her fate..., is inconsolable in his bereavement, would fain accompany her, but wrapped up in blind selfishness, never once contrasts her conduct, which he so much admires, with his own.... No words of reproach passes the lips of Alcestis; but her parting appeal to him, to spare her children the unhappiness of a stepmother, speaks expressively.... There is no mistaking in her comparative coldness of her adieu to him, a sense of the forfeiture he has incurred of that respect without which love lives not. She dies on the stage like Hermione, and her sorrowing husband forthwith prepares her solemn funeral, rejecting his father's contribution, as he regards him as the impersonation of cowardice and selfishness. It is when he returns from the entombment, and stands before the doors of his widowed household, that his nobler heart recovers, and he passionately avows that too late he learns his wife has the nobler and the better fate; he has forfeited happiness and fame together, his dwelling must henceforth be unbearable, and elsewhere he can only expect the vituperation he utterly deserves. The Chorus comforts him, and urges the reparation of funeral honor. In the meantime, Hercules brings back Alcestis veiled, rescued by his arm from the already closed clutches of Thanatos, hateful to God and man. Hercules pretends that his companion is a prize won in games, and offering to leave her with Admetus, and even referring to renewed wedlock,

draws from him expressions soothing to the revived queen, as those that Paulina draws from the penitent Leontes. Yet, like Leontes gazing at the statue, he looks until the force of resemblance raises him to the highest pitch of agitation. At length, by gradation like that in Shakespeare's play, the form of his wife is unveiled, and he recognizes her and falls on her neck. However, she still stands speechless; the purifications due to the infernal gods must first be performed, and a three days' interval elapses before he may hear her voice; and thus in her silent presence the play concludes.

The elevated dignity and majesty thus expressed in the figure of Alcestis, the vindication of the self-devoted womanhood from the selfish neglect of a stronger power, but an inferior nature, is admirably realized, and is parallel in the reparation accorded to Hermione, who suffers with dignity as well as patience, and preserves herself not from consideration for a husband who has forfeited his nobler title, but for the sake of a daughter lost, but promised by the Oracle to be found. The silence of Alcestis is not more satisfactory and expressive than the circumstance that, in the single short speech of Hermione, her words recognize and address alone her recovered daughter. She extends her hand to Leontes, and when he embraces her in joyful astonishment, full forgiveness is sealed by her frank embrace and entire reconciliation. 'She hangs upon his neck;' but it is when the recovered Perdita kneels that her mother's voice is heard again, and then, as if in the same awe of the powers of death from whom Hermione and Perdita seem, like Alcestis, to have been recovered, the scene hastily closes and the play is at an end." (Furness 357-8)

Works Cited

Anders, H.R.D. *Shakespeare's Books: A Dissertation of Shakespeare's Reading and the Immediate Sources of His Works.* New York: AMS, 1904.

Athenaeus. *The Deipnosophists Books XIII - XIV.* Trans. Charles Burton Gulick. Cambridge: Harvard U, 1937.

Bate, Jonathan. *Shakespeare and Ovid.* Oxford: Clarendon, 1993.

—. "Dying to Live in *Much Ado about Nothing.*" *Surprised by Scenes: Essays in Honor of Professor Yasunari Takahashi.* Ed. Yasunari Takada. Tokyo: Kenkyusha, 1994. 69-85.

Bergeron, David M. "The Apollo Mission in *The Winter's Tale.*" *The Winter's Tale: Critical Essays.* Ed. Maurice Hunt. New York: Garfield, 1995. 361-79.

Chaucer, Geoffrey. *Love Visions: The Book of the Duchess* and *The Legend of Good Women.* Trans. Brian Stone. New York: Penguin, 1983.

Euripides. *Alcestis.* Trans. Richard Aldington. *The Complete Greek Drama.* New York: Random House, 1938. 677-722.

Faas, Ekbert. *Shakespeare's Poetics.* Cambridge: Cambridge UP, 1986.

—. *Tragedy and After: Euripides, Shakespeare, Goethe.* Kingston: McGill-Queen's UP, 1984.

Farnell, Lewis Richard. *Greek Hero Cults and the Ideas of Immortality.* Oxford: Clarendon, 1921.

Frey, Charles. *Shakespeare's Vast Romance: A Study of The Winter's Tale.* Columbia: U of Missouri P, 1980.

Furness, Horace Howard, ed. *The Winter's Tale — A New Variorum Edition of Shakespeare.* New York: Dover, 1964.

Gesner, Carol. *Shakespeare & The Greek Romance: A Study of Origins.* Lexington: UP of Kentucky, 1970.

Haigh, A.E. *The Tragic Drama of the Greeks.* Oxford: Clarendon, 1896.

Hoeniger, F. Davis. *Medicine and Shakespeare in the English Renaissance.* Newark: U of Delaware P, 1992.

Jones, Emrys. *The Origins of Shakespeare.* Oxford: Clarendon, 1977.

Kail, Aubrey. *Medical Mind of Shakespeare.* Sydney: Williams, 1986.

Kerényi, C. *Asklepios: Archetypal Image of the Physician's Existence.* Trans. Ralph Manheim. Bollingen Series LXV-3. Princeton: Princeton University, 1959.

Knight, G. Wilson. *The Crown of Life.* Oxford: Oxford UP, 1947.

—. *The Sovereign Flower.* London: Methuen, 1958.

Lyons, Albert S. and Joseph R. Petrucelli. *Medicine: An Illustrated History.* New York: Abrams, 1978.

Magri, Noemi. "Italian Renaissance Art in Shakespeare: Giulio Romano and *The Winter's Tale.*" *Great Oxford: Essays on the Life and Works of Edward de Vere.* Ed. Richard Malim. Tunbridge

EARL SHOWERMAN

Wells: Parapress, 2004. 50-65.

Martindale, Charles and Martindale, Michelle. *Shakespeare and the Uses of Antiquity*. London: Routledge, 1990..

Nutall, A. D. "Shakespeare and the Greeks." *Shakespeare and the Classics*. Ed. Charles Martindale and A. B. Taylor. Cambridge: Cambridge UP, 2004. 209-22.

Ovid. *Metamorphoses — The Arthur Golding Translation of 1567*, ed. John Frederick Nims, Philadelphia: Paul Dry, 2000.

—. *Heroides and Amores*. Trans. Grant Showerman. Cambridge: Harvard University Press, 1914.

Pafford, J.H.P., Ed. *The Winter's Tale — The Arden Shakespeare*. London: Methuen, 1963.

Plutarch. *The Lives of the Noble Grecians and Romans*. Trans. by John Dryden. 1924. New York: Modern Library, 1942.

Poole, Adrian. *Tragedy: Shakespeare and the Greek Example*. Oxford: Blackwell, 1987.

Race, William. *Pindar*. Boston: Twayne, 1986

Root, Robert Kilburn. *Classical Mythology on Shakespeare*. 1903. New York: Gordion, 1965.

Smith, Hallet. Ed. *The Winter's Tale*. The Riverside Shakespeare. Boston: Houghton, 1974.

Sokol, B.J. *Art and Illusion in The Winter's Tale*. Manchester: Manchester UP, 1994.

Theobold, William. *The Classical Element in the Shakespeare Plays*. London: Banks, 1909.

Versluis, Arthur. *Shakespeare the Magus*. St. Paul: Grail, 2001.

Yates, Frances A. *Majesty and Magic in Shakespeare's Last Plays*. Boulder: Shambala, 1978.

—. *Shakespeare's Last Plays: A New Approach*. London: Routledge, 1975.

From Russia with Love:

Shakespeare's *Love's Labour's Lost*
in the Context of Russian-English Relations,
1553-1603

Rima Greenhill, Ph.D.
Senior Lecturer in Russian Language, Stanford University

Although not officially one of three so-called "problem plays," *Love's Labour's Lost* (*LLL*) is probably the least understood, liked, and performed play in the Shakespeare canon. Its linguistic complexity may be the reason for this. The density of plays on words, malapropisms, turns of speech, multiple meanings, and topical allusions is unusual even for a Shakespearean play. The play has been grossly underappreciated. Bernard Shaw said he tolerated *LLL* for Shakespeare's sake rather than for its own merit while William Hazlitt admitted that if he had to part with any of Shakespeare's comedies, it would be this one (61). The present work argues that Russian-English relations, from their beginnings until Queen Elizabeth's death, hold the key to unlocking the multi-layered meanings of *LLL* and the hidden historical figures within it.

Historical Background

The history of relations between Russia and England begins in the 1550s. The year 1553 marks the beginning of a mutually profitable relationship that was at the same time both frustrating and comical.

Prior to the 1550s, very few Westerners had any knowledge of life in Russia. The few outsiders who had dealings with Russia in those early days were merchants of the Hanseatic League, members of the German diplomatic service, and Italians, mainly Venetians, in the service of the Vatican.

During the 16th century, England was not yet "ruling the waves." English merchants, spurred on by a domestic demand for spices, were eager to find their own source of this profitable commodity in the East. The first expedition to find the northwest passage to China was sponsored by a group of London Merchants in 1553. Richard Chancellor, the pilot general of the expedition, sailed on the *Edward Bonaventura*. He was a protégé of John Dee, who trained Chancellor as a navigator, and who provided maps for the journey. Two additional ships, the *Confidencia* and *Esperanza*, were commanded by Sir Hugh Willoughby. Unaccustomed to the hardships of the northern climate, the ships became separated. *Confidencia* and *Esperanza*, with Willoughby and his crew, perished when they were forced to spend their winter on the freezing Scandinavian coast. The *Bonaventura* survived by taking refuge in the White Sea and unwittingly ended up on the shores of Russia—or Muscovy, as it was then called.

Ivan IV

DISCOVERING SHAKESPEARE: A FESTSCHRIFT IN HONOUR OF ISABEL HOLDEN

At this time, the despot Ivan the Terrible ruled Russia. Richard Chancellor and the Tsar met in Moscow; Chancellor carried home a treaty granting English merchants full freedom to trade in Ivan's Russian domains without having to pay duty or taxes of any sort. Chancellor realized that although Muscovy was not China, it represented a potentially large commercial opportunity. In addition, from Russian territories, English traders would be able to enter the heart of Asia and from there, hopefully, find a route to China. Ivan too was satisfied, for, as we shall see, he had his own complex agenda. This accidental "discovery" of Russia led to the chartering of the English Muscovy Company two years later. It opened a period of bustling commercial and diplomatic relations between England and Russia that was to last for almost a century.

Stamp of the Muscovy Co.

Osip Nepea, the first Russian ambassador to England, who arrived in London in February 1556/7, must have made quite an impression at court. Attired in furs with claws and teeth, he probably helped to foster among the sophisticated English courtiers the idea of Russians as barbarians. Ivan was hoping that Ambassador Nepea would persuade Queen Mary to place an embargo on all trade with his enemy Poland. He would later request the same thing from Elizabeth. At the same time Poland was asking England to ban all trade with Russia. Mary, just as Elizabeth after her,

ignored these requests. Both queens tried to avoid being dragged into the politics of the region, their primary concern being to ensure that England obtained a monopoly of all Russia's trade with the west.

In 1557, the last year of Mary's reign, England sent the accomplished traveler, Anthony Jenkinson, to Moscow to secure the monopoly. Ivan took an immediate liking to Jenkinson and the latter was able to secure an agreement permitting the Muscovy Company to establish ports in Kazan and Astrakhan, and to trade without having to pay any customs or duties whatsoever. Subsequently, Ivan granted to the English not only the monopoly of all trade into Russia via the White Sea, but also permission to trade with Persia and China through Russia. England gained a lucrative relationship with Russia denied to other European countries.

The partnership, however, was one-sided, mainly profiting England, or so it seemed, for Elizabeth granted only minor privileges to the Russian ambassadors who began to arrive at the English court from 1557 onwards. She, like the Princess in *LLL*, was determined to secure as much as she could for the English merchants and to concede as little as she possibly could to Russia: "There's no such sport as sport by sport o'erthrown, / To make theirs ours, and ours none but our own" (5.2.153-154).

At the time, England's commercial interest in Muscovy was driven by an import-export crisis. Prices of foreign commodities had risen sharply, while demand for English products (especially woolen cloth, "the honest kersey" as Shakespeare would put it in *LLL*) fell dramatically. Although a trade agreement with Russia would not supply a source for spices, Russia did offer a wide array of cheap raw materials, such as tallow, wax and hemp. In addition, as a northern nation, Russia offered a much better market for England's wool than the southern trade in the warmer countries of the Mediterranean.

Despite the dangers of sea travel and the occasional hiccup in negotiations, the first fifteen years of Russian-English relations could be called the honeymoon years. However, problems began to surface as soon as talk of marriage, quite literally, began.

Jenkinson must have been a charismatic diplomat to have won Ivan's confidence, for Ivan gave him special messages to carry back to the Queen. These messages outlined what Ivan wanted in return for the concessions he had granted the English.

One such message was a letter proposing a closer alliance, asking that England and Muscovy might be "joyned as one." He wanted Elizabeth to be "ffrend to his ffrends and enemye to his enemies and so p. contra"(Morgan and Coote 236-8). Ivan, who was surrounded by his enemies—Swedes, Poles and Tartars—also requested navigators, boatwrights, and various military supplies. Additionally, Ivan suggested that he and Elizabeth exchange mutual pledges to provide each other refuge. By this time, Ivan must have realized that he was hated so much by his subjects that his life was in jeopardy (*Russia at the Close* 172). Jenkinson also carried a secret *verbal* message for the Queen, in which Ivan asked her to marry him.[1] Elizabeth supplied craftsmen and even ammunition, but gave no reply to the question of a political alliance, and she did not respond in any way to his proposal of marriage.

In the meantime, it came to Elizabeth's attention that rival traders had been allowed to use the Baltic port of Narva. She was also informed that Russia had imposed new restrictions on Muscovy Company merchants. A new ambassador, Thomas Randolph, was issued instructions "to confirm, maintain and strengthen the Company's position in Russia" (Willan 100).

When Randolph arrived in Russia in 1568, he was treated coldly and made to wait four months for an audience with the Tsar. Finally, Randolph made a furtive midnight visit to the Kremlin disguised as a Russian (at Ivan's request) and spent three hours with the paranoid Tsar. Ivan arranged secret meetings with other English ambassadors as well, namely Jenkinson and later Jerome Horsey,

requesting they appear in Russian attire. This practice is reflected in the masque of the Muscovites in Act 5 of *LLL* where male courtiers appear dressed as Russians to court the ladies of France.

Randolph had been instructed by the Queen to inform Ivan that he could come to England. However, as was later revealed in a letter from Ivan to Elizabeth, much to Ivan's chagrin, Randolph's "talk with vs was about Marchaunts affaires, and nothing touching ours" (Morgan and Coote 312). Ivan had expected a reply to the verbal message Jenkinson had conveyed to the Queen regarding Ivan's proposal of marriage.

Despite Ivan's frustration, he nevertheless confirmed the White Sea trade monopoly for the English. Another year passed and Ivan was still kept waiting. Elizabeth's answer never came. She had no intention of marrying him but delayed her reply to buy time.

On 28 October, 1570, angry Ivan sent Elizabeth a shockingly rude letter in which he called her "an old maid" who was unable to rule without her merchants' intervention in the country's affairs. Earlier that year, Ivan

Ivan's 1570 letter

ransacked the city of Novgorod, putting to death—by roasting over slow fires, drownings and various innovative forms of torture—virtually the entire population of this great city. In July 1570, Ivan tortured and put to death 200 of his noblemen and closest former associates, claiming they were collaborating with those accused in Novgorod. Among the victims were his loyal State Treasurer and Chancellor who were skinned alive and dismembered, respectively. Costard's words to Armado about the latter's tendency to "heavily punish" and "lightly reward" his close associates (1.2.144-146) apply, accordingly, particularly well to Ivan.

Gruesome accounts of Ivan's violent rampages and unspeakable tortures must have reached the ears of Elizabeth and her courtiers through her ambassadors and traders. In *LLL* the punishment ordered for a woman who dared to come within a mile of the new contemplative court of Navarre is "on pain of losing her tongue" (1.1.122). This kind of cruelty must have sounded abusive even to English ears used to hearing of their own country's gruesome practices of punishment of traitors and religious dissenters. To men in the know, ambassadors and visitors to Russia such as Thomas Randolph, Jerome Horsey, Jerome Bowes, Giles Fletcher[2] and later the compilers Richard Hakluyt and Samuel Purchas, it seemed quite familiar.

In response to Elizabeth's failure to accept his proposal of marriage, Ivan imposed taxes on the English merchants. Although they amounted only to half of those imposed on other countries' traders, Elizabeth thought it prudent to send another ambassador to persuade Ivan to reverse his decision. Daniel Sylvester, who served as a translator during Randolph's mission, was dispatched. In 1575, Sylvester arrived in Moscow and discovered that Ivan had abdicated in favor of the nephew of one of his ex-wives. Ivan was pretending to be a courtier while pulling the strings behind the scenes, a situation analogous to that of the Duke's unexpected withdrawal in *Measure for Measure*.

Sylvester was given an ultimatum and told that unless Ivan received a satisfactory reply from Elizabeth, all foreign trade would be given to the Germans and Venetians. Sylvester sailed back to London and returned to Russia with the Queen's reply. Elizabeth's answer will remain a mystery, because upon Sylvester's return a thunderbolt hit his house in Kholmogory, killing him and burning all his papers. Ivan apparently interpreted this as a divine warning, since the same death was once predicted for him, and he at once, as a consequence, removed all the restrictions that had been placed on the English merchants.[3]

Meanwhile in England, the explorer Martin Frobisher was eager to test the theory of Humphrey Gilbert that there existed a Northwest passage to the Orient between today's Canada and the Arctic Sea (Wooley 100). Frobisher made three disastrous Arctic voyages—particularly the last one in which Edward de Vere, 17th Earl of Oxford, the single heaviest investor in Frobisher's third voyage, incurred losses equivalent to 1% of the entire Royal Exchequer budget (Wooley 312).[4] Frobisher's investors had "gold fever," fired by the fortunes already made by others in trade with Russia.

After the failures of Frobisher's trips it became even more important to maintain good relations with Muscovy. However, a new approach was necessary. The Queen still needed to keep Ivan's interest piqued. Prolonged marriage negotiations, of the type she maintained with other suitors, were out of the question. But as Elizabeth was only four years younger than Ivan, in the early 1580's the Queen was a bit too old to play the blushing bride. What she needed was new bait.

Elizabeth had learned from her ambassadors that Ivan was more notorious for replacing wives than even her own father of infamous memory. Indeed, Ivan, at the time he was soliciting Elizabeth's hand, was living with his seventh wife, Maria Nagaya, but was still longing for a match with English royalty. Elizabeth decided to capitalize on his desire.

In 1581, Ivan requested military supplies from Elizabeth, including gunpowder, saltpeter, lead and brimstone. The Queen responded by sending thirteen ships loaded with war materials. Along with armaments, Elizabeth sent one of her private physicians, Robert Jacob. When the doctor reached Russia, he persuaded Ivan of the attractions of one of Elizabeth's ladies-in-waiting, Lady Mary Hastings. She was the daughter of the second Earl of Huntingdon and a distant relative of Elizabeth. It is very likely that the doctor was instructed by Elizabeth to present this idea to Ivan.

Elizabeth's plan worked. In the autumn of 1582, in a great rush to beat the winter weather, Ivan dispatched a new ambassador to England, Fyodor Andreyevich Pisemsky. Pisemsky's mission, in addition to asking for more armaments, was to meet Lady Mary and return to Russia with her portrait. It is this meeting that found its reflection in *LLL*.

Playing the game Ivan used to play with her ambassadors, Elizabeth did not admit Pisemsky into her presence for four months. When they finally met, she informed him that he could not see Mary until she was fully recovered from an attack of smallpox, and her face, which was "full of O's" (5.2.45), had healed enough to be painted. It is obvious that Elizabeth had no intention of giving away petrified Mary to the monster who had no qualms about "putting away" his wives. Eventually the Queen asked her new ambassador, Jerome Bowes, who accompanied Pisemsky back to Russia in 1583, to convey to Ivan that due to Mary's weak constitution she would not survive the journey, and her friends and family could not bear to part with her.

The ploy succeeded by extending this drama-cum-comedy for another year. Everyone except Ivan benefited from this international romantic interlude: Elizabeth saved face, the Muscovy Company was kept in business, Lady Mary escaped a fate worse than death, and Shakespeare wrote a comedy about it. As for Ivan, he never discovered that he had been offered a "second-hand" bride, for at one time, Lady Mary had been engaged to a very handsome, talented, and dashing young man, a longtime favorite of the Queen herself—Edward de Vere, 17th Earl of Oxford.

Elizabeth's words about keeping Mary at home provoked Ivan's anger and caused some ugly scenes witnessed by Bowes, the fifth and last English envoy Ivan was to welcome. Miraculously, Bowes managed to secure new privileges for the Muscovy Company. No doubt, this was because Bowes mentioned that Elizabeth had other female relatives who were as yet unmarried. Ivan declared he would go to England, marry one of them, and bring her back home to Russia.

These hopes were never realized because a year later, just one year after the Russian ambassador Pisemsky's return from England, Ivan was dead. As Ivan had murdered his eldest son, Ivan, in a fit of rage, his second son, the simple-minded Fyodor, ascended the throne upon his father's demise. Boris Godunov, one of Ivan's trusted councilors, became the Lord Protector and the real power behind the new Tsar. So skilled was Godunov, in fact, that in 1598 Godunov himself replaced Fyodor as Tsar, marking the end of the House of Ryurik from which had come Ivan and his issue.

The death of Ivan was followed by an anti-English reaction in Russian foreign policy and effected a reversal of roles as Elizabeth was then forced to act as suitor to the new Russian government in order to maintain England's trading monopoly with Russia. Godunov responded positively, as he saw England as a valuable trading partner but saw no reason not to conduct business with Dutch traders or with independent English traders who were not part of the Muscovy Company.

Taking a page out of Ivan's book, Elizabeth made a final attempt to bring back the glory of the former days by injecting romance and courtship into her commercial undertakings with Russia. On 11 September 1601, she composed a letter to Godunov suggesting marriage between "the prince your son and one of the daughters of our cousin the Earl of Derby, being of our blood royal."[5]

The proposed bride was the young daughter of Ferdinando Stanley, the 5th Earl of Derby (formerly Lord Strange and rival of the 17th Earl of Oxford as leading patron of the London and Court stages in the 1580s). Godunov wrote back thanking Elizabeth for her suggestion.[6]

Godunov's letter to Elizabeth

His letter was written in April 1604. By then, however, the Queen had been dead for several days.

In England, it was left to James I to resume the careful dance of the English with the Russians. He was not particularly successful. During the first half of the 17th century, the Dutch replaced English traders in prominence and assumed their former privileged positions. In 1649, in a supposed gesture of retaliation for the execution of Charles I, Tsar Alexis Romanov revoked the special privileges granted to the Muscovy Company and placed severe restrictions on its operation. English competitors were virtually eliminated from the Russian marketplace. This brought to a halt ninety-six years of very close association between the Russians and the English. English curiosity and insatiability for all things Russian, particularly during the first fifty years of contact, would never again be matched, and

the memory of their once close relationship gradually faded away.

Love's Labour's Lost (1598)

To use the words of the curate Nathaniel in *LLL*, much "ink" has been "drunk" and much "paper" has been "eat" (4.2.25) in an attempt to determine when this comedy was written, and to lament over its inexplicable passages while praising its linguistic agility and humor.

The majority of Shakespeare scholars, however, see *LLL* as either Shakespeare's earliest comedy or as an exploratory play (Carrol 65) because of its high proportion of poetry to prose. They believe the date of its publication reflects the time of its writing, sometimes conceding a possible earlier date of 1595-6. On the other hand, those who accept the author of the Shakespeare canon to be Edward de Vere have connected the play's characters, topical allusions and contemporary wordplay to his life and experiences that point to a date as early as 1578 (Clark 13).

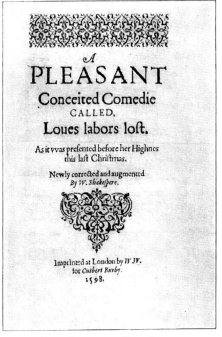

LLL is so rich in topical allusions that interpretation of who each character represents depends, in large part, on when, and by whom, one believes the play was written. The list of allusions range from John Lyly's book *Euphues, the Anatomy of Wit* (published in 1578) to the French Wars of Religion of the 1590s.

LLL has been called Shakespeare's most long-winded play (Carrol 3). My favorite criticism, however, is that uttered by Harley Granville-Barker, a playwright, actor, director, and a close friend of Bernard Shaw:

> Here is a fashionable play; now by three hundred years, out of fashion. Nor did it ever, one supposes, make a very wide appeal. It abounds in jokes for the elect. Were you not numbered among them you laughed, for safety, in the likeliest places. A year or two later the elect themselves might be hard put to it to remember what the joke was. (30)

In other words, it is a play for a specific and select audience and is very time-sensitive.

The record of the performances of *LLL* in the sixteenth and early seventeenth century is itself a testimony to the play's contemporary appeal for Queen Elizabeth, her ministers, and her envoys to Russia, as *LLL* was performed at the most critical points in the history of Russian-English relations. The scope of this paper does not allow for deliberations on the timing of the play's revisions, but an analysis of the play points to the fact that they mirror the fluctuation of friendship and animosity within the Russian-English entendre. It is significant, for example, that *LLL* was considered "an olde one" (Chambers 332), when it was shown to the new Queen in 1604. It is also relevant that during periods of no contact between the two countries, there are no recorded performances of *LLL*. Thus, from 1642 to 1830, following the break in relations between Russia and England commencing with the overthrow of the monarchy and the establishment of the Puritan Protectorate,

there is no record of any performance of this play in England.

Hidden allusions.

Examples of how the play's characters' words and actions reflect the context of Russian-English relations not only add to an understanding of the play but also reveal hidden references and allusions that have hitherto been either unexplained or passed over by other scholars.

The English Court was introduced to the Russians and to Russian life through the Russian envoys. In Act 3, Scene I, before asking Costard to carry his letter to Rosaline, Berowne makes a series of puns on the word "envoy." The word can have several meanings: first, it can mean an agent sent with messages; second, it can denote the concluding stanza of a poem, the lines that send the poem out into the world; and third, it can refer to the final bit of business or the epilogue to a play—meanings that Shakespeare found relevant to his comic subtext. Here is one particular pun on the word "envoy" used by Costard to illustrate how Shakespeare incorporated Russian sources into the play:

> Costard.... Let me see: a fat l'envoy—
> ay, that's a fat goose.
> Armado. Come hither, come hither.
> How did this argument be-
> gin?
> Moth. By saying that a costard was
> broken in a shin. Then called
> you for the l'envoy.
> Costard: True, and for a plaintain;
> thus came your argument in;
> Then the boy's fat l'envoy, the goose
> that you bought,
> And he ended the market.
> (3.1.105-111)

Noting that a *costard* was a kind of apple and was also used as slang for *head* (OED) and that *plantain* is a herb widely used as a blood coagulant, we can translate this heretofore incomprehensible exchange as a reference to a certain incident wherein Ivan devised a novel form of punishment for one of his secretaries who was discovered stealing money and hiding it inside a cooked *goose*. At a *market* place, Ivan commanded his henchmen to cut up a "goose." But the goose he commanded them to cut up was the embezzling secretary; Ivan ordered that the offending secretary's legs first be lopped off about the midst of the shin; his arms were then to be severed above his elbows; the "dressing" of the goose was then to be finished by chopping off the secretary's head—that he might thereby receive the right fashion of mimicking in his death a goose ready dressed (*Russia at the Close* 55). In this context, prescribing plantain, a conventional ointment for bruises and scrapes, would be like prescribing a bandaid for a bullet in the heart. According to the OED, another meaning of envoy at that time was—appropriately enough for such a circumstance—a "catastrophe, denouement." Not too surprisingly, this startling story, in all its elements, must have made a strong impression on Shakespeare, for he alludes to it several times in the play.[7]

Jerome Horsey

No one probably did as much traveling in the Elizabethan Age as Jerome Horsey (d. 1626), who kept going back and forth between Russia and England. Horsey was the man who took the place of Anthony Jenkinson and earned the love and trust of both the Russian and English monarchs.

There are several embedded references to Horsey in *LLL*. For example, in Act 3 (3.1.48-49) Don Armado employs Costard to carry a letter on his behalf to Jaquenetta. Moth, in his usual ironic manner, replies to Armado's request with the following words: "A message well sympathiz'd—a horse to be embassador for an ass" (3.1.51-2). The word "horse" clearly alludes to Horsey and the word "ass" possibly is an uncomplimentary reference to Ivan. Ivan, after all, certainly had made an ass of himself in the eyes of the English court more than once.

The second reference to Horsey is in the sonnet-reading scene. It is very cleverly disguised:

Berowne: When shall you see me write a thing in rhyme?
Or groan for Joan? Or spend a minute's time
In pruning me? When shall you hear that I
Will praise a hand, a foot, a face, an eye,
A gait, a state, a brow, a breast, a waist,
A leg, a limb—
King: Soft! Whither away so fast?
A true man or a thief, that gallops so?
Berowne: I post from love. Good lover, let me go.
(4.3.178-185)

This passage becomes clearer when we recollect a particular historical event, for I believe it refers to Ivan's request for an English bride in 1581. Having had no satisfactory response from Elizabeth with regard to his proposal that she marry him, Ivan decided to find another candidate. And of course, he needed supplies for his military campaigns as well. At the time, Jerome Horsey was an agent of the Muscovy Company. As mentioned earlier, Ivan had asked him to deliver secret messages to the Queen (*Russia at the Close* 189).[8] In order to gain time, Ivan decided to send Horsey over land rather than have him travel by sea. Horsey was given two messages (one about the munitions and one about a bride) in a wooden vodka flask, which, in Horsey's words, was "not worth three pence" (*Russia at the Close* 189).

Horsey rode across Europe on horseback with "400 Hungers ducketts in gold sewn in" his boots and his worst garments, and with the vodka flask attached to the horse's mane (*Russia at the Close* 189). While riding through Lithuania, he was captured twice and kept "as a spie" (*Russia at the Close* 190), but managed to get out of the tricky situations by claiming he was trying to escape from Russia as fast as he could (*Russia at the Close* 191).[9] Taking a ship from Germany, upon his arrival in London he did his best to air out Ivan's "spirited" messages, but when they were handed over to her Majesty, the Queen noticed they still smelled of vodka, or "aqua-vita," as Horsey put it. It was this message that set the Lady Mary negotiations into motion.[10]

The cadence that can be heard in Berowne's words—"a hand, a foot, a face, an eye, / A gait, a state, a brow, a breast, a waist, / A leg, a limb" is (listen to yourself as you read it quickly aloud!) the sound of horses' hooves galloping at top speed. The King's words, "Whither away so fast?" suggest, therefore, that the speed of Berowne's words should increase, for he lists the above-mentioned body parts in order to mimic the sound of a horse's gallop, recalling Ivan's insistence that Horsey impart his message to the Queen by traveling quickly, overland and by horseback, rather than by ship.

In *LLL*, trade, diplomacy, and romance go hand in hand, just as they did in real life. The Russian ambassador Fyodor Andreyevich Pisemsky was instructed to press Ivan's suit with Elizabeth for the hand of Lady Mary Hastings.[11] He arrived in London in September 1582, but was not allowed to see the Queen and it was months before he met with her. In the meantime, he was entertained by royal hunting parties. This is reflected in *LLL*'s Act 4 where there is a hunting scene—and clearly a staged one. The forester instructs the princess where she should stand in order to get the best shot. The princess has an exchange with the forester[12] and concludes with a phrase which has baffled scholars: "A giving hand, though foul, shall have fair praise" (4.1.22-23). I believe this suggests a reference to Elizabeth having to thank Ivan profusely for the presents he had sent to her with Pisemsky—gifts such as sables, gold cloth, and many other items of luxury. Although she knew Ivan was "foul," Elizabeth had to thank him and reciprocate.

Ambassador Pisemsky was finally presented to Lady Mary on 18 May 1583, in the garden of York House. Lady Mary was accompanied by a large group of courtiers

and young ladies, and she sat under a canopy not unlike the tent the King provided for the Princess and her ladies in *LLL*. There is only one account of the events of that day, and we find it in Horsey. According to him:

> Her majesty caused that lady to be attended one, with divers great ladies and maieds of honnor and yonge noblemen, the number of each apointed, to be seen by the said ambassodor in Yorcke Howse garden. She put one a staetly countenance accordinglie. The ambassodor, atended with divers other noblemen and others, was brought before her Ladyship; cast down his countenance; fell prostrate to her feett, rise, ranne backe from her, his face still towards her, she and the rest admiringe at his manner. Said by an interpritor yt did suffice him to behold the angell he hoped should be his masters espouse; comended her angellicall countenance, state and admirable bewty. She after was called by her famillier frends in court the Emporis of Muscovia. (*Russia at the Close* 196)

Let us now examine four quotations from *LLL* that mirror the meeting at York House. Act 5 opens with the words of Holofernes: "*Satis quod sufficit*" (5.1.1); so says he to Sir Nathaniel, without any indication as to what this comment refers. However, in looking at the above citation from Bond's edition of *Russia at the Close of the Sixteenth Century*, we see that this is virtually word for word what, rendered via the interpreter, the Russian envoy said upon having seen Mary: "... *yt did suffice him* to behold the angel he hoped should be his master's espouse" (emphasis added). This implied the proverbial "enough is as good as a feast" in both Russian and Latin. In the next scene, the King warns Moth:

> ... 'an *angel* shalt thou see;
> Yet fear not thou, but speak auda-
> ciously'.

The boy replied, 'An *angel* is not
evil;
I should have feared her had she
been a devil.' (5.2.105-106;
emphasis added)

The first two lines are also a reference to
Pisemsky's comparison of Mary with an
angel.

But why should Moth be frightened?
Here is one more quote from Horsey's account
of Pisemky and Mary's meeting:
The ambassador (...) was brought
before her Ladyship; *cast down his
countenance; fell prostrate to her feett*,
rise, ranne backe from her, his face still
towards her, she and the rest admiringe
at his manner. (emphasis added)

Pisemsky fell down and hit his forehead on the
ground before Mary Hastings. This Russian
custom was performed by a sovereign's loyal
subjects and indicated their subjection and
obedience, as can be seen in the illustration
of Palm Sunday in Moscow.

Palm Sunday in Moscow

Pisemsky's antics must have made him
look like a man possessed by the devil. He did
not just fall down and bang his head on the
floor, but he repeated the ceremony twice, getting up and running back while facing Mary
(custom dictated that he shouldn't run with
his back to the monarch) and then collapsing

on the floor again. In *LLL*, Boyet reports that
the men's preparation for their roles as Russians involved some sort of fall: "The fourth
turned on the toe, and down he fell. / With
that they all did tumble on the ground ... "
(5.2.114-5).

Hidden Characters
Maria

When considering who the characters of
the play represent, it is tempting to suggest
that Maria, the French lady who is the Princess's maid of honor, represents a very English
Lady Mary Hastings. Longaville addresses
her in Act 4 as "O sweet Maria! Empress of
my love" (4.3.53); this certainly evokes the
words of the Russian ambassador "Emporis
of Moscovia" when referring to Lady Mary
Hastings.[13]

Don Adriano de Armado

We are introduced to Don Armado in Act
1 as "a knight from Tawny Spain" (1.1.171-
2). There are many foreigners in the play, yet
Armado seems the most foreign of them all.
Critics have argued that he
represents everyone from
Antonio Perez, secretary of
Philip II, to Edward de Vere
himself, but I would like
to argue that Don Armado
was, at least originally, a
Russian.

1. He is not only a
braggart, but a liar as
well. The king says, "I
love to hear him lie."
(1.1.173).

Virtually every account of
a 16th-century traveler to
Russia mentions untrustworthiness as one of
the defining character traits of the Russians.
At the English Court, Ivan's envoy Pisemsky
was caught lying several times. For example,
he had to lie about the birth of Ivan's son,
Dmitrij (born 19 October 1582) to Ivan's 7th
wife because, at the time, he was in London

negotiating a marriage to Mary Hastings. Pisemsky, in denying the birth of Dmitrij, said it was just a rumor spread by the enemies of Russia, although at the time of his departure to England in September he must have known that Ivan's wife was eight months pregnant.

2. The fact that Armado is not a Spaniard becomes apparent when we consider his religion. He is clearly neither Catholic, nor Protestant. He is a heathen. Note Moth's sarcastic aside in the following exchange:

Armado: I hate to be crossed.
Moth: He speaks the mere contrary: crosses love not him.

(1.2.33-34)

Another allusion to Armado not being a Christian is found in Act 5:

Princess: Doth this man serve God?
Ber: Why ask you?
Princess: 'A speaks not like a man of God his making.

(5.2.522-524)

The English thought that tyranny in Russia was caused in part by heretical religious practices, a topic to which Giles Fletcher dedicated many pages in his *Of the Russe Commonwealth*, published in 1591 (and found in Bond's edition of *Russia at the Close of the Sixteenth Century* (London: Hakluyt Society, 1856).

However, Armado is not just any Russian. Before us, in *LLL*, is a representation of the Russian Monarcho, alias Ivan the Terrible (had he come, as Shakespeare imagines it) to the English court. As noted earlier, Ivan's frantic search for personal security had induced him to request an agreement for mutual asylum with Elizabeth. The Queen ignored this request for as long as she could. Finally, however, she had to yield and offer sanctuary to Ivan, without reserving the right for herself, so as to maintain the status quo vis-à-vis the English commercial interest in

Russia. The Queen must have feared that Ivan might act on her promise of asylum and show up one day in England. The writer who called himself Shakespeare knew of Ivan's mercurial temperament, and of Ivan's reputation as a womanizer and braggart who saw himself as "a soldier, a man of travel, [one] that has seen the world" (5.1.100).

Armado thinks himself a great and worldly warrior, but in fact he is an object of mockery for everyone, just as was Ivan, no doubt, at Elizabeth's court. Armado tries to win women, as did Othello, with the tales of his heroic exploits on the military field. Armado, for example, says to Jaquenetta: "I will tell thee wonders" (1.2.133). "With that face?" responds she. Such a response might not seem surprising; according to eye-witnesses, Ivan had a face of an "angry warrior" and used to foam at the mouth like a horse when he spoke (Madariaga 353).

Here are additional textual examples that reveal Ivan hiding behind the Spanish bravado of Don Armado. Let us consider Don Armado's character:

3. He is besieged by "sable-coloured melancholy" (1.1.226), sable furs being the most popular gifts Ivan sent to Elizabeth, as well as the luxury item of Russian export to England.

4. He is as paranoid as Ivan. He is suspicious of others and is the one who sniffs out Costard's misdemeanor which he calls "treason," the "villainy abroad" (1.1.185-6) in the "north-north-east" from the king's curious-knotted garden (1.1.238-9).

Russia lies north-north-east in relation to the curiously knotted garden of Elizabeth's Richmond Palace. (The Elizabethans were just awakening to geographical directions through the collections and publications of explorers' maps.) Furthermore, Ivan's two other strongholds, Vologda and Aleksandrovsk, the latter being the head-quarters of the infamous *oprichnina* where Ivan used to inflict unbear-

123

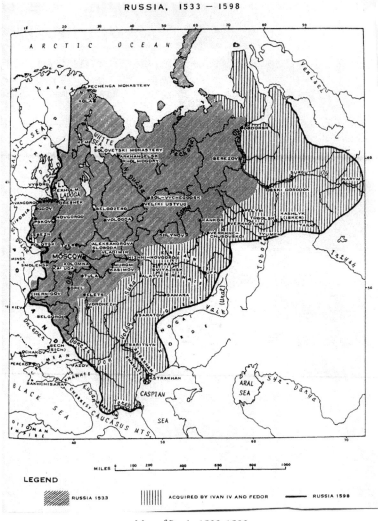

RUSSIA, 1533 — 1598

LEGEND

RUSSIA 1533   ACQUIRED BY IVAN IV AND FEDOR   RUSSIA 1598

Map of Russia 1533-1598

able punishments on all those he suspected of treason, lay north-east of Moscow.

Armado tells the King that he wants to "commend" his "black oppressing humour to the most wholesome physique" of the king's "health-giving air." I believe there is a hint here of Ivan's desire to reach England and of his hope that it will be a source of his regeneration from the oppressive air of his own country. Perhaps Ivan could be jokingly called the first Russian dissident.

    5. Armado is in love with Jaquenetta, "a base wench."

Ivan's seventh wife was Mariya Nagaya, a woman of Tartar origin and a daughter of one of Ivan's courtiers. Tartars, however, even if they were of noble birth, were seen as inferior to Russians. Note that in his letter to Jaquenetta Armado speaks of himself as a king and of Jaquenetta as a beggar (4.1.65-84). Furthermore, Ivan was notorious for marrying women who were below him in social standing. His third wife was a daughter of a Novgorod merchant; his fourth one was "a beautiful girl of humble origin" (Grey 70); his fifth one, like his last one, was a daughter of a Tartar lord.

6. Jaquenetta is the only other character with a Spanish name in the play, implying that she is from the same geographic location as Armado, i.e., from Russia.

7. Armado is always chasing women. Compare Costard's comment in reference to him: he is dressed in a philosophical observation of human nature: "It is the simplicity of men to hearken after the flesh" (1.1.213-4). Armado begets a child with Jaquenetta and at the same time is flirting with the Princess:

> "I do adore thy sweet grace's slipper" (5.2.622).

It was reported by a number of eyewitnesses that Ivan organized "bride parades" and used to take with him on his many travels and military campaigns fifty women to satisfy his libido. Ivan himself admitted to Jerome Horsey that he was a ravisher of virgins (*Russia at the Close* 199).[14]

8. Armado is concerned with envoys and salve. "Doth the inconsiderate take salve for l'envoy, and the word l'envoy for a salve?" (3.1.79).

Ivan suffered from pain in one of his legs and from the degeneration of his joints (supposedly caused by rheumatoid arthritis). To gain relief, he took long baths and used various ointments that contained mercury.

9. Armado says: "Devise, wit; write, pen, for I am for whole volumes in folio." (1.2.176-7)

Armado's letters are long-winded and cumbersome, just as were Ivan's letters to Elizabeth. Like Ivan, Armado is verbose and speaks with "high-born words" (1.1.171). Talking about Ivan's will, the historian Isabel de Madariaga says that "like nearly all of Ivan's writings, it is extremely verbose, quoting extensively from the Old and New Testaments" (353). Armado,

too, loves to identify with historical and biblical figures who have been in love:

> Armado: Comfort me, boy. What great men have been in love?
> Moth: Hercules, master.
> Armado: Most sweet Hercules! More authority, dear boy, name more. And, sweet my child, let them be men of good repute and carriage.
> Moth: Samson, master (…)
> Armado: O well-knit Samson, strong-jointed Samson! (…) I am in love too. (1.2.63-73)

10. Armado is secretive, like Ivan; Ivan used to convey the most important matters (such as requests for munitions and brides) in his verbal messages to the Queen: "… but, sweet heart, I do implore secrecy" (5.1.102).

11. The physical appearance of Armado is provided by Holofernes: "His humour is lofty, his discourse peremptory, his tongue filed, his eye ambitious, his gait majestical and his general behaviour vain, ridiculous and thrasonical." (5.1.9).

Holoferne's description of Armado echoes the foreign ambassadors' accounts of Ivan's physical appearance and behavior (Madariaga 353). In the 1960s, during the repairs to the cathedral where Ivan was buried, his body was exhumed and M. M. Gerasimov, the Soviet expert on facial reconstruction, was asked to create a bust of Ivan which, according to Ivan's biographer, "does suggest the real man, with the eagle nose of the Paleologues, the high brow, sensual mouth and dominating countenance which one would expect. His eyes have been described both as small, and as large; they were light-coloured, bright, and flickered rapidly from place to place." (Madariaga 353). As such, it appears to be the description of the same man Holofernes is describing.

Ivan by Gerasimov

Costard

In *LLL*, Armado is seen in exchanges with the clown, Costard. Costard seems very fond of Moth and says he would buy him some gingerbread (a favorite Russian snack) if he had some money. Costard is Armado's constant rival for Jaquenetta's affection. When Costard is delivered to Armado as his prisoner, Armado promises to punish him. Costard replies, "I am more bound to you than your fellows, for they are but lightly rewarded" (1.2.145-6). And we know how Ivan "rewarded" his close associates. The double meaning of "I am more bound to you," indicates their familial relationship. Here is a hint that Costard represents Ivan's eldest son whom Ivan killed in a fit of rage in 1581. When Costard is taken away, he says, "It is not for prisoners to be too silent in their words and therefore I will say nothing" (1.2.152-157). What does this sentence signify? Ivan used to bring along his son to observe the suffering of prisoners. For example, he took his son, Ivan, then aged 16, to watch the massacre of the inhabitants of Novgorod in 1570. If we acknowledge that Costard is Ivan's son, then Ivan "Junior" knew all too well how "not silent" his father's prisoners were. Ivan was known to enjoy listening to his victims' moans and screams during the agony of torture. Also, the father and son were reported by several foreign visitors as having shared the same women, the scenario re-enacted by Costard, Armado and Jaquenetta in *LLL*.

Honorificabilitudinitatibus and other words.

The longest word in *LLL* is "honorificabilitudinitatibus" (5.1.142), which can be translated as "the state of being loaded with honours." This is pronounced by Costard in reference to Armado. Why is it relevant if Armado represents Ivan? Although Ivan called himself Tsar and Autocrat of the whole of Russia, in the courts of European countries he was considered to be "on a par with the Italian princes, below the Electors of the Empire but above the dependent dukes and republics" (Bobrick 144). In order to inflate his importance, he was excessively preoccupied with the minutiae of his titles. This was recorded by many foreign visitors to his court in the sixteenth century, such as Antonio Possevino as well as Giles Fletcher, who were often infuriated by it.[15] Other kings did likewise, of course, but no one outdid Ivan. Elizabeth, for example, rather succinctly used to address herself as "the Queen of England, France, Ireland, and others." In contrast, here is how Ivan began his letters to Elizabeth:

> We, the great emperor and the Great Duke of the whole of Russia, of Vladimir, Moscow, Novgorod; tsar of Kazan, tsar of Astrakhan; sovereign of Pskov and Great Duke of Smolensk, Tver, Yugorsk, Perm, Vyatka, Bulgaria and others; sovereign and Great Duke of Lower Novgorod, Chernigov, Ryazan, Polotsk, Rostov, Yaraslave, Belozero, Liflandia, Vdorsk, Obdorsk, Kondinsk, ruler of all the Siberian lands and Northern countries and others.

In *LLL*, Ivan's insistent demand for the enumeration of the imposing array of his titles is parodied by Berowne who adopts the following titles for Cupid:

> This Signor Junior, giant dwarf,
>   Dan Cupid,
> Regent of love-rhymes, lord of
>   folded arms,
> Th'annointed sovereign of signs
>   and groans,
> Liege of all loiterers and malcontents,
> Dread prince of plackets, king of
>   codpieces,
> Sole imperator and great general
> Of trotting paritors . . .
>
> (3.1.175-182)

Berowne makes Cupid a military commander, just like Ivan, and more. In this passage, he ironically identifies Cupid with Ivan, which is a reference to Ivan's love exploits. Cupid's army is just like Ivan's. Horsey described Ivan's army as consisting of the dregs of humanity. The words "dread prince" are exactly how the words 'Ivan the Terrible' translate into Russian. "Grosnyj," Ivan's epithet, means "dread" in Russian (that is, dreaded by his enemies), the title Ivan received after his conquest of the Kazan Khanate in 1552.

As if this weren't enough, Shakespeare teases us with more clues. Cupid is the "sole imperator." Not only does the word, of course, mean "emperor," but the word "imperator" is the word for "emperor" in Russian! One may argue that the term *emperor*, which takes its origin from Latin, was not interchangeable with the term *Tsar* until the reign of Peter the Great, but it must be borne in mind that the English Court and English ambassadors to Russia always referred to Ivan in their correspondence to the Queen as "the Emperor."

The word *emperor* is not the only Russian word to make an appearance in *LLL*. Costard greets everyone with "God dig-you-den-all!" (4.1.45). As commentators have observed, the use of this greeting has but a single occurrence in Shakespeare. It is possible that this greeting could be a corruption of a colloquial expression, "God give you good evening," in which the word "den" is an adumbration of the greeting "Good even," contracted to "gooden" (Richardson)? However, the word "den" also means "day" in Russian. If there were one word the English Court would be familiar with, it would be this one, since it would be heard time and time again from the lips of visiting Russian ambassadors who would greet everyone with the daily greeting of "Dobryj den!"—literally "Good day," although, notably, what it actually means, to the Russian, is "Good afternoon." Shakespeare is exhibiting his linguistic sophistication here. What he is doing here is playing and punning on two words, one Russian and one English, which are homonymic doubles when standing on their own but, when used as part of a greeting, taking on a subtle differentiation in meaning in each respective language. The point is that we know that Costard delivers Berowne's letter in the afternoon, while it is still light and while the Princess and her ladies are getting ready for the impending hunt. The fact that the delivery of letter had to take place in the afternoon was conveyed quite explicitly by Berowne:

> Costard: When would you have it
>   done, sir?
> Berowne: This afternoon. (3.1.150-
>   151)

The fact that it must be done in the afternoon and not later is stressed a *second* time:

> Costard: I will come to your worship
>   tomorrow morning.
> Berowne: It must be done this after-
>   noon. (3.1.156-157)

The solitary occurrence of the greeting "God dig-you-den-all" in Shakespeare shows that Shakespeare knew what he was doing with it. As explained above, I believe, therefore, that Costard is conceived as a Russian and modeled on Ivan the Terrible's son who, had Ivan "Senior" carried out his threat of coming to England together with his sons, would have also been present at Court. It is therefore most appropriate that it is should be he who delivers this pun which, until now, has been lost on modern audiences and commentators but was, no doubt, appreciated and relished by those knowingly watching the early performances of *LLL* at Court.

Costard is not the only character in the play who weaves Russian words into his conversation. Shakespeare hides them even in Holofernes' speech and passes them off as bad Latin or fake Italian, as in his comment on Venice (in the 1598 Quarto): "Venetia, Venetia, Chi non ti vede, non ti pereche." Although the publishers of the 1598 Quarto were known for their lack of errors, the word *pereche* was assumed by later editors either to be Shakespeare's own mistake or a printer's misprint. It was changed to *pretia* in later editions. Let us look at this word more closely.

The Russian verb *perechit'* means "to contradict, to oppose someone in speech." To our ears, however, the Slavic word pereche (the aorist form[16] of the infinitive *perechit*) sounds just like an Italian word. So, in English, this would be "Venice, Venice, who does not see you, does not oppose you," a takeoff on a common saying: "Venice, Venice, who does not see you, does not love you," as we are informed in the line that follows. This jest may refer to English competition with Venice for foreign trade.

Another so-called misprint is very revealing. According to Holofernes, Armado is a "racker of orthographie" because he pronounces the word "debt" as "det," "half" as "haf," etc. This is abominable to Holofernes who wants everything said as it is written:

... I abhor such fanatical phantasimes, such insociable and point-device companions, such rackers of orthography, as to speak 'doubt' *sine* 'b', when he should say 'doubt', 'det' when he should pronounce 'debt': d, e, b, t, not d, e, t. He clepeth a calf 'cauf', half 'hauf'; neighbour *vocatur* 'nebour', neigh abbreviated 'ne'. This is abhominable,

which he would call 'abominable'. (5.1.17-24)

This statement alone contains *five* hidden allusions to Ivan. Ivan owed the Muscovy Company for English merchandise he had received. The *debt* remained unpaid after Ivan's death (Willan 133). After Anthony Jenkinson left Russia in 1571, having secured trading privileges for England which included an exemption from taxes, Ivan reversed his decision. He demanded that the English pay taxes, but only *half* of what other countries were required to pay. This is the "half" referred to in the passage. Then we hear that he abbreviates "neigh" to "ne"—which, in Russian, as in some other languages, stands for "no" or "not."

As for the word "orthographie," in both the 1598 Quarto and Folio, it was spelled "ortogriphie." The original spelling confirms this word's Russian pronunciation. Russians cannot sound the consonant combination "th" and, consequently, speak it as a "t" or "s." This word, with the "th" preceded by the letter "r," would have been pronounced by Ivan or his Russian contemporaries as "ortogriphie."

As far as being a "racker" is concerned, Ivan, according to numerous reports, tortured not only orthography. With the inclusion of the word "abominable," Shakespeare is signaling here that he knew all about Ivan's crimes.

Shakespeare's inclusion of Russian words and expressions suggest that Shakespeare either was personally interested in the Russian language or he was intimately associated with those who were. Horsey, for example, thought Russian to be "the most copious and elegant language in the world" (*Russia at the Close* 156), and Queen Elizabeth said that she considered Russian to be a beautiful language and thought herself capable of learning it quickly. In fact, she passed this job on to the Earl of Essex (*Russia at the Close* 233).

Shakespeare was clearly fascinated by the Russians. No doubt, he found Ivan's enigmatic personality compelling. It is not a coincidence that Armado/Ivan is a comic double of Berowne/Shakespeare. Shakespeare's attitude toward Ivan is reflected in his treatment of Armado, whom he sometimes mocks and sometimes sees as a man in whom good and bad are in conflict.[17] It would not be an exaggeration to call Shakespeare the first biographer of Ivan, and this becomes apparent in the pageant of the Nine Worthies at the end of Act 5 of *LLL*.

The Pageant of the Nine Worthies — Pompey and Hector

The pageant at the end of Act 5 offers further support for the portrayal of real historical persons in this play. The roles of the Worthies themselves were not assigned indiscriminately. Their parts in the pageant are consistent with the character traits they exhibit throughout *LLL*. This becomes evident upon examining two of the play's leading characters, Costard and Armado, in their assigned roles in the pageant.

Costard, because of his "great limb or joint" (5.1.120) has been given the role of Pompey the Great. As mentioned earlier, Costard represents Ivan "Junior," the son that Ivan murdered in a fit of rage by hitting him over the head with his staff, a fact which found its way into Fletcher's account (*Russia at the Close* 195).

Costard steps out onto the stage and immediately muddles his lines by announcing that he is "Pompey surnamed the Big." Dumaine corrects him, saying that he is Pompey "the Great" and not "the Big." Costard's error, though, is a giveaway that his native language is Russian. The Russian word "great" is translated as "velikij" which also has the meaning of "big." Shakespeare yet again, in this section of the play, displays his linguistic sophistication, for not only is Costard a Russian making a mistake in English but, a few lines later, there comes a subtle hint that he is Ivan's son:

> Princess: Great thanks, great
> Pompey.
> Costard: 'tis not so much worth, but I
> hope I was perfect. I made a little

fault in "Great." (5.2.582-84)

The Russian princes were called "Velikij knyaz"—meaning the "Great Duke"—only if they owned several lands in their name (Herberstein 38).[18] On his majority, Ivan "Junior" asked his father for his own territorial title and lands but was refused due to Ivan's fear even of his own son (Skrynnikov 495).[19] Thus, Ivan was called the "Great Duke of Russia," but his older son remained just the "duke" and never obtained the title of "Great Duke."

As for Armado, in the pageant he portrays "Hector in arms" (5.2.628). As soon as he enters onto the stage, the men start picking on him, trying to prove that he is not Hector:

> Boyet: But is this Hector?
> King: I think Hector was not so
> clean-timbered.
> Longaville: His leg is too big for
> Hector's.
> Dumaine: More calf, certain.
> Boyet: No, he is best endued in the
> small. (5.2.663-67)

Here are two references, one to Ivan's height and build (he was very tall and strong (Madariaga 353), and the second, to his leg, which was swollen, possibly from syphilis.

Also noted is the reference to Hector fighting from his pavilion from "morn till night." Following Jenkinson's journey to Central Asia, a map of Russia, which included all recently conquered territories, was made for Ivan. In the top left corner, Jenkinson depicted Ivan sitting in his tent and wrote Ivan's name below the "pavilion."

Then another custom-made insult is levied at Armado in the second scene of Act V (ll. 653-66) :

> Armado: Sweet Lord Longaville,
> rein thy tongue.
> Longaville: I must rather give it
> the rein, for it runs against
> Hector.
> Dumaine: Ay, and Hector's a grey
> hound.

Jenkinson's 1562 map

Hector, as all know, was a famous runner. The word "greyhound," however, also implies a coward, which is an insult aimed at Ivan's cowardly retreat from Moscow during the advance of the Tartars, as well as his habit of avoiding the front lines of action in battles. (Morozova 127). That Armado understands this as an insult becomes obvious when he suddenly turns serious and defends the honor of Hector—meaning Ivan. He attacks the men who mock him:

> Armado: The sweet war-man is dead
> and rotten. Sweet chucks beat
> not the bones of the buried.
> When he breathed, he was a
> man. But I will forward with
> my device. (5.2.657-660)

Armado then makes a pass at the princess at 5.2.663, although he was chasing Jaquenetta:

> Armado: I do adore thy sweet grace's
> slipper.[20]

To this, Boyet interjects:

> Boyet: Loves her by the foot.
> (5.2.664)

Dumaine rejoins:

> Dumaine: He may not by the yard.
> (5.2.665)

This is a double pun: punning on the yard as a unit of measure for cloth, the main item of English export to Russia, as well as a sexual pun on "yard" as the old English colloquial synonym for the male sexual organ. Shakespeare is implying that Ivan never got "close enough" to Elizabeth during his marriage proposals.

At this point, Costard arrives; he announces that Jaquenetta is two months "on her way" (5.2.669) and reveals that the baby is Armado's. Armado lashes out at him:

> Armado: Dost thou infamonize me
> among potentates? Thou shalt die!
> (5.2.675)

130

And Costard launches an offensive in reply:

> Costard: Then shall Hector be
> whipped for Jaquenetta that is
> quick by him and hanged for
> Pompey that is dead by him.
> (5.2.678)

These words have a profound impact on Armado/Ivan. Reminded that he killed his son, "Hector trembles" (5.2.679).

Next, Costard / Ivan "Junior" gets into a conflict with Armado / Ivan. The men urge them on, invoking Ates, the goddess of bloodshed and strife:

> Berowne: Pompey is moved. More
> Ates, more Ates! Stir them on,
> stir them on! (5.2.685)

Armado challenges Costard:

> Armado: By the North pole, I do
> challenge thee. (5.2.689)

There is a double reference here. First, as a Russian, Ivan is a "northern" man but, secondly, this also alludes to the fact that he killed his son with his staff, or "pole."

Costard / Ivan "Junior," who was much favored by the English (Madariaga 342)[21] and known to want to command his father's army, puns on the word "pole" but chooses a more Western approach to warfare:

> Costard: I will not fight with a
> pole, like a northern man. I'll
> slash, I'll do it by the sword.
> (5.2.691)

Costard starts undressing, getting ready to fight. Moth offers his assistance to Armado:

> Moth: Master, let me take you a
> buttonhole lower. Do you not
> see, Pompey is uncasing for
> the combat. What mean you?
> You will lose your reputation.
> (5.2.698)

This is another hint at Ivan's cowardice. In addition, Armado / Hector refuses to fight in his shirt. When questioned about this, he admits, at 5.2.706, that he has no shirt.

> Armado: The naked truth of it is,
> I have no shirt. I go woolward
> for penance.

Armado/Hector is wearing his woolen outer garments next to his skin as an act of penance. After the death of his son, Ivan was said to have torn his clothes and his beard and to have worn rags for penance (*Russia at the Close* 195).[22] He gave large amounts of money to monasteries to pray for his son's soul. He spent days praying and composing a canon to the Angel of Death. It is not surprising, therefore, that what follows in Shakespeare is the arrival of Mercadé, the Angel of Death, bringing news of the princess's father's death. But his arrival also brings a release from suffering for Armado and gives him the peace of mind for which he has longed.[23]

> Armado: For mine own part, I
> breathe free breath. I have seen
> the day of wrong through the
> little hole of discretion and will
> right myself like a soldier.
> (5.2.719)

The word "right" is a homonymic pun on the word "write," hinting at Ivan's preoccupation with the search for redemption and the attainment of "righteousness" after his son's death.

Ivan "Senior" and Ivan "Junior" are hidden behind the characters of the Worthies representing, respectively, Pompey the Great and Hector. The identities of the three other Worthies are addressed in a separate paper of mine.

Shakespeare's sources and the Authorship question

I suggest that several scenes described in *LLL*, the play's characters and the characters' language, point to events during the year 1581 to the mid-1580's, while the pageant of the Nine Worthies focuses on the years after 1584. Let us consider how Shakespeare might have come by this top-secret information, for it was, indeed, top secret. Ivan's instructions to Ambassador Pisemsky were not to speak of the matter of marriage to Lady Mary unless the Queen was alone or with only a few of her most trusted councilors (SRIIO 38.4). Even if it was gossiped about at a later date, it would have still have remained within the Court. Moreover, as stated earlier, only "familiar" friends of Lady Mary could call her Empress of Russia. Oxfordians will note with satisfaction that Edward de Vere, the 17th Earl of Oxford, was included in this intimate group.

I have mentioned, in this paper, eight ambassadors—two Russian and six English. Time does not permit details, but my research into the background of the English diplomats reveals that they were a special group of people, most of whom held a variety of other high-ranking offices of state both before and after their Russian missions.

The accounts of Chancellor, Jenkinson, Thomas Randolph and Randolph's secretary, George Turberville, were published for the first time in Richard Hakluyt's *Principal Navigations of the English Nation* in 1589 and then collated into a second edition of 1599-1600, but the information Shakespeare could have gleaned from these accounts would have been the description of the journey to Russia, generalities about its barbarity and tyranny, facts about the Muscovite system of governing as well as Russian traditions and mores.

The Englishman who would have had the most "inside" information about sixteenth-century Muscovy was Jerome Horsey, who spent almost 20 years in Russia, from 1573 to 1591. As mentioned earlier, Horsey was the central figure in the story of Ivan's courtship of Lady Mary. He carried Ivan's letter to Elizabeth in his horse's mane across the whole of Europe.

Horsey's observations of Russia supplied the horror stories that found their way into Shakespeare's play. Shakespeare drew on details of Horsey's descriptive image of Ivan for his depiction of Armado. Horsey knew all about Ivan's mercury treatments long before the

Russians themselves found out about them. It was Horsey's report of Ivan's interest in alchemy that, together with Ivan's leg treatments, prompted Shakespeare's mention of mercury in Act 5 of *LLL* (*Russia at the Close* 200).

Horsey's work entitled *Travels of Sir Jerome Horsey, Knt.* gives details of his experiences in Russia until his expulsion from Russia in 1591. We don't know when he started writing his *Travels*, but based on the dedication addressed to Sir Francis Walsingham, it could have been any time up to 1590, the year Walsingham died.

Although Horsey's work was composed long after the events described in it took place, there is no doubt that it was the most abundant source for the Russian material that appeared in *LLL*. But unlike the works of Chancellor, Jenkinson, Randolph and Fletcher, Horsey's *Travels* were not published during Shakespeare's lifetime. They remained in manuscript form and were only edited for the first time in 1856 by Edward Bond in his *Russia at the Close of the Sixteenth Century* to which source so much of this paper's citations are indebted. Some scholars might argue that Shakespeare could have read Fletcher's work *Of the Russe Commonwealth*, published in 1591, but while this might account for some of his material, it would not explain how Shakespeare knew the exact details of Pisemsky's speech and actions at York House, Horsey's ambassadorial assignments, and so many Russian words and expressions. These, as well as many other allusions in *LLL*, must have come directly "from the horsey's mouth."

In conclusion

I have no doubt that *LLL* was an in-house satire written for the Court audience of Queen Elizabeth, its title, at least in part, a reference to Ivan the Terrible's frustrated efforts to marry Elizabeth. I believe it was rewritten and updated several times, with new material being conveyed to England over the years by sources such as Horsey and Fletcher. The topical jokes and allusions refer to real historical events and personalities; and the Russian references, obvious and implied, are based upon the events and diplomatic circumstances of Russian-English relations. The English and Russian personages subsumed under and hidden behind the characters would have been understood only by those aristocrats and courtiers close to the seat of royal power. Clearly, Shakespeare was privy to this information.

The theatre-going public of late sixteenth century would not have—could not have—picked up on, or appreciated, any of these embedded subtleties better than directors or audiences of today who are unaware of this play's origins. Public audiences could laugh at bearded fat men, comically dressed as Russians with their antics and foreign manners, just as they do today. It did not afford the slightest revelation to audiences of this play's origins (indeed, it further subverted it) in the year 2000 when the masque of the Muscovites was replaced by a sexy dance routine in Kenneth Branagh's film version of *LLL*. But as with *Hamlet*'s play-within-a-play, the masque of the Muscovites reflected the real stage of the Elizabethan Court.

Lighthearted and frivolous as it appears, *LLL* is one of the more complex, intricate, linguistically agile and historically revealing of Shakespeare's plays and is deeply steeped in Russian-English diplomatic and economic history. Indeed, if Ivan the Terrible was called the "English Tsar" by his Russian ministers,[24] I think we can safely call *LLL* Shakespeare's "Russian play."

Notes

[1] According to Horsey, it was Dr Eliseus Bomelius of Westphalia who suggested the idea to Ivan (*Russia at the Close* 187).

[2] Randolph's, Bowes' and Fletcher's missions to Russia took place in 1568-9, 1583 and 1588 respectively. Horsey spent 18 years (1573-1591) living there and traveling between Russia and England.

[3] His decision might have something to do with the fact that during one of Ivan's raids on Pskov, a holy man predicted and told Ivan directly that Ivan would die from lightning as a punishment for his cruelty towards his people (*Russia at the Close* 161).

[4] This calculation is based on the estimates of royal income during Elizabethan times by Penury Williams in *The Later Tudors* (Oxford: The Clarendon Press, 1995), p. 147, and quoted in Woolley, p. 312.

[5] Hatfield MSS, Cal. Xi, 388.

[6] PRO SP102/49, No. 5. Cotton Nero B.xi.

[7] Note also Boyet's opening of the "capon" and its "carving" as well as the phrase "I am ready to serve" in Act 4 (4.1.56-58). Then, a few lines later, Costard again uses l'envoy in connection to the "goose" story: "O! Marry me to one Frances. I smell l'envoy, some goose in this" (3.1.118-19). Prof Felicia Londré, in her article "Elizabethan Views of the Other" thinks this refers to the coming of the French envoy, Simier, in 1579 to seek Elizabeth's consent to marry Francois, Duc d'Alençon, since "oi" means "goose" in French (Londré 338). However, this can also refer to the Russian "goose" story that made such a strong impression on Shakespeare. Clearly, what Costard is hinting at is that should Elizabeth marry Duc d'Alençon, there is bound to be bloodshed.

[8] In his *Travels*, Horsey recollects how Ivan "Sent for me, and told me he had a message of honor, weight and secracie, to imploie me in, to the Quens Majesty of England, pearceavinge I had ateyned to the familiar phrase of his language..." (*Russia at the Close* 185).

[9] Horsey had many amazing incidents to narrate at court after this adventure. Once he was stopped and taken into custody by a Livonian commander who was about to kill him until he discovered that Horsey was the man who had rescued his daughter when she was trapped in Russia. Horsey's fortunes were immediately reversed, and he was hailed as a hero, rewarded and sent on his way again. (*Russia at the Close* 191)

[10] After Horsey delivered Ivan's vodka-reeking message to the Queen, instead of sending Ivan a bride, she sent him Dr. Robert Jacobs (or Dr. Roman as he was later to be called by the Russians). Dr. Jacobs was to play a very special role, as it is generally believed by historians that Ivan began to press him on the issue of an English marriage to someone other than Elizabeth. However, it is more probable that the doctor was instructed by Elizabeth to raise this topic in conversation with Ivan. It would have served Elizabeth well to use delaying tactics to prolong England's

beneficial relationship with Ivan. By now, Elizabeth was far too old to persuade even an ass like Ivan that she was herself considering marriage proposals, as she would have been 48 years old in 1581. In any event, in October 1580, Ivan had married Maria Nagaya, his seventh wife. (The marriage, however, albeit to a Tsar, was not officially sanctioned as the Russian church only allowed one—even a Tsar—three legal marriages. This, of course, did not stop Ivan from choosing new wives, although it was more difficult to officially celebrate each occasion of marriage when he did. An English bride would have made wife Number Eight.) Ivan, knowing about Elizabeth's father's marriage record, must have thought that she, however, unlike the Russian Church, thought nothing of such marital pursuits. Moreover, all readers of English history know what happened to Henry VIII's wives, so in retrospect it may seem to them that Ivan was more merciful than Henry because, though he married more, he sent the no-longer-desired wives not to the headsman but to a nunnery. What he did that was particularly invidious, however, and which was, to some extent, worse for others connected to the monarch's displaced queen, was to spare the ex-wife her life but destroy her family. This was, in a way, more cruel than killing the wife herself, as according to Russian religion, a person has to have as many family members as possible praying for them to attain the fullness of salvation. By destroying his wife's family, Ivan was denying his displaced wife access to heaven and making her life a living hell—perhaps even to the extent that she might believe she would go to hell after death due to too few prayers being offered on her behalf.

[11] Pisemsky also had another objective in coming: he had to revive Ivan's old demands for a lasting alliance between the two kingdoms.

[12] See *LLL* 4.1.14-19.

[13] The conclusion that Maria in *LLL* represents Lady Mary Hastings was also reached by Ruth Lloyd Miller in her 1990 article, "Oaths Foresworn in Love's Labour's Lost" published in *The Oxfordian* (Vol. IX) in October 2006, as well as by Mark Anderson (*Shakespeare by Another Name* 16, 260). Felicia Londre also makes the connection between Lady Mary Hastings and Longaville's exclamation "O sweet Maria, empress of my Love!" in her study of the play (337). Note: I would like to express my gratitude to Mark Anderson

for all our stimulating conversations which sparked my interest in this subject matter. I would also like to thank Bonner Miller Cutting for sending me a copy of her mother's article.

[14] "The Emperowr began griviously to swell in his coddes, with which he had most horrablie offended above 50 years together, bostinge of thowsand virgens he had deflowred and thowsands of children of his begettinge distroied." (*Russia at the Close* 199)

[15] There is an amusing story about papal nuncio Antonio Possevino who had an audience with Ivan in 1582. So as not to be outdone by Ivan's imposing list of titles, when asked by Ivan about the Pope's health, Possevino replied: "Our Most Holy Lord, Pope Gregory XIII, Shepherd of the Church Universal, Vicar of Christ on Earth, Successor to St. Peter, Lord of Many Realms and Regions, Servant of the Servants of God, greets your Highness and give you his blessing." (qtd in Bobrick 308)

[16] The aorist, notes the *OED*, is "an archaic form of the past tense without reference to duration or completion."

[17] The King calls Armado "[a] man of compliments, whom right and wrong / Have chose as umpire of their mutiny." (1.1.166-167)

[18] "The title or word "Knyaz" was often to be heard. Russians have always used it, adding "veliki" to mean "great" or "grand" as in "grand prince" or "grand duke" for those who have more than one duchy under them. But those who have but one use the title "Knyaz" without any addition." (Haberstein 38)

[19] Some chroniclers, as earlier noted, suggest that Ivan suspected his eldest son of intriguing against him (Skrynnikov 495).

[20] In Armado's letter to Jaquenetta,, Armado signs off with the words: "I profane my lips on thy foot…" (4.1.82-83). It was customary to kiss the Russian monarch's foot when taking leave of him. Horsey admitted to doing the same when he was parting with Ivan.

[21] Horsey described the death of Ivan "Junior" as Russia's greatest loss, "the hope of their comfort, a wise, mild and most woorthy prince of heroicall condicion, of comly presence, 23 years of age, beloved and lamented of all men" (qtd in *Russia at the Close* 195). Fletcher, too, said that Ivan Junior was "of the best towardnesse" of Ivan the Terrible's sons (qtd

in *Russia at the Close* 21). Elizabeth herself was apparently very upset by the fact that her doctor could not attend to the young man (Madariaga 342.)

[22] Horsey tells us that Ivan "tore his hear and byrd like a madd man, lamentinge and morninge for the loss of his sonn." (qtd in *Russia at the Close* 195)

[23] Compare this with Armado's wish, earlier in the play, for the peace of mind of the king and the princess. (5.2.528)

[24] This is how Andrey Shchelkalov, one of Ivan's Anglophobic councilors, referred to Ivan while announcing his death to the English ambassador, Sir Jerome Bowes, in March 1584.

Works Cited

Anderson, Mark. *Shakespeare by Another Name.* New York: Gotham Books, 2005.

Bobrick, Benson. *Fearful Majesty: The Life and Reign of Ivan the Terrible.* New York: Putnam's, 1987.

Carroll, William C. *The Great Feast of Languages.* Princeton: Princeton UP, 1976.

Chambers, E.K. *William Shakespeare. A Study of Facts and Problems.* Oxford: Clarendon, 1930. II: 332 (Cope's letter to Burbage)

Clark, Eva Turner. *The Satirical Comedy 'Love's Labour's Lost.'* New York: William Farquhar Payson, 1933.

Granville-Barker, Harley. *Prefaces to Shakespeare. Love's Labour's Lost.* Rpt. Portsmouth, NH: Heinemann, 1995. 30.

Grey, Ian. *Ivan the Terrible,* London: Hodder & Stoughton, 1964.

Hazlitt, William. *Love's Labour's Lost."* *Love's Labour's Lost: Critical Essays,* New York: Garland Publishing, 1997. 61-63.

Herberstein, Sigmund von. *Description of Moscow and Muscovy.* Ed. Bertold Picard. Trans. J.B.C Grundy. New York: Barnes and Noble Inc., 1966.

Grey, Ian. *Ivan the Terrible.* London: History Book Club, 1966.

Londré, Felicia Hardison, "Elizabethan Views of the 'Other': French, Spanish, and Russians in *"Love's Labour's Lost." Love's Labour'sLost: Critical Essays.* Ed. Felicia Hardison Londre. New York: Garland, 1997. 325-341.

Madariaga Isabel de. *Ivan the Terrible: First Tsar of Russia.* Yale UP, 2005.

Morozova, Lyudmila. *Dva Tsarya: Fyodor I Boris (Two Tsars: Fyodor and Boris),* Moscow: Russkoe Slovo, 2001.

Novitsky, G. Anglijskie puteshestvenniki v moskovskom gosudarstve v XVI veke (*English Travelers in the 16th c. Muscovy*), Leningrad, 1937.

Pendergast, John. *Love's Labour's Lost: A Guide to the Play.* Westport, CT: Greenwood Press, 2002.

Richardson, Charles. *A New Dictionary of the English Language.* London: W. Pickering, 1839.

Russia at the Close of the Sixteenth Century. Comprising the treatise "Of the Russe Common Wealth by Dr. Giles Fletcher and The Travels of Sir Jerome Horsey, Knt., now for the first time printed entire from his own manuscript. Ed. Edward A. Bond. London: Hakluyt Society, 1856.

Sbornik Russkogo Imperatorskogo Istoricheskogo Obshchestva (SRIIO) (Collection of the Russian Imperial Historical Society), St. Petersburg, vol. 38, 1883.

Skrynnikov, R. G. *Tsarstvo terrora (The Reign of Terror).* St. Petersburg, 1992.

Willan, T. S. *The Early History of the Russia Company 1553-1603.* Manchester: Manchester UP, 1956.

Woolley, Benjamin. *The Queen's Conjurer: The Science and Magic of Dr. John Dee, Adviser to Queen Elizabeth I,* New York: Henry Holt, 2001.

Elliott and Valenza's Stylometrics Fail to Eliminate Oxford as Shakespeare

Richard F. Whalen and John M. Shahan

To try to winnow down the list of claimants put forward as the author of the Shakespeare canon, the Claremont Shakespeare Authorship Clinic at Claremont McKenna College used computerized stylometrics to compare text from Shakespeare plays and poems to text from three dozen other writers who have been proposed as the true Shakespeare. Teams of undergraduate students were directly involved in the work of the clinic from 1987 to 1994. Their faculty advisers were Ward E. Y. Elliott, Professor of American Political Iinstitutions, and Robert J. Valenza, Professor of Mathematics and the Humanities. They continued the clinic's work after 1994 and updated its findings in a long article in the fall 2004 issue of *The Tennessee Law Review*.

Their principal target was Edward de Vere, the 17th earl of Oxford, whom they describe as "today's leading claimant to be the 'True Shakespeare'" in their article, "Oxford by the Numbers: What are the Odds that the Earl of Oxford Could Have Written Shakespeare's Plays and Poems?" Their 129-page article includes fifty-six pages of charts and graphs. This paper expands on our one-page rebuttal published in the same issue of the law review.

To see if Oxford's verse resembled Shakespeare's, the clinic ran fifteen validated tests of the thirty-eight comparison tests they had developed for computer runs on a VAX processor (342 - 43). Their inputs for Oxford were sixteen lyric poems totaling 3,042 words and blocks of 3,000 words from Shakespeare poems and plays. The inputs for Oxford — half of them actually songs — are judged by Steven May to be Oxford's canonical works, not just "possibly" or "probably" by him (*The Elizabethan Courtier Poets* 270).

According to Elliott and Valenza, Oxford's verse "failed" seven of the fifteen stylometric tests; the seven tests were modal distance, grade level, relative clauses, lines with feminine endings, enclitic microphrases, proclitic microphrases and "bundles of badges" ("Oxford by the Numbers" 370 - 76). They concluded that, "in terms of quantifiable stylistic attributes, Oxford's verse and Shakespeare's verse are light-years apart. The odds that either could have written the other's work are much lower than the odds of getting hit by lightning" (323). Failing seven out of fifteen stylometric tests is, in their opinion, "far too many to look like Shakespeare to us or to our computer" (376). They even argue that failing just one test would be a "silver bullet" that would eliminate Oxford (337, 373). Passing tests doesn't count. Their computer calculated that the odds that Oxford did not write the works of Shakespeare range from four hundred thousand to one to a quadrillion to one (370).

The inputs for Oxford are invalid, however, because they mix genres—apples with oranges, in clichéd parlance. Although Elliott and Valenza refer to the sixteen verse inputs for Oxford as "poems," in actuality, half of these "poems" are songs while half are poems in a variety of verse forms. The songs first appeared in *The Paradise of Dainty Devices*, an anthology of songs collected by Richard Edwards before he died in 1566 but which was not published until 1576. Disle, the printer, described them as "ditties… made to be set to any song in five parts or sung to instrument" (qtd in Rollins 3-4). Elliott and Valenza, however, did not treat Oxford's songs and poems separately when they compared them to blocks of Shakespeare narrative, lyric and dramatic verse, even though they acknowl-

DISCOVERING SHAKESPEARE: A FESTSCHRIFT IN HONOUR OF ISABEL HOLDEN

edge at one point that the songs in *Paradise* "could be song lyrics, not poems proper, and, hence, not suitable for comparison with poems" (392). In fact, they were songs, and despite their own caveat, Elliott and Valenza used the songs — half their sample — as if they were poems for testing purposes with poetic works by Shakespeare.

The mishandling of genres by Elliott and Valenza by neglecting to compare songs to songs and poems to poems, casts serious doubt on the validity of their findings. The stylometric differences their research model generated might well stem from differences in genre, not from the verse being from different writers. Even if a re-analysis of the inputs changed the outputs, however, other input problems are so serious that the results of re-analysis would not suffice to salvage their conclusion regarding Oxford.

The second input problem — and perhaps the most fundamental — is Elliott and Valenza's assumed composition dates for Oxford's verse. No one knows in what month or in what year he wrote the sixteen songs and poems used as inputs, but they were not all, as Elliott and Valenza assumed, written between the ages of twenty-two and forty-four (323, 394). As Nina Green, an independent scholar of primary-source historical documentation, has noted, Oxford must have written the eight songs in *The Paradise of Dainty Devices* before age sixteen ("Oxford's Poems" 1 - 2). This is because the printer stated in his prefatory epistle that Richard Edwards had collected its contents before he died in 1566, the year Oxford turned sixteen. Hyder Rollins of Harvard University, the modern-day editor of the anthology, had come to the same conclusion (lix).

Steven May implicitly tries to support Elliott and Valenza in another article in the same issue of the law review by pushing the composition dates of the songs well into Oxford's twenties. May argues that Oxford wrote the eight songs *after* Edwards' death in 1566, when Oxford turned sixteen, and, of course, before *Paradise* was printed in 1576,

when Oxford was ten years older. May styles them "jaded love complaints," implying that no teenager could have written them ("The Seventeenth Earl of Oxford" 231). However, he gives no examples; nor does he describe them this way in his earlier writings about them. Nina Green suggests that this subjective judgment is highly questionable, pointing out that two of the songs do not deal with love at all, and none of the other six contains any sentiments that would merit the epithet "jaded" ("Does the Early Work" 1 - 2).

May notes that one of the other songs in the anthology — not by Oxford — was sung before the queen in 1574, as if to imply that it, and all of the other songs, including Oxford's, may have been written shortly before 1574, when Oxford was twenty-four; but this performance in no way precludes pre-1566 dates of composition for any of the songs ("The Seventeenth Earl of Oxford" 231).

May also finds the texts of the eight songs to be "fairly corrupt," suggesting that the printer got them "second-hand rather than from court circles tapped by Edwards [before he died]" (231). This, too, is highly speculative. Rollins describes the song collection as "carefully printed" (lix). He does not call any of them, including Oxford's, corrupt, nor would it follow that they could not have been written by 1566. May, accordingly, has no basis for assuming that manuscripts circulating in court pre-1566 would have been error-free. In sum, the printer said that Edwards collected the eight songs before he died in 1566; Rollins agrees, and no solid evidence contradicts these authorities.

Of Oxford's eight poems, one is in the prefatory material to Thomas Bedingfield's translation from the Latin of *Cardanus' Comforte*, published by Oxford in 1573. Bedingfield sent his manuscript to Oxford with a cover letter dated 1 January 1572, when Oxford was twenty-one. The 26-line poem says nothing about *Cardanus* or the meaning of the book or Bedingfield, so it is quite likely that the short poem on the rewards of reading versus the toil of writing had been written some time earlier, that is, by age twenty-one or younger (May, *The Elizabethan Courtier Poets* 270).

The dates of composition of the remaining seven poems in the data base for Oxford are very problematic. They turned up in print in the 1580s and 1590s. May judges that they date primarily to the 1570s because of the range of subject matter and variety of execution, which seem, to him, experimental (53 - 54). That sounds right to us. Given May's assessment, and the lack of any firm anchors in time, these seven poems could as easily date to the early 1570s, or even the late 1560s. Oxford was in his early twenties and late teens in those years. This is supported by Elliott and Valenza's finding that there are "no signs of testable stylistic change" among Oxford's sixteen works — that is, the eight songs of his early teens and the eight poems ("Oxford by the Numbers" 394). They claim that this shows that Oxford's style did not change between the ages of twenty-two and forty-four. A more likely explanation is that their dates are wrong, and the sixteen songs and poems were all written during Oxford's teens and twenties.

As noted, Elliott and Valenza generally assume that Oxford wrote all sixteen poems and songs in the year of first publication, or not more than one or two years earlier, hence between the ages of twenty-two and forty-four. This assumption is not supported by the evidence, and it contradicts what is known about the practices of Elizabethan aristocratic poets. They circulated manuscript copies privately among relatives and friends, and saw them published only years or decades later, if at all. May himself makes this point (*The Elizabethan Courtier Poets* 59, 67-8, 270).

Hence, there is no valid basis for Elliott and Valenza to assume that Oxford wrote all of his songs and lyric poems between the ages of twenty-two and forty-four. The best evidence indicates that he wrote the eight songs by age sixteen, the short poem in Cardanus' Comforte by age twenty-one or earlier, and the other seven works sometime in his

twenties (per May's assessment). It is entirely possible that he wrote all sixteen during his teenage years. By contrast, it was not until 1593, when Oxford was forty-three, that the first published work to be associated with the name William Shakespeare appeared. How can Elliott and Valenza be so sure that Oxford's early writing style did not develop into Shakespeare's more mature style over a period of two decades or more?

Another problem with inputs concerns the "baseline" that Elliott and Valenza constructed for texts from the Shakespeare canon. Their enormous odds against Oxford are for the 3,042 words in the Oxford poem block relative to Shakespeare's own most discrepant 3,000-word block in their Shakespeare baseline ("Oxford by the Numbers" 370 - 71). In other words, they compared the odds that the most discrepant 3,000-word block in their baseline of Shakespeare's own works was written by Shakespeare, against the odds that Oxford's 3,000 known words were written by Shakespeare.

This might seem reasonable, until one realizes that Elliott and Valenza's Shakespeare baseline was purged of its most discrepant blocks to create what they called a "clean" baseline ("Oxford by the Numbers" 335 - 37). Surely a "clean" baseline must be better than a "dirty" one, but what does this really mean? It means that nine plays and two poems, normally included in the canon, were excluded because they were thought to have been "co-authored" with someone else, or to have been of "doubtful" authorship. However, among the criteria for "doubtful" works is that they were "discrepant" on Elliott and Valenza's measures. It is circular reasoning to exclude works because they are "discrepant" on stylistic tests, and then reject alternative claimants by comparing their writings to the "most discrepant block" in a baseline that has been purged of discrepant blocks.

The nine plays excluded are the three parts of *Henry VI, Titus Andronicus, Henry V, Timon of Athens, Pericles, Two Noble Kinsmen,* and *Henry VIII.* These nine plays include four of the five earliest plays, and four of the eight latest plays written, according to the Riverside edition's late dating (47 - 56). Excluding so many early and late plays (which tend to be the outliers at both the upper and lower ends of the range on stylistic measures) creates a homogenous baseline that closely conforms to Shakespeare's mid-career style. Such a baseline is ill-suited to identifying works which he may have written early, or which for some other reason do not conform to the author's mid-career norms. It would tend to concentrate the distribution of scores closely around the mean and reduce the standard deviation, making it more difficult for a comparison sample of works by another claimant to pass Elliott and Valenza's tests. It would also exaggerate the degree of confidence in rejections — that is, the odds against them having been by Shakespeare.

By purging their baseline of eleven works, including four very early plays, Elliott and Valenza biased their study in favor of rejecting candidates, like Oxford, whose known writings predate Shakespeare's mature works by decades. At the very least, they ought to have used baselines both with, and without, the nine plays and two poems that they excluded. There is also the additional issue that Elliott and Valenza used only the First Folio versions of Shakespeare's plays (published in 1623) and excluded all of the earlier quarto versions. These early quarto versions could easily be the works that are stylistically most similar to Oxford's known works.

Yet another significant input problem is whether Oxford's sixteen known works are a representative sample of his writings. They total 3,042 words, which Elliott and Valenza sometimes contradictorily call a "comparison sample" and sometimes the "whole corpus" ("Oxford by the Numbers" 347, 372, 373, 376). In fact, they are neither a true "sample" of a larger body of work, nor are they the "whole corpus." They are the works that Steven May considers to be definitely by Oxford — rather than by someone else — and thus "canonical." (*The Elizabethan Courtier Poets*

270) However, May also argues that "[i]n all likelihood these sixteen . . . poems amount to no more than a good sampling of de Vere's total output in light of the contemporary praise of his writing. Both Webbe (1586) and Puttenham (1589) rank him first among the courtier poets, an eminence he probably would not have been granted, despite his reputation as a patron, by virtue of a mere handful of lyrics" (1980, 12). Elliott and Valenza, however, ignore May's caveat and treat Oxford's known verse as representative.

Several of Oxford's contemporaries praised him as an accomplished and prolific poet and playwright. In 1578, Gabriel Harvey praised Oxford, saying "witness how greatly thou dost excel in letters. I have seen many Latin verses of thine, yea, even more of English." In his Discourse of English Poetry, William Webbe described Oxford as "the most excellent" of the courtier poets (qtd in Ward 55 - 56). In *The Arte of English Poesie* George Puttenham wrote that "I know very many notable gentlemen in the Court that have written commendably, and suppressed it again, or else suffered it to be published without their own names on it: as if it were a discredit for a gentleman to seem learned." Later, he was more specific, writing that many courtiers have "written excellently well as it would appear if their doings could be found out and made public with the rest, of which number is first that noble gentleman, Edward Earl of Oxford" (61).

Oxford was also known for writing plays. In *Palladis Tamia* of 1598, Francis Meres rated him among "the best for comedy" (qtd in Chambers 2: 194 - 95). None of his comedies, however, are in Elliott and Valenza's comparison sample because none survive (under his own name). Long after he died, Oxford's reputation was still such that Henry Peacham, in a chapter on poetry in his *Compleat Gentleman* of 1622, placed him first on a list of seven Elizabethan poets who, in Peacham's appraisal, above others, "honoured poesie with their pens and practice" (108).

As May suggests, it is unlikely that

Oxford received such praise if that praise is based only on the sixteen works in Elliott and Valenza's sample. He must have written many more, and much better, works. The contrast between this praise and the works in their sample ought to have alerted Elliott and Valenza to the likelihood that they were working with a very incomplete, non-representative sample. The validity of their comparison sample was critical to making a meaningful comparison between Oxford's and Shakespeare's works. They should have considered this issue, and they ought to have addressed it in their article when describing the selection of their Oxford comparison sample — *especially* since the issue was mentioned by Steven May, whom they cite as the authority for their Oxford sample.

Finally, there is a metaphor problem. Elliott and Valenza's research design cannot rule out the possibility that any stylistic differences between Oxford's youthful verse and Shakespeare's mature verse, first published two decades later, could be entirely due to Oxford's stage of development as a writer. The correct response to such a design issue would have been to discount stylistic differences as possibly due to developmental factors, and focus on similarities. Elliott and Vanenza did the opposite. Here is how they described what they did, and their rationale for doing it:

> Fitting (Cinderella's) tiny slipper does not prove you are Cinderella nearly as conclusively as not fitting the tiny slipper proves you are not Cinderella. . . . Hence, our distinguishing stock-in-trade has been "silver bullet" negative evidence that tends to disprove common authorship by showing differences, rather than "smoking gun" positive evidence used by most other analysts to prove common authorship with similarities. . . . " ("Oxford by the Numbers" 337)

The test of a metaphor is the extent to which it holds up when looked at in the real world

situation to which it is supposed to apply. The "Cinderella" metaphor fails the test. It assumes that both foot sizes and writing styles are immutable, neither of which is true. Suppose, for example, that, rather than a foot, we have a footprint, and the footprint is size four. Elliott and Valenza would have us conclude that the footprint cannot be Cinderella's because she wears a size-five slipper. But what if the footprint was made two years ago? It makes no difference to Elliott and Valenza; if the footprint is size four, it cannot be Cinderella's. Having size four footprints "proves" you are not Cinderella only if her feet were always the same size and never had to grow to reach maturity.

Elliott and Valenza want people to think that in their small sample of Oxford's youthful verse, they have measured Oxford's "foot" and concluded that it is not Shakespeare's "shoe size." What they really have is something more analogous to a few very old, small footprints —much smaller than Shakespeare's shoe size two decades later. Given the design of their study, it is impossible for Elliott and Valenza to conclude, by any logical argument, that the writer who produced those few small "footprints" could not have grown, over two decades, into Shakespeare's "shoes."

The Cinderella metaphor, rather than supporting an emphasis on differences, shows why it is inappropriate to use in this case. Just as tiny feet grow over time, writing styles develop over time. Emphasizing differences creates an illogical bias to reject any candidate for whom no valid comparison sample exists. Labeling differences "silver bullets," and calling them their "stock-in-trade," hardly constitutes a scientific rationale for such a bias. Fairy tale metaphors that do not correspond to reality are no substitute for rigorous thinking about the kind of conclusions that can, and cannot, be reached using writings that are not comparable in genre, time of composition, or scope of sample.

The inputs that Elliott and Valenza used in their study do not warrant the unqualified conclusion they reached for Oxford. Their

Shakespeare baseline was not representative and was biased because it excluded nine plays and two poems. They did not compare Oxford's songs to Shakespeare's songs, nor did they compare a clean, "unconfounded" sample of Oxford's poems to Shakespeare's poems. They incorrectly assumed that publication dates during Elizabethan times were always close to dates of composition, and they consequently assumed that Oxford's youthful verse was representative of his mature poetry. They ignored consistent praise by Oxford's contemporaries that he was among the greatest of Elizabethan poet-playwrights. The contrast with the works in their sample ought to have alerted them to the likelihood that they were working with an incomplete, invalid sample, and that any differences between Oxford's and Shakespeare's verse could be developmental. They ought to have concluded that although they found little stylometric support for Oxford, he was not a fully testable claimant, and so could not be eliminated. The study, therefore, lacks validity and cannot be said to possess meaningful authority; its conclusions, assessed by scientific standards, must, accordingly, be rejected.

Works Cited

Chambers, E. K. *William Shakespeare: A Study of Facts and Problems*. 2 vols. Oxford: Clarendon Press, 1930.

Elliott, Ward E.Y. and Robert J. Valenza. "Can the Oxford Candidacy Be Saved?" *The Oxfordian* 3 (2000): 71 - 97.

—. Letter. *The Oxfordian* 6 (2003): 154 - 163.

—. "Oxford by the Numbers: What Are the Odds that the Earl of Oxford Could Have Written Shakespeare's Poems and Plays?" *The Tennessee Law Review* 72/1 (2004): 323 - 453.

Green, Nina. "Does the Early Work of Edward de Vere, 17th Earl of Oxford, Reveal That He Wrote Songs as well as Verses?" *Edward de Vere Newsletter* 18 (1990): 1 - 2.

—. "Oxford's Poems." *Edward de Vere Newsletter* 18 (1990): 3 - 4.

Harvey, Gabriel. Address before the Queen at Audley End. (1578). In notes by R. L. Miller her 2d edition (1975) of *A Hundreth Sundrie Flowres* (1573) edited by Bernard M. Ward. (1928): 65 - 66.

May, Steven W. *The Elizabethan Courtier Poets: The Poems and Their Contexts*. Asheville, NC: Pegasus, 1999.

—. "The Poems of Edward de Vere, Seventeenth Earl of Oxford, and of Robert Devereux, Second Earl of Sussex." *Studies in Philology* 77:1 (1980).

—. "The Seventeenth Earl of Oxford as Poet and Playwright." *The Tennessee Law Review* 72:1 (2004): 221- 54.

Peacham, Henry. *The Compleat Gentleman*. London: Constable, 1622.

Puttenham, George. *The Arte of English Poesie*. 1589. Eds. Gladys Doidge Willcock and Alice Walker. Cambridge: Cambridge University Press, 1970.

The Riverside Shakespeare. Gen Ed. G. Blakemore Evans. Boston: Houghton Mifflin, 1974.

Rollins, Hyder. Introduction. *The Paradise of Dainty Devices*. 1576. Ed. Richard Edwards. Cambridge: Harvard University Press, 1927.

Shahan, John. Letter. *The Oxfordian* 4 (2001): 154-165.

Webbe, William. "Discourse of English Poetry." 1586. *Ancient and Critical Essays*. Ed. Joseph Haselwood. London: Triphook, 1811.

Pale as Death:

The Fictionalizing Influence of Erasmus's "Naufragium" On the Renaissance Travel Narrative[1]

Roger Stritmatter, Ph.D., and Lynne Kositsky, M.A.

Abstract

Erasmus' *Colloquia Familiaria* (1518) was one of the most influential books for Renaissance culture. Although condemned by the Sorbonne in 1526 for its satiric barbs against moral laxity in the Church, and eventually placed on the Tridentine Index, the popular pedagogical manual went through many editions during its author's lifetime. "Naufragium," a dramatic dialogue of a shipwreck, was perhaps the most vividly dramatic and readily available of such descriptions in Renaissance letters. Its influence on popular fictions such as Rabelais's *Gargantua* and Shakespeare's *Tempest* has long been acknowledged. But it also exhibits a previously undocumented influence on popular, ostensibly non-fictional travel narratives by, for example, Robert Tomson (pub. 1598-1600), Francis de Ulloa (pub. 1598-1600), and William Strachey (pub. 1625). We investigate the fictional nature of Renaissance travel narratives and explore implications of the appropriation of "Naufragium" for source studies of Shakespeare's *Tempest*.

Genre theorists have long known that the early modern travel narrative, like the modern ethnography, was constructed not from the unmediated experience of actual travelers but by a process of filtering factual events through literary conventions and idioms, characteristically resulting in a text which reflected both the practical needs of the author for colorful material and the ideological preconceptions of his society. The travel narrative was also a lucrative genre, and the temptation to appropriate what experience did not supply was strong. "I am extremely astonished," writes Peter Martyr in an early edition of his *De Orbe Novo*, the first book to describe the voyages of Christopher Columbus,

> that a certain Venetian, Aloisió Cadamosto, who has written a history of the Portuguese, should write when mentioning the actions of the Spaniards, "We have done; we have seen; we have been"; when, as a matter of fact, he has neither done nor seen any more than any other Venetian. Cadamosto borrowed and plagiarised whatever he wrote, from the first three books of my first three Decades. (pt. 4 of 7)

This circulation of ideas and rhetorical elements was not limited to the theft of the work of one travel narrator by another who might never have left his native port, and the consequences could be enduring. In fact, cultural historians long have recognized a close association between travel narratives and the development of early fiction. Tropes, narrative techniques, and topoi—commonly held beliefs about people, places or things—

circulated across the boundary between the fictional and the authentic, and "particular items of description, and even particular turns of phrase bec[a]me established and persist[ed], often through centuries" in the literature of the exotic (George 65). This process is relevant to the disposition of one of the most vexed and longstanding debates in early modern source studies, namely the identification of sources for Shakespeare's *Tempest*, a play conventionally dated, almost solely on the basis of an alleged source, to 1611.

The traditional belief that the play's "new world" ambience results from the influence of William Strachey's account of the 1609 wreck of Sir George Somers in the Bermuda Islands has recently been defended by the appeal to a positivist faith in the transparent and unquestioned priority of the "factual" over the "fictional":

> it is *obvious* that Shakespeare could *only* have borrowed from Strachey, Jourdain, and *A True Declaration* rather than the other way around; *this was not another work of fiction* Shakespeare was basing his play on, but three independent accounts *of actual events*. (Kathman; pt. 3 of 6; emphasis added)

But the cultural historian understands that Kathman's reification of the *actual events* of the Bermuda pamphlets neglects the epistemic problems posed by the free circulation in early modern texts of elements back and forth across the boundary between fictive and "factual" narratives.

Our own study of *Tempest* chronology and sources has already suggested the necessity of a twofold revision of the traditional perspective:

1) Strachey's *True Reportory* (f.p. 1625): the only Bermuda narrative believed since 1892 to have exerted a significant influence on *The Tempest*—although describing events of June 1609-July 1610—was almost certainly not completed until some time after the play's November, 1611 performance record. (Stritmatter and Kositsky [see "Shakespeare and the Voyagers"])

2) Characteristics of *The Tempest* traditionally attributed to the influence of Strachey's *True Reportory* are more likely the consequence of Shakespeare's close familiarity with 16th century travel narratives, especially Richard Eden's *Decades of the Newe Worlde* (1555, 1577), from which the dramatist drew numerous elements. (Stritmatter and Kositsky, [see "'O Brave New World'"])

To these may be added a third telling sign of Strachey's curious fusion of the historical and the fictional, namely the frequent and detailed discrepancies between his own account of the wreck of Sir George Somers' ship and those of other writers recording the same events. Indeed, a close comparison of Strachey's account with those published earlier in Jourdain's *Discovery*, *True Declaration*, and Riche's *News from Virginia*, reveals intriguing discrepancies which go beyond style and recall Strachey's documented practice of embroidering his narratives with material from other sources: only Strachey mentions St. Elmo's Fire, praying sailors, or the cutting down of the main mast. Judging by other accounts, one may reasonably question if these events really happened during Somers' visit to the Bermudas in 1609—or whether, on the contrary, they represent Strachey's fanciful elaboration of an account tailored to enhance salability in a readership hungry for adventure. Figure One illustrates that none of these storm scene elements common to Strachey and Shakespeare are found in other contemporaneous descriptions of the Gates' wreck. Not only is the cutting down of the main mast not mentioned in the three other sources, but Jourdain explicitly says that Gates arrived in Bermuda "with all the tacking of the ship and much of the iron about her" (qtd. in Wright 107), and *True Declaration* states that all the furniture and tackling of the ship was

Strachey	Other Bermuda Pamphlets
The sea touching the sky	No
The lightening of the ship by tossing provisions overboard	No
Sailors praying	No
The (probable) splitting or breaking up of the ship	No
The (probable) overturning of the ship	No
The cutting down of the main mast	No
St. Elmo's Fire	No
Figure One: Comparison of storm elements in Strachey and the other Bermuda pamphlets.	

subsequently removed in port in Bermuda.

Subsequent Virginia publications revisit the shipwreck of 1609 with clear reference to the Jourdain account and *True Declaration* but strangely fail to incorporate any of the seven storm elements in *True Reportory* missing from the other narratives. Most striking are the omissions from Smith's 1624 account of *The Generall Historie of Virginia, New England, & the Summer Isles*. Smith's account of "The first English ship knowne to have beene cast away upon the Bermudas, 1609" includes copious details from the earlier narratives, particularly Jourdain's. Smith, like Jourdain and Strachey, depicts Sir George Somers as being on watch during the storm; only Strachey, however, includes the colorful detail of the St. Elmo visitation. Strachey even states that "divers" men on board "observed [St. Elmo] with much wonder and carefulness" (qtd in Wright 12-13), so it is difficult to understand how such a memorable event did not find its way into any other contemporaneous narratives and why it was not repeated in secondary accounts until after the publication of *True Reportory* in 1625.

The omission is particularly glaring in view of the often iterated claim for the wide dissemination and influence of Strachey's "letter" in manuscript, including various hypothetical and typically vague "chains of custody" resulting in Shakespeare's access to it (Wright xi, Bullough 8:239, Kinney 166, Kathman np). Suggestively, all the *True*

Reportory storm elements missing from and/ or contradicted by other Bermuda narratives, including the reference to St. Elmo's fire, are present in Desiderius Erasmus' well-known dialogue, "Naufragium" ("The Shipwreck"), a work published as early as 1523. "Naufragium," we suggest, formed an influential storm template or paradigm that circulated in the literary milieu of Renaissance Europe.[2] During the 16th century, the Colloquies were translated into almost every European vernacular, even Old Irish, and through these numerous translations (as well as many Latin imprints) the book exercised a pervasive influence on many later Renaissance writers. Given this influence, it would not be surprising if "Naufragium" has left a detectable presence not only in Shakespeare's *Tempest* but also on several 16th-century travel narratives. Our research suggests that these narratives appropriated elements of rhetoric, language, and theme from "Naufragium"— and in the process employed Erasmus' fictive constructs to color their ostensibly factual narratives with a gloss of literary plausibility. Such a perspective has profound implications for our understanding of the inter-textual relations of Strachey with both his sources and his imitators. Ironically, even *True Reportory*, like Cadamosto, may be a palimpsest, assembled as much from other texts (including Erasmus' fictive dialogue) as from the author's own experiences in Bermuda.

To test the proposition that elements of

DISCOVERING SHAKESPEARE: A FESTSCHRIFT IN HONOUR OF ISABEL HOLDEN

the *Tempest* storm supposedly derived from Strachey actually belong to the common heritage of the early modern storm scene, we examined the treatment of storms in seven Renaissance and two ancient sources. We traced the occurrence of eleven motifs, ten of which are found in Erasmus' dialogue, including (1) a storm accompanied by St. Elmo's fire; (2) the lightening of a ship by throwing cargo overboard; (3) a master pilot pale from fear; (4) the cutting down of a mast; (5) praying sailors; (6) a mother with child introduced to enhance pathos; and (7) a ship that leaks, splits, and overturns (Appendix A). While not all of these elements can be found in every Renaissance storm account, and while some combinations of them might be seen as commonplace occurrences of any shipwreck, their widespread diffusion (sometimes in unexpected permutations that reveal definite patterns of literary influence) suggests three conclusions: (1) many *Tempest* elements supposedly derived from Strachey actually have a much greater currency than has often been supposed; (2) it seems likely that Erasmus's "Naufragium" exercised a wide influence, well beyond its documented inspiration on Rabelais (see Gilman) and Shakespeare's *Tempest* (Bullough 8: 334), including on supposedly factual travel narratives, offering an intriguing illustration of the transmission of early modern influence across the Maginot line between

nent early modern and ancient shipwreck texts. The results illustrate the wide diffusion of elements of the *Tempest* shipwreck scene *in antecedent* shipwreck literature. In particular, the association of shipwrecks with St. Elmo's fire appears to have been a commonplace by the early 16th century, occurring in accounts of shipwrecks in such writers as Ariosto, Tomson, de Ulloa, and Gilbert, as well as in "Naufragium," Strachey and the *Tempest*. Appendix B demonstrates specific examples of this "storm set" in Ariosto, Erasmus, and Strachey. St. Elmo's fire, as illustrated in Appendix B, is definitely associated in nature with climactic disturbances, and by the 16th century it had become, in both fictional and ostensibly factual narratives, an emblematic harbinger of shipwrecks, a literary symbol used to charge a storm scene with special emotional and figurative intensity, being considered "a token of drowning" (Eden 217v).

While it is difficult to rule out the *a priori* possibility that St. Elmo's fire actually accompanied the events recorded by De Ulloa, Tomson and other 16th-century travelers, additional elements of Tomson's storm scene, for example, confirm that his narrative was constructed with the Erasmian template before his eyes. Both texts include a pathos-inducing description of a woman and child cast into the sea during the shipwreck (Figure Two).

Tomson	Erasmus
I do remember that the last person that came out of the ship into the boat, was a woman black Moore, who leaping out of the ship into the boat with a yong sucking child in her arms (qtd. in Hakluyt 344).	Amongst all the rest, there was none more quiet, and free from feare, then a certain woman, who had an infant sucking upon her breast (G3v).
Figure Two: The suckling child in his mother's arms.	

fiction and "history"; and (3) several features of Erasmus' narrative *unambiguously confirm* its unmediated influence on *The Tempest*.

Appendix A provides a synopsis of the results of our survey of a number of promi-

While it is outside the purview of this brief survey to analyze in detail the patterns of influence linking "Naufragium" to these 16th-century travel narratives, let us examine some previously unconsidered instances of the

"Naufragium"	*Tempest*
A bal of fire, which…is to the shipmen a most fearful signe of hard successe….by and by the fiery globe sliding downe by the ropes…roled it selfe along the brimmes of the ship, and falling from thence down into the middle roomes…(Gr-v)	Ariel. Now in the beak, now in the waist, in the deck, in every cabin,/ I flamed amazement. Sometime I'd divide/And burn in many places – on the topmast/The yards and bowsprit would I flame distinctly… (1.2.196-200).

Figure Three: St. Elmo's Fire

"Naufragium"	*Tempest*
Adolph. At length the Maister of the ship came unto us very pale. **Anto**. That paleness doth presage some great evil (Gr).	Gonz. I have great comfort from this fellow. Methinks he hath no drowning mark upon him – his complexion is perfect gallows (1.1.27-29).

Figure Four: The shipmaster turned pale with fear

"Naufragium"	*Tempest*
An. How religious men are in affliction: in time of prosperitie, men thinke neither upon God, nor any godly man (G3r).	Gonz. The king and prince at prayers, let's assist them, for our case is as theirs. (1.1.52-53).

Figure Five: Prayer

dialogue's impact on the *Tempest* storm scene. Several specific parallel elements connect the two texts, *viz*. St. Elmo's Fire (Figure Three).

A more specific topos connecting Shakespeare's text to Erasmus is the motif of the shipmaster who turns pale with fear (Figure Four). Unlike St. Elmo's fire, this image is found only in Erasmus, Ariosto and Shakespeare. In both Erasmus and Shakespeare, the image becomes a sign moralized by other characters: in Erasmus, the paleness "presages some great evil," and in Shakespeare, Gonzalo interprets the same image as a token of safety for the ship's crew and passengers, since the boatswain's complexion is "perfect gallows"—that is, it signifies he will die by

hanging instead of by drowning.

Perhaps it is unsurprising that in both texts the shipwrecked sailors turn to prayer as a means of salvation, but since this same parallel has been cited as one of great significance by those who have sought to make Shakespeare dependent on Strachey, we illustrate the parallel language that links Erasmus' dialogue to the *Tempest* (Figure Five).

Finally, and most specifically, both texts parody the disposition of drowning passengers not only to pray to, but to *bargain with*, God. The parallel passages illustrate clear traces of *linguistic* as well as thematic influence. "Naufragium" recalls a "certaine Englishman," who "*promised* golden mountains to his Lady

147

of Walsingham, *if ever he came safe to land*" (Burton Gv2), while others "vowed to become Carthusians [and] one who vowed to go to St. Iames of Compostella, barefooted, and bare headed, with nothing upon his bodie but a shirt of male, and begge for vittailes" (G 3) if he were spared. The proto-reformationist Erasmus apparently rejected the logic of such appeals. Later, one of his characters remarks that "I make no covenant with Saints, for what is it else but a formall contract, or bargaine? I will give you this, *if you will doe that for me: I will give you* a Candle, *if I may* swimme to land" (G3r-v; emphasis added). Gonzalo, in the *Tempest*, imitates both the diction and the sentiment of Erasmus' dialogue: "Now *would I give* a thousand furlongs of sea *for an acre* of barren ground—long heath, brown furze, anything. The wills above be done, but I would fain die a dry death" (1.1.65-68; emphasis added).

The suggestion that Shakespeare is indebted to Erasmus for this latter emphasis is not new; it goes back at least to Zachary Grey's 1754 *Critical, Historical, and Explanatory Notes on Shakespeare*. Regrettably, it has been entirely ignored by a Shakespearean discipline uncritically fixed on Strachey as the sole and exclusive source of the *Tempest's* shipwreck and New World imagery.

Although some of the enumerated elements (St. Elmo's Fire and praying sailors, for instance) can be found in Strachey's account of the Bermuda shipwreck, it is evident that Erasmus contains a more dense network of associations with the *Tempest* storm, both of image and theme, than Strachey. Neither the pale pilot whose pallor "signifies" an impending doom, nor the passenger who bargains with the fates, can be found in Strachey's narrative. Moreover, the occurrence of the common elements in a much earlier text indicates the possibility that the similarities between Shakespeare and Strachey are most likely to be the result of *Erasmus* casting his influence over both later texts. Perhaps it will suffice to drive home the probability of this conclusion to mention that of the extant accounts of

the 1609 Somers wreck, only Strachey—the notorious plagiarist— "remembers" that the storm was accompanied by the "fearful sign"of St. Elmo's Fire.

Notes

[1] This paper was also presented at the Annual Meeting of the Renaissance Society of America that convened from March 23-25, 2006 in San Francisco.

[2] Ariosto's *Orlando Furioso* also contains the elements of this template, but they are dispersed among several cantos.

Works Cited

Ariosto, Ludovico. *Orlando Furioso: A Romantic Epic*. Trans. Barbara Reynolds. 2 vols. London: Penguin, 1977.

Bullough, Geoffrey. *Narrative and Dramatic Sources of Shakespeare*. Vol. 8. London, Routledge, 1973. 8 vols.

Eden, Rycharde, ed. *The Decades of the Newe Worlde or West India*. By Pietro Martire d'Anghiera. 1555. Readex Microprint, 1966.

Erasmus, Desiderius. "Naufragium." *Colloquia Familiaria*. Lipsiae, 1829. <http://www.grexlat.com/biblio/colloquia/colloquia_24_Naufragium.html>.

—. *Seven dialogues both pithie and profitable*. Trans. Burton, William. London: Simmes, 1606.

—. "The Shipwreck." *The Colloquies*. 1518. Ed. E. Johnson. Trans. Nathan Bailey. London: Reeves, 1878. 20 May 2005. <http://oll.libertyfund.org/hd_lf046.1.head.163>.

George, Katherine. "The Civilized West Looks at Primitive Africa, 1400-1800: A Study in Ethnocentrism," *Isis* 49.1 (1958): 62-72.

Gilman, D. "French Readers of Erasmus." *The European Legacy* 7.1 (1 February 2002): 79-81, 83.

Hakluyt, Richard. *The Principle Navigations, Voyages, Traffiques & Discoveries of the English Nation*. London, 1589.

Kathman David. "Dating the Tempest." *The Shakespeare Authorship Page*. <http://shakespeare-authorship.com/tempest.html>.

Kinney, Arthur. "Revisiting 'The Tempest'," *Modern Philology* 93.2 (Nov. 1995): 161-177.

Martyr, Peter. *De Orbe Novo*. Trans. Francis Macnutt. 1912. < http://www.fullbooks.com/De-Orbe-

Novo-Volume-1-of-2-4.html>.

Shakespeare, William. *The Tempest. The Arden Shakespeare.* Ed. Frank Kermode. London: Methuen, 1958.

Smith, John. *The Generall Historie of Virginia, New-England, and the Summer Isles: with the names of the Adventurers, Planters, and Governours from their first beginning An: 1584. to this present 1624. Travels and Works.* 1910. Ed. Edward Arber. Vol. 2. New York: Burt Franklin, 1967. 418–419. 2 vols.

Strachey, William. *The True Reportory of the Wracke and Redemption of Sir Thomas Gates.* 1625. Charlottesville: UP of Virginia, 1964.

Stritmatter, Roger and Lynne Kositsky. "Shakespeare and the Voyagers Revisited," *Review of English Studies* 58.236 (November 2007): 447-472.

—. "'O Brave New World': *The Tempest* and Peter Martyr's *De Orbe Novo*." Unpublished MS. 2007.

Wright, Louis B. *The Elizabethan's America: A Collection of Early Reports by Englishmen in the New World.* Cambridge: Harvard UP, 1965.

Appendix A

	Acts	Ovid Book 11	Ariosto	Erasmus	De Ulloa	Tomson	Gilbert	Strachey	Shakespeare
Sea touching sky	No	Yes	Yes	Yes	No	No	Yes	Yes	Yes
Dark as night	Neither sun nor stars	Yes	Yes	No	No	No	No	Yes	The sky… would pour down stinking pitch
Pale Pilot	No	Pilot "sore dismayed"	Yes	Yes	No	No	No	No	Yes
Leaking	No	Yes	Yes	Yes	No	Yes	No	Yes	Yes
Lightening of ship	Yes	No	Yes	Yes	No	Yes	No	Yes	Yes
Sailors praying	No	Yes	Yes	Yes	Yes	Yes	No	Yes	Yes
Splitting of ship	No	No	"gaping wide"	Yes (probable)	No	No	No	Yes (probable)	Yes
Overturning of ship	No	No	Yes	Yes	No	No	No	Yes (probable)	No
Cutting down of main mast	No	Broken mast/struck the topsail	Yes	Yes	Mainmast broken	Yes	No	Yes	Topmast taken down
Woman and child detail	No		No	Yes	No	Yes	No	No	No
St. Elmo's fire	Ship called Castor and Pollux	No	Yes—brief description	Yes	Yes	Yes	Yes	Yes	Yes

Appendix B

Motif	1. Ariosto, Barbara Reynolds translation	Erasmus 1606 translation	Strachey's *True Reportory*
The sea touching the sky	The water rises up almost until It laps the sky (XLI, 13)	About midnight the tempest began to increase more and more…so often as we were heaved up with [the waves of the sea] we might have touched the moon with our fingers…(G1v)	The sea swelled above the clouds
The lightening of the ship by tossing provisions overboard	Boxes and bales, all cargo and all weight Go overboard…From every storeroom every precious crate Of merchandise is given to the waves…(XIX, 49)	But first (quoth [the master]) **the ship must be disburdened**…better it is to save our lives, with the loss of our goods, than to lose both goods and life together. The truth prevailed, **many vessels were thrown over into the sea, full of rich merchandise**. [An] ambassador to the King of the Scots… had a chest full of plate, gold rings, cloth, and silk apparel. [The master continues] It is not fit that all we should be in danger for the saving of thy chest…so the Italian lost his goods…(G4).	[We] **threw overboard much luggage**, many a trunk and **chest** (in which I suffered no mean loss) and staved many a butt of beer, hogsheads of oil, cider, wine, and vinegar, and **heaved away all our ordnance** on the starboard side.
Sailors praying	And noises louder than his words assail The air as voices of the crew unite To mourn their fate in a concerted wail, While crashing waves together join their might. (XLI, 11) And all on board **commend their souls to God** (XLI, 479)	Much loud praying in *Naufragium* by sailors and passengers: Yes, I heard one…promise St. Christopher, a wax candle as big as himself…and this he **cried out as loud** as every he could, for fear he should not be heard, and this he often repeated…(G3)	Prayers might well be in the heart and lips, but drowned in the **outcries** of the officers

Appendix B   (cont'd)

Motif	1. Ariosto, Barbara Reynolds translation	Erasmus 1606 translation	Strachey's *True Reportory*
The (probable) splitting of the ship	The ship in many parts is gaping wide, And hostile water rushes through inside (XLI, 14)	and the master, fearing lest it would be split all in pieces, he bound it together with cables (G3v).	there was not a moment in which the sodaine splitting…was not expected
The (probable) overturning of the ship	Threatening to turn the vessel upside-down (XLI, 14)	Before it could get free from the great ship, [the boat] was overthrown.	or instant oversetting of the Shippe…
The cutting down of the main mast	Rigging and spars and superstructures crash Beneath the elements' hostility, **And what remains the sailors hew and slash and To lighten ship**, and cast into the sea. (XIX, 44) The captain, in a plight so merciless, Un-ships the mainmast to relieve the stress. (XIX, 48)	he commanded al the ropes to be cut, and the maine-maste to be sawen down close by the boxe wherein it stood, and together with the saile-yardes to be cast overboord into the sea (G2v).	we much unrigged our ship..and had now purposed to have cut down the Maine Mast the more to lighten her…

Appendix B (cont'd)

Motif	1. Ariosto, Barbara Reynolds translation	Erasmus 1606 translation	Strachey's *True Reportory*
St. Elmo's Fire	When on the prow they saw St. Elmo's fire. Their jury rig and sail it glowed upon, Instead of on a mast, for there was none. When they beheld that **miracle of light**, The grateful sailors fell upon their knees… (XIX, 50-51)	And in **the top of the mast** stood one of the mariners in the basket…**looking about to see if he could spie any land:** fast by this man began to stand a certain round thing like a ball of **fire,** which (when it appeareth alone) is to the shipmen a most fearful sign of hard success, but when two of them appear together, that is a sign of a prosperous voyage. **These apparitions were called in old time Castor and Pollux…**By and by the fiery globe sliding downe by the ropes, tumbled itself until it came to the master of the ship… it having stayed there a while, it rolled itself along the brimmes of the ship, and falling from thence down into the middle roomes, it vanished away…(G-Gv).	Sir George Somers, being upon the watch, had an apparition of a **little round light,** like a faint Starre, trembling, and streaming along with a sparkeling blaze, halfe the height upon the **Maine Mast,** and shooting sometimes from Shroud to Shroud, tempting to settle as it were upon any of the foure Shrouds …running sometimes along the Maine-yard to the very end, and then returning . . . but upon a sodaine, towards the morning watch, they lost the sight of it, and knew not which way it made. The superstitious seamen make many constructions of this sea fire…the same (it may be) **which the Grecians were wont in the Mediterranean to call Castor and Pollux…**Could it have served us now miraculously to have taken our height by, it might have strucken amazement…

Sir George Somers, when no man dreamed of such happiness, had **discovered and cried** land… |

CPSIA information can be obtained at www.ICGtesting.com
Printed in the USA
BVOW06s1537110813

328283BV00004B/7/P